Teaching Environmental Writing

Environmental Cultures Series

Series Editors
Greg Garrard, University of British Columbia, Canada
Richard Kerridge, Bath Spa University

Editorial Board
Frances Bellarsi, Université Libre de Bruxelles, Belgium
Mandy Bloomfield, Plymouth University, UK
Lily Chen, Shanghai Normal University, China
Christa Grewe-Volpp, University of Mannheim, Germany
Stephanie LeMenager, University of Oregon, USA
Timothy Morton, Rice University, USA
Pablo Mukherjee, University of Warwick, UK

Bloomsbury's *Environmental Cultures* series makes available to students and scholars at all levels the latest cutting-edge research on the diverse ways in which culture has responded to the age of environmental crisis. Publishing ambitious and innovative literary ecocriticism that crosses disciplines, national boundaries, and media, books in the series explore and test the challenges of ecocriticism to conventional forms of cultural study.

Titles available
Bodies of Water, Astrida Neimanis
Cities and Wetlands, Rod Giblett
Civil Rights and the Environment in African-American Literature, 1895–1941, John Claborn
Climate Change Scepticism, Greg Garrard, George Handley, Axel Goodbody, Stephanie Posthumus
Climate Crisis and the 21st-Century British Novel, Astrid Bracke
Colonialism, Culture, Whales, Graham Huggan
Ecocriticism and Italy, Serenella Iovino

Fuel, Heidi C. M. Scott
Literature as Cultural Ecology, Hubert Zapf
Nerd Ecology, Anthony Lioi
The New Nature Writing, Jos Smith
The New Poetics of Climate Change, Matthew Griffiths
This Contentious Storm, Jennifer Mae Hamilton
Climate Change Scepticism, Greg Garrard, Axel Goodbody, George B. Handley
and Stephanie Posthumus

Forthcoming Titles

Reclaiming Romanticism, Kate Rigby
Ecospectrality, Laura A. White
Radical Animism, Jemma Deer
Cognitive Ecopoetics, Sharon Lattig
Eco-Digital Art, Lisa FitzGerald
Environmental Cultures in Soviet East Europe, Anna Barcz
Weathering Shakespeare, Evelyn O'Malley
Imagining the Plains of Latin America, Axel Pérez Trujillo Diniz
Ecocriticism and Turkey, Meliz Ergin

Teaching Environmental Writing

Ecocritical Pedagogy and Poetics

Isabel Galleymore

BLOOMSBURY ACADEMIC
LONDON • NEW YORK • OXFORD • NEW DELHI • SYDNEY

BLOOMSBURY ACADEMIC
Bloomsbury Publishing Plc
50 Bedford Square, London, WC1B 3DP, UK
1385 Broadway, New York, NY 10018, USA
29 Earlsfort Terrace, Dublin 2, Ireland

BLOOMSBURY, BLOOMSBURY ACADEMIC and the Diana logo are trademarks of
Bloomsbury Publishing Plc

First published in Great Britain 2020
This paperback edition published in 2021

Copyright © Isabel Galleymore, 2020

Isabel Galleymore has asserted her right under the Copyright, Designs and Patents Act,
1988, to be identified as Author of this work.

For legal purposes the Acknowledgements on p. viii constitute an extension
of this copyright page.

Cover design: Burge Agency
Cover image © Shutterstock

All rights reserved. No part of this publication may be reproduced
or transmitted in any form or by any means, electronic or mechanical,
including photocopying, recording, or any information storage or retrieval
system, without prior permission in writing from the publishers.

Bloomsbury Publishing Plc does not have any control over, or responsibility for, any
third-party websites referred to or in this book. All internet addresses given in this
book were correct at the time of going to press. The author and publisher regret any
inconvenience caused if addresses have changed or sites have ceased to exist, but can
accept no responsibility for any such changes.

A catalogue record for this book is available from the British Library.

A catalog record for this book is available from the Library of Congress.

ISBN: HB: 978-1-3500-6841-4
PB: 978-1-3502-4327-9
ePDF: 978-1-3500-6842-1
eBook: 978-1-3500-6843-8

Series: Environmental Cultures

Typeset by Newgen KnowledgeWorks Pvt. Ltd., Chennai, India

To find out more about our authors and books visit www.bloomsbury.com
and sign up for our newsletters.

Contents

Acknowledgements	viii
Introduction	1
1 'Where you are': Place writing	25
2 The 'I-me-my voice': The first-person in environmental writing	57
3 'I am not a swift': Approaching non-humans	89
4 Writing 'more in the world': Fact and figuration	117
5 'On the world's terms and not my own': Authenticity, self-reflexivity and otherness	143
Afterword	169
Notes	175
Bibliography	187
Index	203

Acknowledgements

I owe a debt of gratitude to the teachers I interviewed for this project. For their insightful contributions that have been fundamental to this study, I would like to thank Elizabeth-Jane Burnett, Mark Cocker, David Cooper, Miriam Darlington, John Elder, Paul Evans, Sheryl St Germain, Jon Gower, Chris Kinsey, Stephen Moss, Andrew Motion, Jim Perrin, Jonathan Skinner, Mary Swander and George Ttoouli. In particular I would like to thank Laird Christensen at Green Mountain College, Vermont; James Canton at the University of Essex; and the students enrolled at both institutions, who permitted me to interview them and also to sit in on their seminars. I would like to take this opportunity to thank Andy Brown and Nick Groom for their guidance and support in supervising this project in its early stages as a doctoral thesis. I am grateful to Greg Garrard for his encouragement and assistance in the process of writing this book's proposal and I extend my utmost thanks to Richard Kerridge, 'Environmental Cultures' series editor, whose help in preparing this book for publication has been so valuable. I would like to thank all the scholars who have helped me in this process: Sarah Daw, Sophia David, Sharanya Murali and Miranda Cichy with whom I discussed many of the questions raised in this book. My thanks also to Jos Smith, Ben Smith and Luke Thompson for their constructive conversations. Finally, I would like to thank Nigel Tattersfield and Phil Child for reading earlier versions of this book and for their continued support.

The third-party copyrighted material displayed in the pages of this book are done so on the basis of 'fair use for the purposes of teaching, criticism, scholarship or research' only in accordance with international copyright laws, and is not intended to infringe upon the ownership rights of the original owners.

Introduction

We're writing poems about last night's bat.
Charles has stripped the scene to lyric,
while I'm filling in the tale

– Mark Doty, 'Pipistrelle' (2008: 4–6).

In 'Pipistrelle', the prize-winning American poet Mark Doty describes the experience of hearing a bat calling as it flies through the twilit sky. Doty is with companions, but only he can hear the bat as it flits above their heads. 'Only some people can hear their frequencies', explains his friend Charles (Mark Doty 2008: 35). Yet, as soon as Doty tries to put what he has heard into words, he stumbles. 'I could hear the tender cry of a bat', he states before immediately questioning: '*cry* won't do: a diminutive chime / somewhere between merriment and weeping, // who could ever say?' (ibid.: 37–40). To depict the exact sound of the bat appears impossible. While 'merriment' and 'weeping' serve as useful coordinates for Doty's impression of the sound, the issue of whether the bat can feel such emotion distracts, drawing attention to whether this representation is accurate. Indeed, Doty seems to ask whether any representation can be accurate since the only tool we have as writers about the non-human world is a language that is decidedly human. As he continues in this self-reflexive vein to consider the different poems he and Charles are writing about the bat, further questions arise:

> Charles considers the pipistrelle's music navigational,
> a modest, rational understanding of what
> I have decided is my personal visitation.
>
> Is it because I am an American I think the bat came
> especially to address me?

(2008: 49–53)

The language attributed to Charles's depiction appears scientific in nature whereas Doty's is imbued with the self. Is the depiction arrogant, and, if so, is his status as an American citizen to blame?

'Or does that mean I am a son of Whitman, / while Charles is an heir of Wordsworth, // albeit thankfully a more concise one?', Doty continues (ibid.: 56–8). Wrestling with anxieties concerning vocabulary and approach, Doty arrives at the anxiety of influence as he hints that his writing, if not his original perception of the nocturnal creature, is shaped by Whitmanesque epiphany. Later in the poem, Doty's questions take on a more ethical flavour. After suggesting that the bat has visited him personally, he asks whether he needs to 'worry my little aerial friend // with a freight not precisely his?' (ibid.: 65–6). Has Doty imposed a human – or personal – agenda upon the non-human? There seems to be an underlying violence to his use of 'freight' given the small and delicate body of the species. Could Doty's literary imposition upon the bat echo the *physical* imposition humans have made, and continue to make, on environments? There is no satisfying conclusion to the poem, no final line on how we should represent, as writers, environments and their inhabitants. Instead, Doty asks one last question: 'Does the poem reside in experience / or in self-consciousness // about experience?' (ibid.: 67–9). This is the question that has troubled him all along. It highlights the tensions he has encountered when trying to put the bat into words. There is a struggle between an unaffected and unmediated representation and one mediated via the imagination and the writer's self. Having read 'Pipistrelle', we might ask is it possible to create an unmediated representation? Is there a better way of writing about the environment? A more ethical way? Rather than focusing on the encounter as a semi-spiritual 'personal visitation', should Doty have approached the pipistrelle as a scientist might?

What is commonly called 'nature writing' is popular among readers and as a field of academic study. In the United States, the popularity of the genre has been well established since the early twentieth century; in the United Kingdom, the genre has recently become popular again after a period of relative neglect. In this book, I will focus on the emergence of creative writing courses and modules dedicated to nature writing or 'environmental writing' in the last two decades. As I explain later, this new movement in pedagogy has become a popular study specialism, responding to the growth of creative writing degrees both in Britain and in the United States, and to the commercial market for nature writing. This book will be a critical examination of the pedagogical methods that have emerged in this context. I will ask not only how teachers guide their students into creative engagements with environments, but which literary models provide inspiration and what cautions and preferences are repeated, and why? Students wanting to attempt this genre can investigate various literary precedents, from Henry David Thoreau's *Walden* to the penchant for 'edgelands' often exhibited by the 'new nature writing'. Writing about the environment might mean writing with the naturalist's scientific eye, yet it might also mean claiming spiritual communion with nature, praising the natural world as in Mary Oliver's 'praise poems', and also producing elegies for the loss of wild nature as well as protests at its demise.

In creative writing courses dedicated to writing about the environment, first-hand experience is repeatedly prioritized: 'Prepare to enter a whining-free zone for the six days we are in the field', asserts Hal Crimmel as he embraces the idea of the excursion narrative (2014). 'You will be expected to eat, sleep, and work outside in a remote desert canyon environment' (ibid.). Scientific engagements with local landscapes are also encouraged: Michael Umphrey (2008) asks students to become 'apprentices' to place. Assignments are expected on 'the ecology of boundaries between grasslands and forests, on the hydrology of rivers and streams, on the mid-summer feeding habits of grizzly bears' (ibid.). Conversely, other teachers guide their students into Doty's more personal perspective: 'I have the students write in their journals about a place or a time in the wilderness or a park or anywhere they have felt some kind of connection', Jennifer Beigel explains (1996: 111). Teaching at Chatham University, Sheryl St Germain makes a similar appeal: 'I try to focus on – I know this is going to sound kind of Mickey Mouse – but on celebration' (2014a).

Interdisciplinary practice frequently frames environmental writing courses, defining and, indeed, marketing their approach. At Essex University, the Master's course dedicated to 'Wild Writing', launched in 2009, describes, on its web page, how it encourages students to explore landscape 'through a combination of science and literature modules' which will help them to develop their 'own ways of approaching writing about the wild: creative, critical, and scientific'.[1] The latter phrase appears like a short list of ingredients, and yet how are we to define the quantity of each and how are they to be mixed? Too much of a scientific approach might generate writing that is more appropriate to that of a government report than a poem or piece of literary non-fiction. Alternatively, let the writer depend on their creative capacity for similes and metaphors, and the writing they produce might appear too disconnected from the real knowledge of the landscape that it tries to describe. The Master of Fine Arts (MFA) in Creative Writing and Environment at Iowa State University describes itself online as 'an original and intensive opportunity to document, meditate on, mourn, and celebrate the complexities of our transforming natural world'.[2] Continuing the kind of questions Doty asks himself in 'Pipistrelle', we might ask how we are to manage objective versus subjective perspectives on the environment in such writing? Celebration is a mode that recurs across such pedagogy, but should our thoughts and feelings be carefully managed if a piece of writing is meant to take the environment, rather than the self, as its core subject?

In this book, I explore recurring instructions given to students for writing about the environment that address tensions touched on so far: scientific objectivity, personal and local engagements with place, as well as others I will address later, such as an anxiety concerning literary affectation. I draw upon interviews conducted with a range of teachers, predominantly working in higher education, and by guidebooks on the subject published between 1985 and 2017.

While offering an appraisal of such pedagogy as a distinctive development in contemporary thought on environmental literature and education, I am also interested in making an intervention by asking how these recurring instructions could be restrictive. Although it might be said that the chief objective of teaching environmental writing is to foster good writers, other intentions are clearly evident. Many teachers describe a desire to increase environmental awareness in their students: to make their students better ecological citizens. Others, especially those who run postgraduate courses, anticipate their students becoming published environmental writers of the future. For example, Bath Spa University's course advertises itself online to 'any writer inspired by places, people and wildlife, who wants to be published'.[3] By comparing pedagogical approaches to the current theory and practice of ecocriticism – a scholarly field which tests and stretches definitions of nature and traditions of literary representation – I hope to develop new guidance that will not only assist the student in becoming an accomplished writer, but also deepen ecological consciousness and advance new routes into writing about the world we inhabit.

The idea of 'nature' has of course been subject to much scrutiny. In 1976, Raymond Williams referred to 'nature' as 'perhaps the most complex word in the language' (1976: 184). The capitalization of the word, Nature, is often associated with problematic ideologies concerning mastery, mystery and purity. However, 'writing' also deserves enquiry of its own, particularly given the fact that the phrase 'nature writing' is frequently associated with non-fiction. Patrick D. Murphy explains that in America the non-fiction prose essay is often thought to be the 'starting point for the rest of literature' about nature, citing Thoreau as influential upon the growth of this tradition (2000: 4–5). As I discuss in later pages, this privileging of non-fiction extends to the United Kingdom with the success of the 'new nature writing'. The connection between nature writing and non-fiction may not be all that surprising in light of the topics approached so far involving the role of science and, indeed, Doty's anxiety about unmediated rather than mediated practices of representation. Yet, as Murphy suggests, this predisposition runs 'the risk of killing the genre through baking it into a rigid mold' and stifling alternative forms of expression such as fiction and poetry (ibid.: 54).

Understanding the phrase 'nature writing' to be troublesome, I use the term 'environmental writing' throughout this study for two main reasons. The term 'environmental writing' opens the discussion to different forms of writing and aims to do justice to the scope of pedagogical approaches surveyed in this book, some of which appear to push back against ideologies associated with 'Nature'. I use 'environmental writing' as a term which is intentionally inclusive. However, it is important to note that I also use 'environmental writing' as a discrete proposal for the future of pedagogy. In what is perhaps the most extensive taxonomy of 'nature-oriented literature' to date, Murphy describes 'environmental literature' as that which is conscious of environmental issues: compared to nature literature, 'it is concerned more with the depiction of agrarian values than the plot of agrarian life' and 'the intrinsic value of other animals' existence than what encounters with other animals mean to people' (ibid.: 5). Although 'environmental writing' can often strike an activist tone, Murphy's definition suggests a more reflective approach: one that I encourage pedagogy to adopt via dialogue between creative practice and ecocriticism.[4]

The beginnings of environmental writing pedagogy

In the 1960s and 1970s, a growing environmental movement emerged in many countries, perhaps most notably in the United States. There, new environmental legislation was introduced: the Clean Air Acts of 1963 and 1967, and the Wilderness Act of 1964. The question of education wasn't far behind. The US National Environmental Education Act of 1969 was followed by international initiatives as the United Nations Conference on the Environment addressed the importance of environmental education in 1972. Demand for an environmentally inflected pedagogy was growing, encouraging the possibilities of interdisciplinary curricula. From the two disciplines of literature and creative writing, one of the first voices to respond to such calls was Frederick O. Waage in his edited essay collection *Teaching Environmental Literature: Materials, Methods, Resources* (1985). 'New undergraduate curricula that combine tradition and innovation must be designed', declares Waage in his introduction (1985: xii). He argues that 'environment-humanities courses, however structured, embody a vital dialogue between imaginative and active, practical and contemplative, experience', and goes on to suggest that the absence of dialogue between disciplines 'may be a root cause of the decline both of humanities in education and of the ideal of the well-educated person' (ibid.: xii–xiii). Readers today will find these words resonant, since such concerns are now widespread throughout the humanities. Looking back to C. P. Snow's famous 1959 lecture that diagnoses the 'two cultures', Waage makes the case that 'sciences and humanities … must be made more responsive to each other' (ibid.: xii).

Waage's argument finds support in the fact that many commentators have identified a work of environmental literature that seems to marry these two cultures as the catalyst for the emergence of the international movement: Rachel Carson's *Silent Spring* (1962). As scientific journalism concerning the destructive effect of pesticides on American wildlife, Carson's non-fiction, first published in 1962, has continued to receive praise for its unexpectedly 'poetic' style. Waage includes Carson alongside Gilbert White, Charles Darwin, Henry David Thoreau, Walt Whitman, Aldo Leopold, John Muir and John Burroughs and others in his array of exemplary models in which science and the humanities are combined. Included in Waage's edited collection, Paul T. Bryant attempts to define the genre:

> It is not fantasy, it is not fiction, and it is not a scientific report. It is not a taxonomic list or a collection of folklore. And it is neither a moralizing fable nor a philosophical metaphor. The nature writer avoids sentimentality, personification, and teleological assumptions … nature writing must remain true to the objective facts of nature, but at the same time it must present the human response to nature. Thus nature writing must maintain the physical accuracy required of the scientific writer and, at the same time, present the human imagination and emotions with the integrity of the creative writer.
>
> (1985: 93–4)

Though this may seem, at first impression, a reasonable definition, many of the canonical writers listed above would seem to contravene Bryant's rules. Burroughs, for example, deliberately distanced himself from Thoreau's writing, criticizing it for its overly moral tone. Should Thoreau, then, be dismissed as an exemplary model because his work resembles 'a moralizing fable'? How do we police the line between 'fantasy' and human imagination? If environmental writing is 'not fiction', then what about the poetry of Whitman?

The first noteworthy guides on environmental writing were published sporadically and, with the exception of one or two British contributors, were generally a US phenomenon. Following Waage's collected essays, John A. Murray produced *The Sierra Club Nature Writing Handbook* (1995). In its preface, Murray asks the reader to 'think of this book as a field guide. As a set of maps that will help you to explore the country of the imagination' (1995: ix). An escapist flavour emerges: 'In a world of hatred and death and violence we surely need more essays and books with nature as a theme' (ibid.). Despite Murray's favouring of the imagination, he pushes for realism, affirming the need for 'complete fidelity to the truth' in writing about animals, landscapes and experiences in the wild. Published just three years later, *Stories in the Land* (1998), produced by the Orion Society as part of their drive for place-based education, proposes 'a perceptual process of discovery, celebration, and community' for children and adults alike (1998: 15). Alongside the ecocritic and writer John Elder, who edited the collection of essays, teachers included in this book emphasize the potential for outdoor experiences in local environments to enable students to write field journals or environmental magazines. The emphasis is very much on factual accuracy, but when poetry is discussed as a possible form, Lorain Varela loses all sight of this emphasis as she praises poetry's 'magical' properties (ibid.: 87). In this instance, it appears that the creativity associated with the humanities appears completely disconnected to the environmental subject with which it aims to unite.[5]

In attempting to bridge the disciplinary divide, pedagogy concerned with environmental writing often makes explicit gestures towards incorporating scientific methodologies. Bryant describes 'a laboratory period' in which his students write about environments 'in the style of a professional scientific journal', and far more widespread is the adoption of the phrase 'field work' (1985: 98–101). Hal Crimmel's edited collection, aptly named *Teaching in the Field* (2003), recognizes that before the interdisciplinary turn in education, 'there was little written about teaching arts and humanities outdoors ... Only those in the sciences took students on field trips, and they conducted empirical studies on site' (2003: 4). Over the course of almost forty years, Waage, Crimmel and the majority of contemporary teachers of environmental writing have pursued this interdisciplinary move. They have done so in the belief that the opportunity to undertake 'field work' allows students to obtain valuable first-hand experience of an environment. Often, as will be discussed in the forthcoming chapters, field work is associated with naming species, understanding natural processes, and, ultimately, donning the naturalist's hat. However, it should also be noted that the roots 'field work' has in scientific study seem rather forgotten when, at least in a few instances, guidance asks students to simply go outside for a short period and describe what they see.

What Bryant calls the 'objective facts of nature' are not always successfully prioritized, but the aspiration carries a certain moral authority. Empirical observation is valued for its ability to represent environments accurately, to support a critically distanced perspective and create 'grounded' depictions. Such an ethic stands against more mediated portrayals such as Doty's in 'Pipistrelle'. This wariness towards the intrusion of personal or cultural meaning derives, of course, from the long tradition in the West of seeing nature as that which is separate from or even opposed to culture. Bryant himself implies this dichotomy when he defines the subject of nature as 'natural processes or the natural world not affected by human manipulation or at least not primarily determined by such manipulation' (1985: 93). Although conscious that the boundaries are porous, he expects writing about the environment to be as unpolluted by humans as possible. Frequently, the assumption is that too much reliance on the self or on the imagination is anthropocentric and thus antithetical to the ecocentric endeavour of environmental writing. 'Thoreau invented the personal nature essay', David Petersen states in his guide *Writing Naturally* (2001: 6), as he recommends first-person narration. At the same time, however, he warns that using the pronoun 'I' too often can result in a 'sort of auto-infatuation' (ibid.: 80). Though the interdisciplinary project of environmental writing requires a literary perspective, Bryant and Petersen's comments exemplify a concern that this perspective is associated with culture at the expense of nature. Consequently science appears trusted over art, literalness over literariness.

The variety of approaches to be found in historical examples of writing about the environment only serves to increase these tensions. To try and identify an exact canon of such writing is a difficult, if not an impossible endeavour. Waage's list given above, including Darwin and Carson, only takes us so far. 'Environmental writing' as a category can include works of natural history; the Georgic tradition and other pastoral literature; the literature of travel, exploration and empire; Romantic writing; Transcendentalist writing; British rural writing, American excursion narratives and, of course, the 'new nature writing' among much else. In each instance, the boundaries between nature and culture, science and literature are questioned, redrawn and questioned again. In *The Rural Tradition* (1975), W. J. Keith examines writers from the sixteenth to the twentieth centuries who have fought over how to depict the English countryside with many choosing to hide all signs of rural hardship in romanticized accounts.

Raymond Williams says that writers at the turn of the century – and, as one example, he refers to Edward Thomas's *The Heart of England* – 'brought with them from the cities, and from the schools and universities, a version of rural history which was now extraordinarily amalgamated with a distantly translated literary interpretation' (1973: 256). As some sought to challenge these idealized interpretations (we might look to Thomas Hardy as one such challenger), styles of writing became politicized, and this sometimes led to a preference for accounts that were written in a more 'down-to-earth' style and with a greater emphasis on realism.

A commitment to fact and realism may usually seem, Keith states, 'not so much unnecessary as irrelevant to creative writing' (1975: 15). Keith explains his comment by referring to the importance of the imagination to creative endeavour and Coleridge's 'willing suspension of disbelief' (ibid.). 'But the situation of the rural writer seems somehow different' as a 'premium [is] put on truth and accuracy' (ibid.). We might extend Keith's discussion to environmental writing more broadly. As we shall see in Chapter 3, the Nature Fakers Controversy emerged from the belief that 'the line between fact and fiction' had been dangerously compromised by the anthropomorphic tales published under the guise of non-fiction in the early 1900s by several US writers. The instigator of the controversy was John Burroughs – the same John Burroughs who, as noted earlier, criticized Thoreau's writing. Burroughs never went so far as to call out Thoreau as a 'sham' nature writer (as he did of William J. Long and Ernest Thompson Seton), but he questioned whether it was nature that Thoreau was interested in, or himself. Compared to the British naturalist Gilbert White, whom Burroughs considered 'a true observer' of the environments he studied, Thoreau 'had other business with the gods of the woods than taking an inventory of their wares' ([1922] 2006: 113). Of Thoreau, Burroughs said, 'His science is only the handmaid of his ethics', and 'his wood-lore is the foil of his moral and intellectual teachings' (ibid.). The fear of being not a naturalist, but a 'supernaturalist' who, being too concerned with human matters, fails to see the world for what it is, continues in much American writing (ibid.: 135). Tracing its history, Peter A. Fritzell suggests that many contemporary US writers have attempted to counter the Thoreauvian tradition by adopting a scientific, objective stance, 'keeping human subject and natural object separate, and sustaining conventional discriminations between metaphor (or mystery) and fact' (1990: 27).

The anxieties and conflicts that emerge from several centuries of literature about the environment have been valuable subject matter for ecocriticism, the beginnings of which are closely entwined with the beginnings of a pedagogy specifically concerned with environmental writing. Studies such as William Rueckert's 1978 essay 'Literature and Ecology: An Experiment in Ecocriticism' initiated this new approach, and, by 1992, ecocriticism was a large-enough movement to form its own scholarly society, the Association for Literature and the Environment. ASLE began in the United States (the UK division, later UK and Ireland, was founded in 1998), and became a vital point of contact not only for scholars, but also for teachers, with the website collating sample syllabi that ranged from the critical exegesis of environmental texts to classes dedicated to creative writing. Although materials and strategies may well have been shared by those coming from critical and creative contexts, ecocriticism's activist approach to literature also meant that the scholarly field frequently adopted the prescriptive tone customary for teaching environmental writing. In other words, while ecocritics have drawn significant attention to literary representations of environments, asking what relationships humans have with the earth and how these depictions have changed over time, ecocritics have often also charged themselves with the responsibility of deciding which literary styles or forms can, in the words of John Felstiner, 'save the Earth' (2009).

Ecocriticism

Creative and critical approaches to environmental literature grew in close proximity. The ecocritic, the environmental writer and the teacher were often the same person. John Elder, so far discussed as an editor of pedagogical essays, is also known as an accomplished non-fiction author as well as a pioneer in ecocriticism. His book, *Imagining the Earth* (1985), examined poetic celebrations of nature in the Romantic and Transcendentalist traditions – a central topic in early US ecocriticism. Elder's interest lies in how poets move us 'from estrangement to transformation and reintegration' with the earth (1985: 1). He suggests that American poets such as Gary Snyder and Wendell Berry 'advance ... connectedness, through reverence for nature that is rooted in one chosen place' (ibid.: 39). Elder's main objective would seem to be literary analysis, but he also frequently becomes didactic in a way that is consistent with the efforts of teachers – including Elder himself – to encourage students to write on their local bioregion and focus on personal feeling. His readings frequently return to the tension between literalness and literariness, valuing textual 'simplicity and transparency', and at one point proposing a kind of moralistic equation between 'unelaborated' forms of expression and 'groundedness' (ibid.: 54). Predominantly concerned with Thoreau's writing, Lawrence Buell's landmark ecocritical text, *The Environmental Imagination* (1995) moves in a broadly similar direction. Examining the ways in which writers retain objectivity in their depictions, Buell praises elements of nineteenth-century realism and mimetic representation.

In *Sustainable Poetry* (1999), Leonard Scigaj addresses the question of which poetic forms and traditions are most consistent with ecocritical theory. He developed a post-structuralist argument that explores the ways in which poets have demonstrated 'the limits of language' (1999: 38). Hostile to Derrida's *différance*, he offers a riposte in his notion of *référance* that refers 'one's perceptions … to the referential origin of all language' (ibid.). His work stands in contrast to the previous ecocritical concentration of mimetic realism and the aspiration to write 'transparent', unmediated description. David W. Gilcrest, in *Greening the Lyre* (2002), similarly advises a self-reflexive textual awareness. Guided by Scigaj, Gilcrest asserts that 'an environmental poetics informed by linguistic skepticism can serve to establish a more intimate and responsive relationship toward nature' (2002: 133). Yet this scepticism is compromised by his belief in a 'meditative perception' that, contrary to a 'metaphoric perception', corresponds to an ethical 'diminishment of the self or ego' (ibid.: 127–8). Though crucial in trying to establish ecocriticism as a *scholarly* field, these arguments seemed to struggle to move beyond Elder's interest in 'unelaborated' representations presented seventeen years earlier.

Such a potted account of ecocritical thought cannot of course do justice to the work of the scholars who built this emerging movement. For one thing, I have only mentioned American male ecocritics. The account fails to recognize women's voices in the discussion, and, furthermore, fails to engage with developments in Britain, which, though often considered as co-constitutive, featured differences of approach and emphasis from American ecocriticism, which I will discuss later. Nonetheless, the account is at least in part representative of how ecocriticism and a creatively focused pedagogy have shared and promoted a certain aesthetic for writing about the environment. What Elder describes as 'connectedness' suggests that estrangement has little place in depictions of the natural world, whereas plain diction or what Gilcrest describes as 'direct treatment' is almost fetishized in keeping with Murray's pedagogical instruction to write with 'complete fidelity to the truth' (1995: 13–14).

If at first ecocritical and pedagogical thinking developed in strong alignment, there was some divergence later, when ecocritics began to engage with critical theory. Writing in 2003, Dana Phillips criticized Buell's praise of realistic environmental depictions. Phillips warned that 'if ecocriticism limits itself to reading realistic texts realistically, its practitioners may be reduced to an umpire's role, squinting to see if a given description of a painted trillium or a live oak is itself well-painted and lively' (2003: 163–4). Timothy Morton, now hugely influential in ecocriticism and the broader environmental humanities, shares Phillips's mocking view of the rhapsodic tone sometimes taken by ecocriticism (2007). This scolding was a wake-up call for ecocriticism. Phillips and Morton took the scholarly field in a new direction by introducing concepts from critical theory, continuing, to some extent, Scigaj's earlier endeavour. This injection of post-structuralist and post-modernist theory marked a crucial turning point, one that many see as distinguishing 'first-wave' from 'second-wave' ecocriticism.[6] From focusing on depictions of wild nature, ecocriticism in its second wave began to question problematic conceptions and ideologies associated with nature. Much attention was given to exploring 'naturecultures': a phrase used by Donna Haraway to describe the messy entanglement of nature and culture in which the boundaries between bodies – human, animal and technological – are blurred (2003: 12).

First-wave ecocriticism, which had been dominated by a Romantic view of nature, was, in many cases, hostile to the introduction of theory. Given that the beginnings of a pedagogy of environmental writing were bound with those of early ecocriticism, teachers were similarly opposed to this shift. Remembering his experiences as a graduate teaching assistant in the 1980s, Hal Crimmel reveals the division: 'I started taking my class on short field trips – a Saturday morning here, an afternoon or evening there … The other TAs [teaching assistants], mostly theory-addled types, addicted to the latest trends, smiled patronizingly when I shared my experiences' (2003: 3). Reading this, we might ask whether the teacher in the field smiles patronizingly back when those who are 'theory-addled' share their experiences. Not all share Crimmel's hostility to theory, however. Some environmental writing courses currently available in universities include ecocritical texts, and, moreover, texts that might be considered particularly challenging in their philosophical approach. Teaching 'Writing on Location' at Newman University, Elizabeth-Jane Burnett (2019) gives her students short extracts from Timothy Morton's work. She explains how Morton's *Hyperobjects* (2013) – a text that explores the difficulty of representing entities that are vast because of their relation to space and time – complements one week's focus that involves writing exercises on rocks, plastics and deep time, providing new angles for students to pursue (2019). Alongside the creative component, Burnett's students are expected to write a critical commentary in which they are encouraged to make links between the theory and their writing.

The Wild Writing MA at the University of Essex also incorporates an element of ecocritical theory. Taught by Susan Oliver, the module 'Literature and the Environmental Imagination' focuses on texts by writers such as Thoreau and Muir and explores ecocritical readings of them via, among others, Morton and Haraway. The module serves two functions: it is designed for students on the literature MA who seek training in ecocriticism, and the module is also compulsory for creative writing students on the MA in Wild Writing. Compulsory though it may be, compared to Burnett's exercise, it is not entirely clear how this critical lens is intended to influence or benefit creative practice. While James Canton sees the module as an essential part of the Wild Writing course he leads, he signals a division between theory and creative writing as he suggests that engagement with ecocriticism can risk compromising students' creativity (2013). If theory is introduced, might students confuse the role of writer with literary critic? This kind of concern is seen elsewhere. Teaching at Green Mountain College in Vermont, Laird Christensen protests that he already spends enough time thinking about ideas and is thus apprehensive that theory would encourage more inward-looking tendencies (2014c). In turn, many teachers suspect that introducing it to the writing classroom could widen the gap between students and their subject matter.[7] Teaching at Iowa State University, Sheryl St. Germain describes how she and fellow colleagues became 'depressed' about ecocriticism's theoretical concerns and the way in which these imposed a particular agenda on creative writing (2014a).

Pedagogical guides published since the millennium such as *The Alphabet of the Trees* (McEwen and Statman 2000), *Teaching about Place* (Christensen and Crimmel 2008) and *Environmental and Nature Writing* (Prentiss and Wilkins 2016) may be more interested in expanding the canon of environmental literature than their predecessors (such as Waage, Elder and Murray), but they are not influenced by the ecocritical arguments that appeared contemporaneously, such as Scigaj's or Morton's. This disconnection between creative and critical fields means that pedagogy dedicated to environmental writing tends toward many of the first-wave approaches that second-wave ecocriticism (and further waves hence) criticized and, to some extent, abandoned, almost twenty years ago. Is this disconnection necessary? Does theory have to present a threat to creativity and to our engagements with the environment as the teachers I have quoted above suggest?

This book argues that theory presents an opportunity. Indeed, in each chapter I demonstrate how pedagogy is developed and enriched through dynamic conversation with ecocritical thought informed by theory. In response to recurring instructions for students to engage locally and become 'apprentices to place', Chapter 1 introduces Ursula Heise's influential argument in *Sense of Place, Sense of Planet* (2008) that articulates the necessary challenge of engaging globally. Drawing on her theory of 'eco-cosmopolitanism', I suggest ways of developing current pedagogical emphasis on intimate connections with local environments by cultivating awareness of global ecological relations. Likewise, countering the importance placed on scientific language in current pedagogy, in Chapter 4 I examine David Abram's ecocritical argument in *Spell of the Sensuous* (1996) that suggests such language is unhelpfully deterministic. His call for a more metaphorical language that acknowledges and appreciates the material diversity of environments informs an alternative pedagogical approach that challenges the binary between factual and figurative language. Far from being 'theory-addled', the ecocritical pedagogy that I aim to propose is critically-aware, thought-provoking and imaginatively inventive.

The last twelve years have seen intermittent debate concerning ecocriticism, education and the environmental humanities. The influential ecocritic Greg Garrard has led much of this discussion, expressing his concern for the lack of innovation he sees in pedagogical strategy. Garrard claims, as I have here, that this lack of innovation is rooted in 'the commitment of "first-wave" ecocritics to wilderness epiphany [that] skewed their attention toward the methods and assumptions of environmental education (EE)' (2007: 363). Such an emphasis upon epiphany in ecocriticism – which can of course be linked to the role of celebration and spiritual connection in environmental writing pedagogy – comes at the expense of more recent developments in Education for Sustainable Development (ESD) that aim to address key issues such as climate change and biodiversity. Looking for pedagogy that responds to Morton's call for 'ecology without nature', Garrard articulates the need for a second-wave pedagogy to match 'second-wave ecocriticism' and in so doing parallel ESD's more issue-led innovations (2010: 238). Garrard is not a lone voice. Departures in ecocritical pedagogy range from Sidney Dobrin's and Christian Weisser's *Ecocomposition* (2001), Garrard's recent collection of essays by ecopedagogues such as Richard Kerridge and Timothy Morton, *Teaching Ecocriticism and Green Cultural Studies* (2012), as well as *Teaching Climate Change in the Humanities* edited by LeMenager et al. (2017).[8] These works discuss topics such as slow reading, rhetoric and climate change cinema, but the creative practice of environmental writing is missing, or at best reduced to a few paragraphs. Even the new and improved 2008 edition of *Teaching Environmental Literature* edited by Waage, Mark Long and Laird Christensen, which aims to recognize developments since its original publication in 1985, abandons creative practice despite this having been central to its first incarnation.

Environmental writing pedagogy explicitly informed by developments in ecocriticism is limited to a chapter written by Terry Gifford in Hal Crimmel's *Teaching in the Field* (2003), which references Patrick D. Murphy's argument on non-humans as subjects rather than objects, and 'Ecological Creative Writing' by James Engelhardt and Jeremy Schraffenberger in *Creative Writing Pedagogies for the Twenty-First Century* (2015). Wanting to depart from more traditional perspectives, the latter productively counters the possibility of 'pastoral fantasies or wilderness retreat narratives' (2015: 496). At one point anticipating the argument presented in Chapter 1 of the present work between the local and the global, the authors make the valuable suggestion that students might use their connection to place to explore global connections: 'If a student writes about dandelions dotting her lawn, she would then research how the plant likely arrived in North America with the English settlers on the Mayflower' (ibid.: 499). Yet, if such perspectives are limited to a single chapter that aims to convince an otherwise un-ecological creative writing community of the merits associated with ecological engagement, it is clear that more sustained and specific work is needed.

Transatlantic perspectives

Turn to *Writing Naturally*, a guide to environmental writing produced by American non-fiction author David Petersen and you will find, among discussions of American writers such as Annie Dillard and Edward Abbey, discussions of the eighteenth-century British naturalist Gilbert White. Pick up the reading lists belonging to many courses in the United Kingdom and you will find the likes of Rachel Carson, Annie Dillard and, above all, Henry David Thoreau. Look at the number of prizes, journals and publishers dedicated to environmental writing in both countries and it seems both are readily comparable.[9] There can be little doubt that UK and US approaches have influenced and continue to influence one another. Yet a number of factors have made these approaches diverge, including geography, influence, marketplace (both commercial and institutional) and the emergence of the 'new nature writing' in the United Kingdom. Understandably, these differences influence the kind of instruction given in the classroom.

With place occupying such a significant role in writing about the environment, the consequences of *where* these approaches come from cannot be ignored.[10]

Compared to the wild, expansive landscapes of America, the landscapes of the British Isles have obviously been manipulated and managed by centuries of civilization. Reflecting on the difference, John Burroughs wrote that '[William] Wordsworth never knew the wild as we know it in this country – the pitilessly savage and rebellious ... but he knew the sylvan, the pastoral, the rustic-human, as we cannot know them' ([1922] 2016: 131). Is it possible, then, for students exploring British environments to undertake a 'retreat narrative', often deemed an American form in which a first-person narrator immerses herself in the wild? (Roorda 2008). After all, students are likely to encounter dog-walkers, farmers and the encroachments of new suburbs. The populated lands of the British Isles afford a populated environmental writing – from the conversations recorded in William Barnes's Dorset dialect poetry to John Clare's poems protesting enclosure. And yet, as I will discuss in Chapter 1, the search for wilderness perseveres in these inhabited and managed lands through what Jeremy Hooker has termed 'ditch vision' in which 'the bounded is necessarily the way into the unbounded, the wild' (2017: 66).[11]

Alongside place, the question of literary history is also important because as the tradition of writing about the environment in America continued apace, the tradition began to dwindle in the United Kingdom. Anna Stenning and Terry Gifford suggest that this falling-off occurring in the 'mid-to-late twentieth century [was] perhaps due in part to critical association with sentimental escapism, or a lack of philosophical sophistication' (2013: 1). Richard Kerridge expands discussion on this matter, drawing attention to the way environmental writing generated much suspicion in the inter-war period because of its association with 'a nostalgic conservative politics' (2012: 137). Anticipating discussion that follows on teaching ecocriticism, Greg Garrard also makes the point that the 'intermittent misogyny and authoritarianism [of D.H. Lawrence] combined with the fascism of figures such as nature writer Henry Williamson to ensure the marginalization of the environment in literary studies – even as it grew in popular and political significance – for at least two decades' (2007: 362). Robert Macfarlane laments the fact that while the US literary press have treated poets and non-fiction writers such as Barry Lopez, Gary Snyder and Annie Dillard 'midway between celebrities and shamans', the United Kingdom has seen a 'withering away' of such writing (2003). This hiatus in terms of tradition presents itself most obviously in UK curricula: with the exception of Gilbert White, J. A. Baker and of course the 'new nature writing', the texts that students are expected to read are often chiefly by the same American writers as listed by Macfarlane.

The unfashionability of such writing in the United Kingdom clearly contributed to the late development of environmental writing pedagogy in British institutions. Other reasons also present themselves. Whereas the United States saw its first creative writing programme in 1903 in the form of Iowa's Writing Workshop, the United Kingdom took another seventy years to offer its first course at the University of East Anglia.[12] Similarly important are the differing positions of environmental education within universities in the United states and the United Kingdom: the former having a plenitude of 'green universities' that, operating like small liberal arts schools, offer green curricula, while the latter has only one such institution, Schumacher College. It is unsurprising, then, that the early environmental writing pedagogy was primarily an American phenomenon. It is difficult to pin down any particular examples in the United Kingdom except, perhaps, for Ted Hughes's encouragement of animal perspective and landscape writing for children in *Poetry in the Making* in 1967 and the fact that Hughes's work was very widely used in secondary education. And yet, in the late twentieth century, interest in environmental writing was growing in Britain. In its treatment of Romantic literature, Jonathan Bate's *Romantic Ecology* (1991) appears the British counterpart to Buell's focus on Transcendentalist texts in his landmark *Environmental Imagination* (1995). Kate Soper's *What Is Nature?*, published in 1995, as well as Terry Gifford's *Green Voices*, of the same year, in many ways suggest an anticipation of ecocriticism's 'second-wave' given their critiques of hegemonic ideologies concerning the natural world.

With these challenges to conventional understandings of nature came a new climate that revived environmental writing in the United Kingdom. In 2008, the esteemed British magazine *Granta* heralded the arrival of the 'new nature writing'. Among its defining features were a keen interest in man-made environments and responsiveness to ecological threat. Docklands, car parks and cancer biopsies all became relevant subjects, with writers such as Kathleen Jamie and Robert Macfarlane leading the way. Universities in the United Kingdom had already begun to teach ecocriticism (one of the first examples being Richard Kerridge's 'Writing an Environmental Crisis' undergraduate module at Bath Spa University in 1992), but a more creatively focused pedagogy emerged later, partly in response to the commercial success of the 'new nature writing'. In many cases modules and courses have materialized (and continue to do so) in direct response. Programme leader James Canton describes how the 'Wild Writing' Master's course at the University of Essex deliberately 'aimed to recognize that shift in nature writing', establishing itself a year after the publication of the *Granta* special issue (2018). However, a question haunts the 'new nature writing': is it really 'new'? According to Jason Cowley's editorial in *Granta*, the shift is marked by its 'experiment in forms: the field report, the essay, the memoir, the travelogue' and its 'voice-driven' quality (2008). Yet, doesn't 'the field report' echo much of what has already been discussed in terms of non-fiction, natural history and the role of science in writing about the environment? Can a 'voice-driven' approach be described as 'new' when teachers often give their students Thoreau's writing as an exemplary model of such?

Differences between US and UK approaches clearly exist, but in spite of them parallels prevail. This dynamic seems set to continue. Although the term 'new nature writing' is used primarily in the British literary world, and refers to a specifically British resurgence of the genre, the criteria that define the 'newness' are in use elsewhere. In her 2010 article, 'Not Your Grandfather's Nature Writing', Andrea Nolan describes how many American journals such as *Orion* have taken up similar ideas. Although texts from the United States frequently make up Britain's historical shortfall of environmental writing on courses in the United Kingdom, the recognition of 'new nature writing' in America finds that such influence is reciprocated. US and UK perspectives contrast in important ways, and their pedagogical approaches sometimes differ, but there is much to compare in terms of instruction concerning bioregional attention, narrative voice and questions about ethical representation. Pedagogy on either side of the Atlantic encounters the tension between scientific empiricism and the wayward creative imagination that, I shall argue, prompts the need for a new ecocritical pedagogy.

A new ecocritical pedagogy

In the following chapters, I investigate recurrent instructions in environmental writing pedagogy by asking three key questions. Firstly, what has influenced these instructions? Secondly, what argument do these instructions communicate? Thirdly, how might these instructions impede or obstruct other forms of expression? By comparing pedagogical instruction to innovative departures in ecocriticism, each chapter develops new techniques for stimulating deeper environmental thought in students. The fact that canonical works of environmental literature such as Thoreau's *Walden* frequently inform the advice given by teachers suggests that the first place to begin rethinking pedagogy is the reading list. Which literary models can illustrate a new ecocritical pedagogy in which aesthetic conventions are challenged? In answering this question, I shift the focus from non-fiction, which frequently dominates current curricula, to poetry.

When the course title refers to 'nature writing', the expectation is often that the writing will be non-fiction: a lineage from White and Thoreau, through Carson, to contemporary practitioners of the genre. However, reflecting on the place of 'nature writing' for *The Guardian*, Robert Macfarlane (2015a) moves from discussing non-fiction writers to poets without qualification. Similarly, Jason Cowley, when he defines the 'new nature writing' in *Granta*, includes poets such as Seamus Heaney and Sean O'Brien. Despite this flexibility in definitions of the genre, the relevant pedagogy regularly gives preference to non-fiction even when the titles of courses would seem to move away from the term 'nature writing' to suggest a more inclusive approach (for example, 'Wild Writing' and 'Creative Writing and Environment'). Given the fact that both US and UK courses frequently allow students to write poetry as part of their assignments makes this disparity even more impracticable. Why do Annie Dillard and Richard Mabey appear more frequently on course materials than A. R. Ammons or Alice Oswald? How can pedagogy be invigorated by poetry's inclusion?

From the Romantics to the present-day work that is sometimes called 'ecopoetry', the importance of poetry in the history and practice of environmental literature can scarcely be doubted. It still, however, has a hard time competing with the commercial success of non-fiction works associated with 'new nature writing': an issue that is, of course, reflected by the fact that prose generally sells better than poetry. Tutors designing their courses to reflect this commercial success and encourage students to seek it may well overlook poetry. At the University of Warwick, Jonathan Skinner leads an undergraduate module, 'Ecopoetics', with a reading list that includes many American avant-garde poets, reflecting the journal, also titled *ecopoetics*, he founded in 2001. This kind of focus is, however, quite unusual. Rather than poetry leading an environmental writing course, it is more common for poetry to be one focus alongside non-fiction and fiction. Even then, we might ask whether the focus on non-fiction might dominate. I referred earlier in my discussion to the ecocritic, Dana Phillips, who criticized early ecocritics for their approach, which resembled that of 'an umpire's role' (2003: 163). Phillips's comment speaks to pedagogical approaches in which, at least in some instances, there is a risk of reading and valuing poetry for its non-fictional content. In 'Ecosystems of Meaning in Robert Frost's "Spring Pools"' (2006), for example, John Elder partners with a biologist, Glenn Adelson, to produce a reading of Frost's poem that shows how the poem is answerable to ecological fact. Although the authors are careful to explain the relevance of this reading in the light of Frost's relationship to science, they go on to advocate, in a rather troubling manner, their form of reading as an advanced model to be applied to works by other poets.

The tension between literalness and literariness that I have been discussing could well be articulated as a tension between non-fiction and poetry. A search for moral clarity and a fear of fantasy and sentimentality arise from the need to incorporate a scientific perspective that we have seen in early ecocriticism and the pedagogies that were associated with it. This has created an appetite for objective fact and thus a predilection for non-fiction. John A. Murray reminds his students of 'the importance of eliminating half-truths in thought and writing', but poetry sometimes goes by another rule altogether, that of Emily Dickinson's famous line 'Tell all the Truth but tell it slant' ([1868] 1975). And yet, as I will set out to demonstrate, poetry's capacity for 'literariness', manifested through, say, perspective-taking, word play and figurative language, is not a risk but an opportunity to challenge and enrich perception and expression. Through my close readings of twentieth- and twenty-first-century poets – many of whom are not usually considered ecopoets – I hope to demonstrate the value of looking beyond the literary canon often presented through pedagogy. I have selected the poets included in this book because of their self-reflexive stance towards their own representations, and I shall argue that they provide compelling creative models that help introduce a new ecocritical approach to the teaching of environmental writing.

'I went to the woods because I wanted to live deliberately', explains Thoreau in *Walden* ([1854] 2008: 83). *Walden* is often seen, especially in the United States, as the originating text of the environmental writing tradition, and much pedagogical instruction attempts to follow the spirit of that declaration. In Chapter 1, I will investigate the ethical imperatives that are often involved in place-based education in the United States and United Kingdom. I will do this by examining the exercises frequently given to students concerning species identification, tree shrines, map-making and personal memory. Such approaches are clearly valuable in creating a connection with the local, but I go on to question their limitations in the light of Ursula Heise's influential ecocritical argument about the need for perception to be global as well as local. My close readings of Juliana Spahr's experimentalist poetry serve as models for such alternative strategies. A global responsibility lies at the core of Spahr's work. She represents this responsibility in surprisingly intimate forms, demonstrating a poetics that finds the local within the global and vice versa. My analysis of *This Connection of Everyone with Lungs* (2005) reimagines pedagogical map-making exercises on a global scale, while my approach to *Well Then There Now* (2011), which considers webs of connection and causality in the context of colonization, draws attention to particular techniques for the development of an ecocritical approach to environmental writing. As with each chapter in this book, Chapter 1 concludes by proposing a series of new pedagogical exercises involving personal journals, translation and metaphor relevant for students working in a range of forms.[13]

For creating a connection with place, a first-person narrator is often deemed essential. Teachers will often encourage students to use a personal perspective in order to complement scientific content. Consequently, in Chapter 2 I explore the frequent advice given to students to use the first-person in order to convey personal relationships with environments that often extend to spiritual epiphany and, conversely, the fact that many teachers, especially in the United Kingdom, caution their students as to the egoistic risk of writing about the environment through the self. This caution arises again in pedagogical views on polemic. Questioning whether the 'I-me-my-voice' really is 'the voice of choice for nature narration' as David Petersen believes (2001: 99), the chapter turns to Rob Nixon's ecocritical argument in *Slow Violence* (2011). Nixon conveys the limitations of writing from the self by emphasizing the need to look beyond the here and now in order to conceive of ecological change. My close readings of poems by Jorie Graham aim to provide a set of models for the pedagogical use of Nixon's ecocritical thought. A reading of Graham's *Never* (2002) reveals the tensions created by the 'I', in contrast to the 'eye', while in *Sea Change* (2008) and *PLACE* (2012), I examine her projections into future environments. Through these close readings I propose new pedagogical guidance for taking the perspective of others, diminishing the risk of egoistic writing and raising awareness of important ecological changes that occur on time scales greater than our own.

Chapter 3 develops my discussion of perspective-taking. To this end, I examine anthropomorphic approaches to non-human animals and inanimate materials. Teachers often warn students against anthropomorphism, in the fear that the results will be whimsical or representative of appropriative behaviours. In this chapter, however, I argue that it is possible to deploy anthropomorphism's attribution of likeness as a connective device with which to explore differences between humans and non-humans. Influential arguments in ecocriticism help to develop the case: Donna Haraway's discussion of 'becoming-with' and 'non-mimetic sharing' (2008), and Timothy Morton's concept of the 'strange stranger' (2010a). Haraway and Morton develop these ideas to suggest that intimacy and otherness may be experienced concomitantly. I find creative examples in Les Murray's poems in *Translations from the Natural World* (1993), which explore animal experience through attempting animal language. In the second half of this chapter, poems by Roy Fisher are shown to explore agencies belonging to urban inanimate matter. These readings, supported by ecocriticism and new materialist thought, point to the possibility of an ethical anthropomorphism that pedagogy can explore through exercises that range from intertextuality to psychogeography and cross-genre forms.

Chapter 4 takes an in-depth look at the importance given to natural history in environmental writing courses and the resulting preference for scientific language and distrust of figurative language. It exposes the seeming binary in which fact is associated with accuracy and honesty, whereas metaphor is associated with abstraction and the ego. Drawing on ecocritical arguments by David Abram concerning language, materiality and sensuality, I demonstrate how these ethics concerning literary representation may be reconsidered. I give examples of how scientific languages can be problematically reductive, and how, conversely, metaphor conceives of environmental diversity. My close readings of Charles Tomlinson's poems serve as a creative intermediary between pedagogy and ecocriticism, showing how this poet initially prioritized objective accounts of the world before recognizing that these accounts could not do justice to the world's 'facets of copiousness' ('The Art of Poetry', 1966: 4). These readings illuminate the way in which experiential engagements with environments can be enhanced by metaphor. To help students put these ideas into practice, I conclude the chapter with a series of suggested exercises involving etymologies and naming, found poetry and erasure.

The final chapter turns to consider pedagogical calls for authenticity. Authenticity is a difficult term to pin down, but in the context of environmental writing and the examples I discuss, it appears synonymous with terms such as 'accuracy' and 'truth'. An authentic description of the environment, I argue, often attempts to dissolve the boundary between art and non-art. As the desire for textual authenticity demonstrates parallels with outdated and problematic ideas concerning literary realism, it demands the need for alternative thought. As I show, ecocritics who have argued against the value of mimetic strategies in literature are crucial in developing pedagogy. I employ their thought here to show how students may productively reflect on the relationship between language and environment. This chapter, then, looks to Kate Rigby's theory of 'negative ecopoetics' (2004a) in order to replace the idea of 'authenticity' with 'unsayability', and to Timothy Morton's proposal of 'radical kitsch' (2007). The latter provides insight into the ways in which texts deliberately invalidate themselves in order to provoke recognition that the reality of environments lies beyond language. My close readings of Don McKay and Jen Hadfield demonstrate how deliberately forced and often funny anthropocentric representations can function self-reflexively. In this vein, I suggest exercises to productively destabilize voice and place within writing, and draw attention to fruitful ways of using meta-textual techniques, cuteness and cliché.

My research has included a critical survey of 'how to' guides to environmental writing, and an extensive set of interviews with teachers, the scope of which is important to explain. The initial step was to send an invitation to teachers via the ASLE mailing list, asking for relevant syllabi. This international mailing list provided a good initial picture of environmental writing in higher education, particularly in the United States, and I was able to hold Skype interviews with teachers of environmental writing courses at University of Iowa State, and Chatham University, Pittsburgh. I also experienced a four-week class-shadowing period at Green Mountain College, Vermont which included interviews at Green Mountain College and at Middlebury College, Vermont. In the United Kingdom, I benefitted from direct communication with teachers leading postgraduate courses and undergraduate modules dedicated to environmental writing. I carried out interviews with teachers at Royal Holloway (University of London), Manchester Metropolitan University, Bath Spa University, Swansea University, University of Warwick, Newman University, University of Exeter and University of Essex: at the latter two I also class-shadowed.[14] Keen to reflect the fact that the teaching of environmental writing is not an exclusively academic practice, I also conducted interviews with teachers outside higher education who frequently deliver short courses on the subject. During the writing of this book, teachers have moved universities, courses have been handed over, and, unfortunately in the case of at least one example, dropped from the curriculum altogether. Of course, elsewhere new modules and programmes in environmental writing have also sprung up or been reinstated. Consequently, this book is not, and could never be, exhaustive, but what I hope to illuminate through the survey I have made are the principal cultures that often emerge from this relatively recent pedagogical development, a development so new that it has received no critical reflection until now.

If environmental writing is to continue developing as a rich and diverse practice, if it is to keep pace with the ecological challenges of the present and the future, a flexible, self-reflexive and imaginative approach is needed. This book shows how pedagogy can borrow from ecocritical theory in order to respond to this need. I hope to demonstrate that ecocritical argument has the capacity to enrich students' understanding of environments and of the representational opportunities available to them. Through readings of poets who display a flexible, self-reflexive and imaginative approach themselves, the new ecocritical pedagogy that emerges from this study aims to stimulate fresh ideas for thinking and writing about the environment and provides vital assistance to students experimenting in a range of literary forms.

1

'Where you are': Place writing

'Become a monomaniac. Study one thing – one species, one acre of ground, one river, one tree – until it has become either a foreign country to you (fabulously strange) or one of the things you understand best in the whole world (fabulously familiar)', advises Robert Macfarlane in an article entitled 'How to Be a Nature Writer' (2011). Writing about particular places – one garden, 'one acre of ground', one landscape – has become such an established practice that 'place writing' has become a frequent phrase with which to title modules and classes in environmental writing. Yet, as Macfarlane asserts elsewhere while discussing the need to broaden the voices associated with the genre, 'there is no one true way of writing about nature and place. The tradition of such literature has always been ... passionate, pluriform and essential' (2003). While undoubtedly 'there is no one true way', recurring pedagogical prescriptions explored in this chapter suggest particular tendencies in teachers' advice on how to write about place. As I go on to discuss, place is frequently synonymous with 'the local' for many teachers, owing, in part, to particular developments in the environmental movement. Informed by Ursula Heise's ecocritical perspectives on globalization, I intend to show that it is place itself that needs to be understood as 'pluriform' in order for writing to follow suit. It is important to note that my argument does not intend to replace current pedagogical practices, but to extend them by proposing a self-reflexive, self-questioning approach to place that underlines connections between the local and the global.

The popularity of place writing that zooms in to study the details of one particular landscape corresponds to the popularity of place-based environmental movements. Signs of such are not difficult to find: a weekly shop or meal out suggests how commercially significant locally sourced produce has become. The proliferation of farmers' markets in towns and cities similarly speaks of a growing engagement with the local (though whether this is more a lifestyle or environmental movement is less easy to determine). Rejecting political boundaries associated with counties, cities and nations for boundaries that depend on differing ecosystems, the bioregional school of thought has – and continues to – advocate investment in the local. Empowering communities towards sustainable action often involving grass-roots activism, bioregionalism has introduced positive action to daily routines. Gaining ground in 1970s America, bioregional concepts have influenced what has come to be known as place-based education: an educational philosophy that fosters learning that is invested in the local. Championed by John Elder who, in a series published by the Orion Society, described his desire for students to experience 'a perceptual process of discovery, celebration, and community', place-based pedagogies continue to be present in environmental writing classes today with much the same intention (1998: 15).

'I went to the woods because I wanted to live deliberately', writes Henry David Thoreau in a paragraph of *Walden*: a text that has become imperative to many discussions of place writing and environmental writing more broadly ([1854], 2008: 83).[1] His two years spent in Walden Woods, Massachusetts, were an opportunity 'to front only the facts of life, and see if I could not learn what it had to teach' (ibid.). Influential examples of environmental writing published prior to, and during, developments in pedagogy underline attentiveness to localist perspectives of place. Aldo Leopold's *Sand County Almanac* (1949) that explores Sauk County, Wisconsin and Annie Dillard's *Pilgrim at Tinker Creek* (1974), detailing her encounters in Virginia's Blue Ridge Mountains, are two models frequently favoured by teachers alongside *Walden*. Such texts demonstrate the significance of close attention to one place: the comprehension of particular species, their part in the ecosystem, as well as the opportunity to observe seasonal change.[2] But of course, such work does more. Referring to Thoreau's *Walden* as a guiding model, Dillard's project has a distinct Transcendentalist flavour as it attempts 'to discover at least *where* it is that we have been so startlingly set down, if we can't learn why' (1974: 14). Provoking questions of a spiritual nature, Dillard's attention to Tinker Creek affords a meditation on consciousness and perception. Concentrating on one place permits Dillard to see minute details otherwise overlooked: field mice cutting grass stems to reach grain, the oval egg cases that the praying mantis entrusts to the weeds. As her more self-reflexive statements explain, 'The lover can see, and the knowledgeable' (ibid.: 20). Following Dillard's subtle but persuasive examples, one might begin to think that lacking a close relationship to place results in losing our powers of perception which, borrowing Elder's words, cannot be dissociated from experiences of celebration and discovery in an environment.

Sheryl St Germain, who teaches on Chatham University's Master of Fine Arts in Environmental Creative Writing in Pittsburgh, describes how her class is a way of 'introducing people to pay attention to where they are' (2014a). As a strategy of engaging with local place, she asks her students to keep weekly blogs that 'identify where they are: what are the trees? What are the animals? What are the birds?' (ibid.). It might be said that the identification of species has long been understood as a prerequisite to *any* environmental engagement – an opportunity to test a student's ecoliteracy. However, concerning these educators' approaches to place, the ability to differentiate between species more specifically represents an engagement with the local in a way that enacts Dillard's equation between place-based study and perception. St Germain's argument is, after all, similar to that of Allison B. Wallace who, in 'The Place of Drawing in Place Journaling', claims that identifying species through field-guides creates '*placed*' students (2012: 102). Through both writing and drawing, Wallace aims 'to inspire in students a desire to know more about our local biome ... to give them ways to sharpen their powers of perception' (ibid.: 101). As she explains, 'Students must select a specific place on campus that they will visit at least once every week for at least thirty minutes at a time, about which they will compile a "place journal"' (ibid.). While this cues students to engage their senses, Wallace, like St Germain, suggests that an emphasis upon identification remains crucial to fostering consciousness about place: 'A student who goes from saying "bird" to "starling" or "towhee" within a few weeks is already a more attentive, more *placed* student than she was at the start of the course' (ibid.: 102).

Katherine R. Chandler appears less concerned with identifying species to define place in her essay, 'Can't See the Forest or the Trees', and more interested in highlighting a personal relationship with place. As part of her teaching that aims to increase student awareness of their surroundings, Chandler writes 'One activity I now require is for students to adopt a tree as their "tree shrine"' (2003: 114). Although she explains that this term originates with Thoreau's description of particular trees that, in his words, 'were the shrines I visited both summer and winter', Chandler's choice of vocabulary '*adopt* a tree' suggests a stronger sense of stewardship and responsibility (ibid., emphasis added). Once again advising students to keep an ongoing journal, she explains how a relationship is fostered with place as students return to that tree 'For the whole semester' and write about their experiences (ibid.). Comparable understandings of place-based pedagogy as 'romantic pedagogy' – a term Elder uses to describe 'an approach to education that begins with love' (1998: 12) – are evident in the advice given by Ann and Susan Zwinger (2008). A deeply sensual appreciation of wild places, according to the authors, will trigger emotion and thus create memories that will serve to prompt behavioural change.

The fact that Britain lacks the pristine wilderness at the heart of much American writing would seem to suggest differences between US and UK understandings of place and thus place writing. Though paralleling much of America's environmental movement and its encouragement of various localisms, an emphasis on social community emerges from British endeavours that appears distinct. One project led by the charity Common Ground, for example, revitalizes the idea of Parish Maps in order to generate awareness of distinguishable local features. Britain's landscapes are peopled: palimpsests of agricultural industry and habitation. Teaching at Swansea University, Jon Gower communicates this characteristic as he takes his students to Kenfig National Nature Reserve and explains that the key to understanding and appreciating the site is 'in all the people you bump into' (2013). The social aspect of Gower's instruction echoes W. J. Keith, who, nearly fifty years ago, suggested that British writers are often concerned with the countryside and the lives of its inhabitants and possess an 'inveterate suspicion of metaphysics' (1975: 138).

Yet, a solitary, more contemplative engagement with the environment remains in British pedagogy. Echoing the 'retreat narrative' (Roorda 1998) that might be contextualized by Transcendentalism, Gower recalls how a particular student at Kenfig returns to a grassy tussock to sit quietly and write on her own, and reflects on how this Thoreauvian practice 'reaps rewards' (2013).[3] Mark Cocker's *Crow Country* (2008), which studies 'one acre of ground, one species' in Norfolk's Yare Valley and which prompts a field-trip to the Yare Valley on the course at the University of Essex, provides further example. At once as factually rich as Gilbert White's *Natural History of Selborne* in its scrupulous record of rooks, *Crow Country* might, as Dillard consciously notes of her own work, be read as 'a meteorological journal of the mind' in the spirit of *Walden* (1974: 13). After all, Cocker's attachment to place is simultaneously a personal narrative of discovery. Echoing Dillard, Cocker finds that 'enquiring becomes a way of loving'; that 'a reduction of the whole sunlit panorama to a simple vista' can be 'deeply restorative', generating empathy and wisdom (2008: 186). The assertion that metaphysics does not come so easily to British writers is, then, open to question.

The differing scales of British and American landscapes has led Jeremy Hooker to suggest that many British writers demonstrate 'ditch vision' in their portrayals of environments (2017). Rather than grand expanses, this approach studies microcosms of the wild in landscapes otherwise deemed increasingly urban.

Hooker takes his lead from Richard Jefferies who in 'The Pageant of Summer' finds a ditch overflowing with 'Green rushes, long and thick … the white pollen of early grasses … hawthorn boughs … briars … buds' ([1884] 2011: 41–2). The observation leads him to remark, 'So much greater is this green and common rush than all the Alps' (ibid.: 43). Enthusiasm for the overlap between the 'wild' and the human reappears in Richard Mabey's *The Unofficial Countryside* (1973) in which Mabey writes about disused factories, docklands and canals, and in *Edgelands* (2011), in which Paul Farley and Michael Symmons Roberts explore motorways and retail parks. In some cases, such texts have influenced teachers' guidance on how to write about place to interesting effect. David Cooper who teaches on the MFA in Place Writing at Manchester Metropolitan University encourages his students to think about their urban surroundings and sets *Edgelands* as course reading. In contrast to the strategies described above involving tree shrines or even Gower's nature reserve, Cooper describes how one of his students focused on Manchester Airport. Interviewing staff in Air Traffic Control and airport restaurants, the student tussles with the idea of the airport as a 'meaningful' place and as a 'non-place' in her subsequent essay (2018). Although approached with a local perspective, the concept of place becomes something of a paradox. Not only is an airport a potentially indistinguishable place given how one airport is much like another, it also serves as a kind of intermediary place for travel to other, more significant places.

The idea that place might be a relatively fluid or negotiable concept also comes into Stephen Moss's teaching at Bath Spa University. The fact that Moss's designed MA is in both Travel and Nature Writing and is structured as a series of residentials (in Wiltshire, Gloucestershire and Sella, Spain) enables an alternative perspective to those courses that approach place with a localist perspective. The assignment briefs that Moss gives to his students include 'The Meaning of Nationality' (2018c). He asks students to 'consider the fixed and fluid nature of what is means to be a particular nationality or mix of nationalities, especially in the light of current events. This can relate to the concept of nationality and identity in nature as well as the most straightforward idea of nationality in people/society' (ibid.). This spurs thought as to how place might be embodied (or not) by the writer through her sense of belonging. It is interesting that Moss proposes that this self-reflexive study might 'arise from your experience on a trip abroad', implying that one might see their attachment to place differently when situated in a foreign location (ibid.).

Given the commitment many teachers feel to a bioregional ethic, Moss's sampling of different landscapes through the residential structure of the course – and its consequent querying of identity and place-attachment – is rare. Place – and the right to represent it – is often fiercely guarded. In contrast to the value Moss seems to find in travel, Jim Perrin caustically names the 'new nature writers' 'day-trippers' because of the fact that they often hail from metropolitan cities (2014a).[4] A kind of nativist sentiment seems to feature in his belief that such writing 'rings false', whereas, supposedly, writers who inhabit these rural landscapes generate more 'authentic' depictions (ibid.). We might ask how long a writer must live in a landscape before she is qualified to write about it? Two months? Two decades? These questions become more troublesome when we consider them in the context of courses in environmental writing. Teaching at Essex University, James Canton takes a 'regional approach' that draws on the rich literary tradition of East Anglia to embed his students in local environments in a way that Perrin would surely approve of. However, as students discuss their need to learn the names of birds to better appreciate the fens, one international student questions the purpose of the exercise given that, after graduating, she will leave the United Kingdom (2013).

The student's comment raises the issue of the globalized nature of higher education, but, we also might see it raising specific questions over what place writing might be in a time of widespread globalization that influences life on a day-to-day basis. Surely the question of 'where you are' is not as simple as it first seems. Wallace's identification of a bird as representative of place proves problematic in ways that usher in connections between the local and the global: is the plant that a student notes in her 'place journal' a native plant? Where does a student draw a line between their place and other places? Why? Which environmental interactions challenge this boundary? Taking an ecocritical, post-pastoral perspective on the Lake District, Terry Gifford begins to trouble place-based boundaries as he reveals the apparent pristine site to be 'constructed to provide drinking water for Manchester' as one of a few exercises on reconsidering place (2003: 123–4). Perhaps most relevant to the questions posed, in her exercises on place writing SueEllen Campbell meditates upon the invisible factors affecting specific places: 'Things like radioactive wastes … the effects of vanished ice ages, distant wars' (2006: 87). Her intention, after all, is to prompt her students to contemplate the 'layered' quality of place. As noted in my Introduction, the most promising example comes via James Engelhardt and Jeremy Schraffenberger's assertion that 'if a student writes about dandelions dotting her lawn, she would then research how the plant likely arrived in North America with the English settlers on the Mayflower' (2015: 499). The authors also note the value of researching etymologies in order to make similar connections.

How might pursuing these pedagogical perspectives lead students not to thinking of their chosen place *like* 'a foreign country' because of its strange detail (as Macfarlane suggests), but to an awareness of how their place is associated with other countries given its inevitable ties with the rest of the world? Building on Moss's self-reflexive questioning of identity, I wish to suggest a pedagogy that develops existing strategies on the local with new strategies on the global in order to discover that place is an entangled concept; that one representation of place is necessarily a representation of other places. William Blake saw 'a World in a Grain of Sand' ([1863] 2008: 1). Rachel Carson elaborated, 'In every outthrust headland, in every curving beach, in every grain of sand there is the story of the earth' ([1958] 1999: 114). When Annie Dillard contemplates how Spring moves north 'at sixteen miles a day', her place-based focus expands to imagine 'Caribou straggle across the tundra … Somewhere, people in airplanes are watching the sunset … In the montana in Peru, on the rain-forested slopes of the Andes, a woman kneels … Along estuary banks of tidal rivers all over the world, snails in black clusters like currants' (1974: 99). Dillard's arc of thought considers not only the connection between neighbouring continents, but also of connections across the world. Similarly, at the conclusion of *Crow Country*, Cocker defends his study of one species as a hymn to ecology: illustrating the principle 'that everything is connected to everything else' (2008: 187). The popular environmental mantra to 'think global, act local' proves that the connection between scales is nothing new. However, there is perhaps more to be explored that counters the romantic quality of these examples by engaging with the carbon released from Dillard's airplane and, as noted by Schraffenberger, colonial exploration.

In the survey I have carried out, teachers of environmental writing pedagogy have, almost without exception, expressed the hope that their students will finish the course or module with a greater environmental consciousness. Like Chandler's instruction to 'adopt' a tree, St Germain believes that her exercise makes students 'charged for being responsible for that place' (2014a). Understanding that their teaching methods underline place-attachment, there is a hope that students will become stewards, conservationists, perhaps even spokespeople for their environments. It is here that a stronger articulation of the connections between the local and the global can be effective in enriching the kind of responsibility that these exercises aim to achieve. After all, if a local river becomes a student's way of engaging with place, and the hope is for her to become responsible for that river, shouldn't she also think beyond what is in front of her, and consider environments both upriver and downriver? Wallace believes that her exercises on place contribute to the attitudes of 'tomorrow's caretakers of the world' (2012: 103). A reconceptualization of place that makes obvious its connections to other places is needed if Wallace's ambitious assertion is to hold strong. This strategic shift appears particularly necessary given that teachers aim to engage their students with environmental issues that characteristically cross local and global frames. Responding to whether he intends to foster an awareness of human impact on the environment in his classes, Jon Gower states simply, 'I think that's all of it' and refers to the plastic-filled strand line on Kenfig's shore (2013). Though choosing not to draw student attention to the debris, Gower's awareness of such problems as 'huge swathes of the ocean now covered in plastic' provides further opportunity of seeing the global in the local (ibid.).

When it comes to the field of ecocriticism, the first popular texts held local conceptions of place in high esteem: not only do many texts focus on a writer's attachment to place, they also open with the ecocritic describing his or her environs. 'As I write this, I am sitting on the seashore', Timothy Morton mocks, 'The gentle sound of waves lapping against my deck chair coincides with the sound of my fingers typing away at the laptop' (2007: 29). Morton, heralding progress in ecocritical thought, suggests the inherent failure in such authorial attempts to conjure place as immediately and unquestionably 'here'. Through her concept of 'Shadow Places' Val Plumwood similarly dismisses what she calls 'literary rhapsody about nice places, or about nice times (epiphanies) in nice places' (2008: 139). Troubling such perspectives, she describes how our 'ecological footprint' implicates us in countless elsewheres (ibid.). Plumwood's commitment to a 'critical bioregionalism' (ibid.: 140), informed by globalization and an environmental justice perspective, sets a precedent of sorts to Ursula Heise's landmark work, *Sense of Place and Sense of Planet*, which, as its title suggests, signals a movement towards global scales and systems. Corresponding to the analysis of current pedagogical strategies above, Heise identifies how place is associated with 'spatial closeness, cognitive understanding, emotional attachment, and an ethic of responsibility and "care"', and draws a history of such dominant thought (2008: 33). Indeed, concerns about the possible shortcomings of local conceptualizations of place underpin Heise's approach as she suggests there has been an 'excessive investment in the local' that has reached fetishistic proportions (ibid.: 10). Drawing upon influential studies in anthropology and sociology that explore the complex and seemingly contradictory relations between identity and place through concepts such as 'transnationalism' and 'cosmopolitanism', Heise proposes an ecocritical lesson in 'eco-cosmopolitanism'.

Heise's 'eco-cosmopolitanism' considers how environmental commitment needs to be revised in the context of globalization. Her critique of current environmental discourse and its emphasis upon the local touches upon the limitations of pedagogy as she quotes Joan Hamilton's account of a class taught by professor and poet Robert Hass.

> On a balmy September afternoon, about a hundred students at one of the finest public universities in the nation are gathered under a sprawling Monterey pine. 'What kind of tree is this?' a professor asks. Silence. 'How many of you don't know any more than that it's a tree?' Most students raise their hands. They can converse knowledgeably about chlorofluorocarbons and the ozone hole, but most can't tell a pine from a fir, or even an oak. The professor is perturbed. 'I don't think we have a chance of changing our relationship to the natural world if you don't know what's around you', he says.
>
> (2008: 28; cites Hamilton)

As Heise concludes, an understanding of 'larger-scale ecological phenomena such as the depletion of the stratospheric ozone is dismissed here as too abstract a kind of knowledge', whereas, according to Hass, genuine ecological perception 'lies in the local' (ibid.). Yet, as she signals, an understanding of this larger scale is undeniably important. After all, such an understanding provides a significant angle to the pedagogical instruction to write about 'where you are'. Realizing the importance of the local, but also its increasing unhelpfulness on its own in view of global environmental issues, Heise proposes how eco-cosmopolitanism is 'an attempt to envision individuals and groups as part of planetary "imagined communities" of both human and nonhuman kinds' (ibid.: 61).

In her account of recent scholarship on place in global contexts, Heise reviews Mitchell Thomashow's recommendations for fostering 'biospheric perception' in *Bringing the Biosphere Home* (2002). With broad proposals that might be adapted to different disciplines, Thomashow's suggestions begin to problematize place. He questions the relevance of the local in view of students who have relocated to different states in the United States for their education, the unstable quality of place in terms of its temporal nature, and, to some extent, the entanglement of place with other places. Pursuing the latter, he advises such exercises as 'following a cloud around the world, tracing the origins of the air you breathe, tracking today's rain to a distant ocean' as a way of 'using place-based perceptual ecology to interpret the biosphere' (2002: 129). Conscious of the departures he makes, Heise is also rightly wary of Thomashow's reversion to the importance of place. Indeed, his proposal to trace the origins of the air you breathe concludes by stating that through such exercises 'you come to know your place', which would seem ironic if it didn't sound so sincere (ibid.).

Although making important progress by raising awareness of different scales of perception, Thomashow's recommended practice ultimately brings us back to the local in a romanticized manner that Heise believes is incongruent with a more 'pragmatic' perspective of globalization (2008: 41).

The possibilities for representing the global community Heise describes in *Sense of Place* are consequently examined through her refreshingly wide-ranging curation of sources. Visual media such as the Blue Marble image, made available by NASA, and the 'zooming techniques' of recent digital technologies such as Google Earth, go some way in connecting the vast disparity between local and global scales. With these strategies in mind, she goes on to discuss collage and montage as ways of superimposing different places upon one another: literary fragmentation in the science fiction genre as a tool to integrate different localities and imagine their future, and the potential of virtual networks as new sites for recognizing global connections. Her insightful analysis draws together otherwise unrelated matter from different genres in literature as well as art and film. These readings are complemented by pedagogical proposals outlined in her essay 'Developing a Sense of Planet: Ecocriticism and Globalisation' (2011). Here, Heise returns to the same visual materials as a foundation for student learning (the Blue Marble, Google Earth), but goes on to suggest travel narratives, on the basis that they afford an understanding of how 'ecological crises manifest themselves around the globe', (ibid.: 97).

Underlining Heise's approach in *Sense of Place* is her criticism of 'the ethic of proximity' in considering place, which 'relies on the assumption that genuine ethical commitments can only grow out of the lived immediacies of the local that constitute the core of one's authentic identity' (2008: 42). Explaining how her approach differs from previous ecocriticism and environmental thought more broadly, she states that identities are unstable, being 'at their core made up of mixtures, fragments, and dispersed allegiances' (ibid.: 43). Might there be a text that demonstrates methods with which to navigate away from the significance placed upon the local, which, as Thomashow and Heise agree, is disrupted by factors such as contemporary migration, and give new prominence to these dispersed allegiances? How might this afford engagements with places that are not 'natural', not abounding with species ready to be identified, but suburban or urban? How might certain literary forms and devices question identity and consequently allow an opportunity to study places other than our own immediate locale? To create a bridge between current environmental writing pedagogy and ecocritical pedagogy, creative strategies that question and expand a sense of place are needed. With Heise's emphasis on identity, what kind of text might invite readers to develop their understanding of place and realize their own global connections no matter where they find themselves?

Juliana Spahr, a poet, critic and editor from the United States, responds to political and environmental issues through a keen sense of global connection in her experimental writing. Concerned by the exclusivity arising from the importance placed upon the individual in contemporary Western society, Spahr's work demonstrates how apprehending connections between personal, local and global frames complicates our self-identity and identification of our surroundings to produce more informed approaches to being 'placed' in the world. Having studied under Charles Bernstein and Susan Howe at the State University of New York at Buffalo, Spahr's work reveals certain Language School traits. The influence of Modernism is clear in both Spahr's choice of subject and style: she echoes explorations of the local and the global in the context of nineteenth-century imperialism and draws upon the concerns of particular literary styles as symptomatic of imperialism, demonstrated, for example, by Gertrude Stein.[5] Spahr's pursuit of the complex entanglements of place through avant-garde poetics and confessional poetry, alongside experiments with metaphor, permit a sustained exploration of style and device that, following the subsequent close readings, I will develop into a series of prompts for students to reimagine place in their writing.

'We come into the world': Connections to the global

The question of how we self-identify – of how separated, or how connected we are with the rest of the world – compels Spahr's poetic practice. In an interview with the poet, Michael Boyko draws attention to her understanding of connection as he asks her about the 'complicated relationship' between the pronouns 'we' and 'I' in much of her work (2005b). Evoking the kind of spatial connections to be analysed, Spahr explains how her use of 'we' presents a global community and how 'becoming individuals, becoming distinct and disconnected, is part of the problem' (ibid.). Spahr's suggestion that an engagement with smaller scales has the potential to produce disconnection rather than connection has implications for the kinds of pedagogical approach I have discussed so far in terms of their emphasis on local place. Moreover, her comments anticipate the importance of perceiving global connections. Beginning with Spahr's use of pronouns prompts exploration into how the local might be connected to the global, in a manner that recalls Heise's interest in the 'zooming techniques' of Google Earth. As a way of developing current pedagogical proposals, these pronouns offer students a first step in interrogating the idea of 'what's around you'. Indeed, Spahr's description of 'we' as a 'global community' presents a whole of which the personal, local 'I' is a part. This speaks strongly to the subject of spatial connection as this 'I' that exists in any part of the world is, according to Spahr, connected to the rest of the world.

Spahr's poem 'Gentle Now, Don't Add to Heartache', collected in *Well Then There Now* (hereafter known as 'Gentle Now') illustrates her response to Boyko by playing with pronouns and their associations with different forms of self-identity. Formed of five sections, the poem begins with the line 'We come into the world' and describes how 'we' begin 'to move between the brown and the blue and the green of it' (2011: 124).[6] Focusing more narrowly, sections two and three of Spahr's poem then describe a stream.

> We came into the world at the edge of a stream.
> The stream had no name but it began from a spring and flowed down a
> hill into the Scioto that then flowed into the Ohio that then flowed into
> the Mississippi that then flowed into the Gulf of Mexico.
>
> (2011: 124)

Beginning like an origin myth with 'We come into the world' means that the scale of this stream is hard to pin down. As this stream is said to be 'a part of us and we were a part of the stream and we / were thus part of the rivers and thus part of the gulfs and the oceans' (ibid.), the mythic quality of the stream continues: the stream is a life-giving entity, at once a figurative and literal symbol for communality. Spahr moves from the metaphysical to the physical specifics of the stream as, through a smaller lens, she turns her attention to the sycamore trees along the banks and 'the long pendulous polygamous / racemes of its small green flowers' (ibid.: 127). By focusing in from the 'world' – its broad swathes of browns, blues and greens evoking Heise's reference to the Blue Marble image – Spahr attends to the parts that form the whole. 'We' are connected to entities at all scales: 'We' are 'part of the rivers and thus part of the gulfs and the oceans' and later, 'Our hearts took on the shape of whirligigs [beetles] swirling across the water' (ibid.: 125, 127). As Spahr explains in the interview with Boyko mentioned previously, ' "We" is humans and animals and plants ... I wanted everyone to be there in the poem. I wanted "we" to include those who read it' (2005b).

The stream becomes a pedagogical site for Spahr as she describes 'This is where we learned love and where we learned depth and / where we learned layers and where we learned connections / between layers' (2011: 126). The shifting of scale in the poem implies that such lessons on love and depth are likely to go beyond any one, fixed location. An 'emotional attachment, an ethic of responsibility and "care"' that Heise rightly identified and criticized in place-based environmentalist thought becomes more expansive in Spahr's poem. The utopian quality of Spahr's representation of a global community, or 'world citizenship' as described by Heise, might make the exercise seem unhelpfully idealistic. Yet, the nature of these connections begins to change in section four of the poem, and, as it does so, Spahr elaborates upon the potentially detrimental consequences of identifying at smaller scales. Beginning, 'It was not all long lines of connection and utopia', the stream becomes polluted and, as 'we' previously took on the stream's qualities and shapes, so we let in 'soda cans and we let in cigarette butts and we let in pink / tampon applicators' (ibid.: 130). As this pollution degrades the environment and creates the loss of certain species, the global community of 'we' disintegrates. Spahr writes with a new pronoun: 'I replaced what I knew of the stream with Lifestream Total / Cholesterol Test Packets, with Snuggle Emerald Stream Fabric / Softener Dryer Sheets' (ibid.: 132). The 'I' demonstrates a dislocation from the collective 'we'. With this comes distortion as natural entities are replaced by chemical products of the same name, upon which the 'I' appears dependent. At the conclusion, the 'I' has forgotten her connection to a wider non-human community. This environmentally destructive individualism is accentuated by the way attention turns away from the stream and towards one another. The detail and beauty first found in the environment can now only be found in 'each / other's breast, the folds of each other's elbows' (ibid.).

Spahr reverses such connections so that we are led from the personal towards the global in *This Connection of Everyone with Lungs* (2005a): a collection comprised of two long sequences that chart US political events between 2001 and 2003 (hereafter known as *This Connection*). Connection is explored slightly differently here: the expansiveness of the macrocosm is stressed, while its relation to the microcosm is understood to be paradoxically intimate. The poem that gives the collection its title is 'Poem Written after September 11, 2001'. Despite referring to the events of 9/11, Spahr only alludes to these events at the conclusion of the ten-page poem. Indeed, the poem concerns itself with building a series of connections from the local towards the global in order to show 'how connected we are' through the air that everyone breathes (ibid.: 9). This makes the later introduction of materials from the twin towers into the air – 'sulphur and sulphuric acid and titanium and nickel and minute silicon particles from pulverized glass and concrete' – all the more disturbing as it is suggested the materials have impact beyond local and even national environs (ibid.: 10). Unlike 'Gentle Now' that opened with the world, Spahr begins the poem at a very small scale.

> There are these things:
>
> cells, the movements of cells and the division of cells
>
> and then the general beating of circulation
>
> and hands, and body, and feet
>
> and skin that surrounds hands, body, feet.
>
> This is a shape,
>
> a shape of blood beating and cells dividing.
>
> (2005a: 3)

Each of these 'things' is a part that represents the whole figure. Having created this supposedly human 'shape', Spahr continues the list

> But outside of this shape is space.
>
> There is space between the hands.
>
> There is space between the hands and space around the hands.
>
> There is space around the hands and space in the room.
>
> (ibid.: 4)

Although space quite literally dislocates the parts upon the page, the repetition in the lines and their increasing scale provokes connection. This connection is then heightened as Spahr states that 'this space goes in and out of everyone's bodies' (ibid.). Paradoxically, then, the parts become connected through space as 'everyone with lungs breathes the space in and out' (ibid.).

A synecdochic relationship between the part and the whole underpins this increasing scale in Spahr's poem that moves far beyond the notion of personal space. This increasing scale can only be represented through extensive quotation of the text:

> As everyone with lungs breathes the space between the hands and
> the space around the hands and the space of the room and the
> space of the building that surrounds the room in and out
>
> As everyone with lungs breathes the space between the hands and
> the space around the hands and the space of the room and the

space of the building that surrounds the room and the space of
the neighborhoods nearby in and out ...

As everyone with lungs breathes the space between the hands and
the space around the hands and the space of the room and the
space of the building that surrounds the room and the space of
the neighborhoods nearby and the space of the cities and the
space of the regions and the space of the nations and the space
of the continents and islands and the space of the oceans and
the space of the troposphere and the space of the stratosphere
and the space of the mesosphere in and out.

(ibid.: 5–8)

Evoking a child-like style of narration, Spahr's repetitive use of 'and' creates a chain of parts and wholes. Although the space of the room appears to be contained and isolated, it becomes a part of a greater whole; 'the space of the building'. Yet, juxtaposing this 'building' against the 'neighborhoods' recognizes yet another relation in which the building is just a part, and so on, until Spahr reaches the mesosphere. Such lengthy repetition mocks any common usage of the sentence: as has been noted by Christopher Arigo, reading the poem aloud leaves a reader breathless 'as if the scale of events and connections is too much to bear' (2008).

In making these connections, Spahr's work challenges the pedagogical emphasis upon place that often accompanies emphasis upon the personal narrative 'I' explored in the next chapter. An example of such teaching can be seen in St Germain's writing exercise entitled 'Map-Making' that aids her intention to introduce students to 'where they are' and foster responsibility for that place. Make a 'visual map of a place that is important to you, and where you've spent a lot of time', she instructs, emphasizing the need to map 'the emotional details ... where you experienced your first kiss, or buried your dog' (2014b).[7] The students are then expected to write a story or poem that follows the map. This strategy that attends to place through the personal 'I' clearly has the potential to develop feelings of care as it recognizes a personal investment in place. While it could be argued that memory-mapping activities like these aim for a kind of place-stewardship that might serve as a model to care for other places beyond a student's immediate environs, these connections are worth highlighting and clarifying so that a more complex sense of place can come to the fore. As a personal investment has the potential to neglect broader notions of community – such as those proposed by Spahr – such exercises foster an understanding of place that could, at its very worst, echo the irresponsible move from 'we' to 'I' that Spahr parodied in 'Gentle Now'. This is clearly not the intended outcome, but it remains a tension that deserves consideration. Could emphasizing personal investment in place, while not foregrounding its potential connection to other places, have the potential to foster a kind of NIMBYism in which environmental stewardship and more selfish attitudes to place become difficult to tell apart?

By thinking about the site of your first kiss, St Germain suggests a heartfelt engagement with the local, but 'emotional details' could, of course, include fear, anxiety and apathy. Is there a street or wooded park where students might feel uncomfortable on their own? How does one aspect of a student's place change at night? Though such questions might seem to compromise feelings of place-*attachment*, ignoring them altogether could risk a crude, incomplete map. The individualistic nature of the map-making exercise might similarly be reconsidered. How might that badly-lit street evoke different emotions in a woman, a man, a person of colour? How might the tranquil, unspoiled hill by the lake be viewed by a person with a disability compared to an able-bodied person? In a prompt on perspective, St Germain asks her students to 'experiment writing about the same place from different perspectives—that of a child's, an immigrant's, a tourist's, a native's etc.' which initiates reflection on more plural understandings of place (2014b). In *Environmental and Nature Writing*, Sean Prentiss and Joe Wilkins go a step further in providing a list of questions that aim to guide deeper understandings of place that include the following: 'What are the neighboring areas like? What are the politics of the area? Do you know the median income for your area? Do you know the racial makeup?' (2016: 64). Pursuing these enquiries has the potential to prompt reflection on place as multi-faceted, complex: sites of privilege and disadvantage. In moving beyond a personal viewpoint of place, such questions might be co-opted to initiate the kind of work undertaken by Spahr in which one's backyard is understood to be part of a larger community.

'Poem Written after September 11, 2001' is, to some degree, an attempt to see outside of the nation state at the time of the attack on the World Trade Centres, to remember connections between countries that might otherwise be compromised by fear and hostility. Moving between neighbourhoods to islands and the mesosphere, Spahr shows how the places that educators ask their students to describe are only part of a larger conception of place. By creating the part/whole sequence between the 'space around the hands' and the 'space of the mesosphere', that parallels the connections between 'I' and 'we' in 'Gentle

Now', Spahr presents a much larger map than that expected from St Germain's students. This has repercussions when considering the responsibility that educators hope to foster. Spahr's form of connection – the act of breathing – is a shared act that while provoking perception to extend from local place to other places, also raises the possibility of extending feelings of responsibility. Many place-based approaches suggest that focusing upon the local goes hand in hand with defending the local environment from threat. Although this is an admirable ambition and, as demonstrated by many community grass-root campaigns, one that can often be achieved, the approach might be made more reciprocal. Studying Spahr's poem prompts thought on the way in which the local environment might be at threat *and* how it might be threatening to other places. An oil spill from another country's offshore rig might threaten the coastline here, but doesn't a weekly rubbish collection, transported from here to a landfill in another county, threaten elsewhere? Seeing both sides of this situation are surely necessary to enrich a student's understanding of responsibility.

Spahr's focus upon the act of breathing in terms of this connection of everyone with 'lungs' applies both to humans and animal non-humans – however, Spahr's use of 'hands' that begins each stanza suggests that the responsibility for this global community is solely with humans. Spahr's repetition of this body part echoes the traditional synecdoche of 'hands' as representative of human agency ('all hands on deck') and so emphasizes the potential for certain actions to have consequences upon 'everyone with lungs'. Spahr's impersonal phrasing – '*the* space between *the* hands' (emphasis added) – rather than 'this', 'your' or 'my' hands – affords the opportunity to participate in a similar way as Spahr's use of 'we' in 'Gentle Now' that aimed for reader participation. Spahr introduces 'sulphur and sulphuric acid and titanium and nickel' from the twin towers at the poem's conclusion, but the interdependent structure that Spahr builds in the poem encourages thought on other causal relations. The hand turning the key in the ignition in order to drive to the shops is no longer a local place-based activity, but representative of greater global activity in terms of climate change. Likewise, the particulates generated by a power plant are brought into spatial proximity not only with one's own breathing – of polluting 'the space around the hands' – but also of polluting 'the space of the nations … the troposphere'.

The practice of relating the microcosm to the macrocosm responds to Heise's interest in how environmental commitment might be premised 'no longer primarily on ties to local places but on ties to territories and systems that are understood to encompass the planet as a whole' (2008: 8). Yet, these ties must be strong if they are to stretch to unknown places and their inhabitants.

Like Katherine R. Chandler with her 'tree shrine' exercise, St Germain aims to cultivate a relationship to place in her exercise on intimacy that complements her map-making prompt. She asks her students to 'try to articulate the precise nature of the feeling of intimacy you might have with a place. How is it like or unlike the relationship you might have with another human, or an animal?' (2014b). To some extent, Spahr has already illustrated a feeling of intimacy on a global scale; 'Gentle Now' conveyed 'we' as a global community and 'Poem after September 11, 2001' pursued this conceptualization of community by foregrounding the connections between spatial frames through the intimate medium of breath. However, in *This Connection*, Spahr heightens this sense of intimacy and, in doing so, accentuates such connections.

Spahr's 'Note' to 'Poems Written from November 30, 2002 to March 27, 2003' conveys a self-reflexive awareness of how connections to other places affect her own life and thus her own responsibilities. Referring to her time teaching at the University of Hawai'i during the US invasion of Iraq, Spahr explains:

> I felt I had to think about what I was connected with, and what I was complicit with, as I lived off the fat of the military-industrial complex on a small island. I had to think about my intimacy with things I would rather not be intimate with even as (because?) I was very far away from all those things geographically. This feeling made lyric—with its attention to connection, with its dwelling on the beloved and on the afar—suddenly somewhat poignant, somewhat apt ... more useful than I usually find it.
>
> (2005a: 13)

In an interview with Jos Charles, Spahr explains that she left university with the thought that 'I was an experimental poet. And I was, thus, against lyric and confessionalism' (2015a). Echoing the intimacy in the aforementioned relationships between 'I' and 'we', 'the space around the hands' and 'the space of the continents', 'December 2, 2002' begins 'As it happens every night, beloved, while we turned in the night sleeping uneasily the world went on without us' and goes on to list particular events:

> While we turned sleeping uneasily at least ten were injured in a bomb blast in Bombay and four killed in Palestine
>
> While we turned sleeping uneasily a warehouse of food aid was destroyed, stocks on upbeat sales soared, Australia threatened first strikes, there was heavy gunfire in the city of Man, the Belarus ambassador to Japan went missing
>
> (2005a: 24)

Those experiencing night in another time zone are quite literally unconscious of political and environmental events happening elsewhere. Yet this disconnection becomes questionable as Spahr goes on to state, 'Beloveds, our world is small and isolated' (2005a: 25). Spahr's use of the term 'world' is uncertain. It is a common phrase used to describe personal space: for the room or even the bed in which 'we turned sleeping' and in this way underpins a sense of isolation. Simultaneously, however, Spahr's 'world' refers to the actual globe that being 'small and isolated' increases the importance and possibility of global connection and community. By suggesting both understandings of 'world' Spahr brings them closer together to propose both the limitation and possible expansion of an individual's relationship with other places.

Tender and unsettling by turns, 'December 8, 2002' develops these connections. Spahr initially presents a simple, sensual scene in which lovers are looking at clouds 'out the window from our bed as we lie there in the / morning enjoying the touch of each other's bodies' (ibid.: 35). However, this scene becomes more complex as Spahr explains a few lines later

> This is an attempt to speak in praise of the firm touch of yours
> hands on my breast at night and its comfort to me.
>
> An attempt to celebrate the moments late at night when yous
> wake up with kindness
>
> (2005a: 36)

Distorting the previous reference to a lover by making the pronoun plural radically changes the nature of the intimacy Spahr conveys. In the conclusion of 'Gentle Now', we saw the way in which she commented upon disconnection from the larger, non-human world through an intimate focus on the human body. Yet, the intimacy between the speaker and 'yous' reverses that argument. Rather than an intimacy between two people, Spahr suggests an intimacy between herself and a number of others. Initially these 'yous' might return her intention to involve the reader. Yet, this inclusive use of 'yous' more strongly evokes the range of figures in Spahr's previous poem such as 'four killed in Palestine' and the 'Belarus / ambassador'. This use of the lyric continues to be manipulated to explore connections between her personal world and the world of others elsewhere as she writes 'All I know is that I couldn't get out of bed anymore at all without / yous in my life. // And I know that my ties with yous are not unique' (ibid.: 38). With a strange literal quality, the poem acknowledges the impossibility of continuing life in a personal 'world' and thus draws attention to the interdependency shared by all.

'I hold out my hand. / I hand over / and I pass on. ... Some call this mothering', Spahr writes in her most recent collection *That Winter the Wolf Came* (2015b: 53). Collected in this volume that meditates upon environmental and social systems inextricably linked to oil economies, 'Tradition' provides further illustration and development of St Germain's writing prompt to imagine relationships with places in light of relationships between people. Unlike the previous poem's portrayal of large-scale connection through the interactions between lovers, 'Tradition' explores a parental bond. 'I hold out my hand and take engine / oil additive into me and then I pass on this engine oil additive to / this other thing that once was me, this not really me', writes Spahr (ibid.: 53). This 'not really me' stands for the child who is later described as being passed 'a breast cup filled with sound insulation panels and imitation wood' (ibid.: 54). Echoing the pollutants detailed in 'Gentle Now', 'Tradition' tells of chemicals transferred to the child through breast milk. Yet, subtly there is a sense that this 'not really me' stands for more – perhaps even the rest of the world. It is difficult to know whether Spahr is writing figuratively or literally when at one point she mentions 'Not really me is a ram perched on a cliff above a stream' (ibid.). With the conclusion of the poem in which 'not really me' sings a 'song of rebuke', it becomes possible to read the process of 'handing over and passing on' not simply in terms of a mother's breast milk transferring chemicals to a child, but of how each one of us is physically involved in a causal chain of pollutants and, as the title of the poem ('Tradition') suggests, how these interactions with the world might be continued across generations (ibid.: 57).

There is a shared understanding that, as Jon Gower stated, environmental writing courses should foster consideration of human impact upon the environment, but certain concerns seem to hinder progress. As St Germain explains of her programme, there is 'a part in the class that is political and looks at particular issues ... but I don't want them to feel depressed in this class' (2014a). Fearing other consequences, Jim Perrin, who up until recently was a consultant for Bath Spa's MA and who teaches outside higher education, associates writing about environmental issues with polemic and argues: 'Once you start taking a polemical slant I think you're in danger of losing your closeness to subject, losing your attentiveness' (2014a). Spahr's work has already made some valuable suggestions in light of Perrin's concerns. Juxtaposition in 'Gentle Now' modelled ways of using detail and thus 'closeness to subject' ('the long pendulous polygamous / racemes of its small green flowers') when apprehending ecological connection, threat and, ultimately, an inclusive, connected community. More recent examples ('December 8, 2002' and 'Tradition') find a rather more unexpected understanding of 'closeness to subject' in terms of sexual and familial relations and demonstrates that such closeness facilitates, rather than counters, engagement with some of the most pressing environmental issues we face today. How might pedagogy lead students into thinking, let alone writing, about environmental issues without the sheer enormity of the situation leading to creative paralysis?[8] While the conclusion to this chapter will propose a series of prompts and exercises to complement these readings, in the next section I explore the techniques Spahr employs to represent the ecological impact of colonization.

Connection and causation

Exploring the specific context of colonial Hawai'i, Spahr's work goes on to speak of particular issues in terms that navigate away from polemical styles and feelings of depression, emphasizing, if anything, a curious fascination with the causal chains associated with environmental change. Having moved to Hawai'i in 1997 for a teaching position, Spahr describes how she took offence at the nature poetry written by tourists visiting the islands: 'Much of it is written by those who vacation here and it is often full of errors. Rob Wilson calls these 747 poems' (2011: 69). Included in Spahr's afterword to her poem sequence 'Things of Each Possible Relation Hashing against One Another' (hereafter known as 'Things of Each') published in *Well Then There Now*, Spahr explains that

> even when it got the birds and the plants and the animals right it tended to show the beautiful bird and not the bulldozer off to the side that was destroying the bird's habitat. And it wasn't talking about how the bird, often a bird which had arrived recently from somewhere else, interacted with and changed the larger system of this small part of the world we live in and on.
>
> (2011)

Spahr describes how this style of poetry parallels the practice of botanical artists who accompanied explorers of Hawai'i and who 'made drawings of isolated plants against white backgrounds' (ibid.). Beth Fowkes Tobin states that these drawings 'reinforced the concept of plant transfer by erasing local habitat, plant physiology, human use, and cultural significance' (1996: 275). Drawing from Tobin's study, Spahr concludes that these artists were 'a crucial part of colonial exploration' (2011: 69). In turn, Spahr suggests that the '747 poems' are not only naïve, but also potentially symptomatic of an appropriative attitude towards the environment.

It could be said that a certain solipsism underlies Spahr's criticism. Spahr indulges in chastising these tourists and privileging her own, supposedly more ethical position – and this while being a tourist of sorts herself, albeit one who stayed in Hawai'i for just over six years. Yet, it is worth investigating Spahr's position – not least because of this awkward tension. After all, Spahr's description of 'a bird which had arrived recently from somewhere else' (although vague in this instance) suggests connections between the local and the global that challenge pedagogical exercises that help students define place through particular species. Allison B. Wallace believes that differentiating between a starling and a towhee creates more 'placed' students, yet says nothing of how starlings first came to the United States from Europe. Spahr's noting of the arrival of a bird that has 'changed the larger system' of the islands alludes to the larger issue of non-native species in Hawai'i that have dominated native species since their colonial introduction in the eighteenth century. Spahr takes the colonization of Hawai'i as the subject for her poem 'Things of Each'. Her concentration on the interactions and change resulting from the imposition of one spatial frame onto another provides a level of detail and complexity that develops her earlier approach of ties and systems in *This Connection* and thus affords further strategies for reconsidering pedagogical approaches to place.

The poem begins with 'the view from the sea / the constant motion of claiming, collecting, changing, and taking' (2011: 55). At first it seems as if it is the sea's currents and tides that are changing the shore. Yet, 'the view from the sea' introduces a more human presence to the poem that is developed as Spahr goes on to describe 'the arrival to someplace else' (ibid.). The 'view from the sea' coupled with 'the arrival' suggests incoming ships. The following lines that repeat 'the arrival to someplace differently', and later, 'what we know is like and unalike', suggest that this view from the sea is a different perspective from 'the view from land' (ibid.: 65). Spahr's 'view from the sea' conveys the arrival of Captain Cook to Hawai'i in 1778 that provoked the further arrival of Protestant missionaries and whalers from the United States in 1820. Her statement that 'what we know is like and unalike' anticipates her lines that repeat with variation: 'it is as the problems of analogy / it as the view from the sea' (ibid.: 56). In describing the arrival of settlers as presenting 'the problems of analogy', Spahr suggests those arriving from other lands disregarded what was 'unalike' both in terms of the ecosystem and culture they encountered. Illustrating Heise's interest in ecological misunderstandings and conflicting viewpoints inherent to global interactions, Spahr proposes that those arriving from other lands wrongly assumed the land in Hawai'i to be similar to their own.

Necessitating some knowledge of the history of Haiwai'i, Spahr goes into further detail in describing how

> that is what the problems of the analogy are
> the problems of the sight from the sea
> and the problems of the introduction of koa haole …
> the problems of the analogy are still
> as the sight of the sea
> as the introduction of factories and animals, foreign, exotic
>
> (2011: 56-7)

Spahr understands analogy as a device that posits similarity and, evoking pedagogical concerns of the ego in the next chapter of this book (and anticipating similar criticisms of metaphor and anthropomorphism in later chapters), she understands its potentially imposing and appropriative consequences. Working from this basis, she suggests that despite Hawai'i presenting much in the way of contrast to the Western world, Western settlers transferred their own notion of commercial business and their own dietary requirements that in turn would introduce new species and agricultural methods to the islands. What might at first appear to be a local species, like the koa haole or mongoose, is revealed as a species entangled in other spatial frames.[9] Moreover, Spahr suggests that these species are only parts of causal chains that continue to change life on the islands and thus produce even further entanglement.

Spahr's earlier description of how 'the view from the sea' enacts a '*constant motion of claiming, collecting, changing, and taking*' comes to the fore as she names particular species introduced to Hawai'i by the explorers (emphasis added). The 'introduction of mongoose' mentioned by Spahr was made in order to help control the rat population, which had increased dramatically with the introduction of sugar plantations (ibid.). Further change resulted from these changes as the mongoose devastated the native bird population because of its diet of bird eggs. Her expression, 'Analogy from analogy', acknowledges how it is not only the human settlers that make sense of the islands through their own perspectives and behavioural habits, but also the non-native species introduced by the settlers. Spahr's understanding of the problems of analogy leads her to the 'opening of the things sewn together' (ibid.: 59). Indeed, she probes Hawai'i's seemingly stable environment – exemplified by the aforementioned perception of 'the beautiful bird' – to find a series of interactions between entities brought together from divergent spatial frames.

Spahr's understanding of analogy not only continues to influence the content of her poem but also the form. In 'Things of Each', Spahr goes on to present a series of analogies:

> like the wing of the butterfly and the bird
> like hummingbird the aspirations and the aspiration of the
>   butterfly
> like the language of humans of nature and hummingbird the
>   language
> as newt the wing under the amphibians and lizards under the
>   reptiles
>
> (2011: 59-60)

This series of connections evokes a biological definition of analogy as presenting a superficial resemblance between unrelated species. In comparing species of different origins, Spahr forces connections in a way that echoes 'the problems of analogy'. The result is strange; yet it is not only the connections between species that are strange, but also the syntax that conveys such connections. The latter is in fact supported by a particular manipulation that she uses which self-consciously enacts the 'problems of analogy'. She explains in her afterword, 'I put the drafts through the altavista translation machine (world.altavista.com) and translated my English words between the languages that came to the Pacific from somewhere else: French, Spanish, German, and Portuguese' (ibid.: 71). The process with which 'Things of Each' is written enacts analogy as the online translation machine finds a word supposedly analogous to another in a different language. As the outcome of this process presents grammatical discord, Spahr emphasizes the distortive effects arising from the belief that spatial frames can be alike. In this way, her poem illuminates Heise's call not only for an understanding of connection between spatial frames, but more precisely, of how these connections shape each other around the world.

For young schoolchildren, a common activity that engages thought on connection is to hold hands and pretend to be various animal herbivores and carnivores. Such has become a regular feature of education – environmental or otherwise – in teaching pupils about food chains and ecological systems more broadly. In other classrooms, and with other age groups, connection is frequently of a benign, and often semi-spiritual, nature. These exercises seek to foster an understanding of relation and respect. Margot Fortunato Galt's exercise (2000) provides one such example within environmental writing pedagogy. In 'Nature as Teacher and Guide', Galt guides her students towards thinking about equality. Galt begins by explaining how environmental entities are often structured through a hierarchical pyramid and so echoes previous pedagogical exercises on food chains. She contrasts the pyramid with a circle and claims, 'When we think of living things on a circle, we see that they are all connected, all related', and 'On the circle, every place is equal and every place is important' (2000: 250). Describing how this circle of life comes from 'Many Native American cultures', Galt presents N. Scott Momaday's poem 'The Delight Song of Tsoai-Talee' as a poetic model of connective environmental thinking (ibid.: 249). Momaday's poem begins: 'I am a feather on the bright sky / I am the blue horse that runs in the plain / I am the fish that rolls, shining, in the water' (ibid.: 253 cites Momaday 1–3). This metaphorical identification between 'I' and a range of environmental entities continues in a similar vein until Momaday concludes with 'I stand in good relation to the earth … You see, I am alive. I am alive' (ibid.: cites Momaday 20–4).

Galt asks her students to draw their own circles and, around these circles, note environmental entities of varying scales and from places not necessarily familiar. She then asks her students to draw a line between any two points on the circle and 'describe how one part of the circle teaches something to another part', or to write, in the style of Momaday that 'I am' connected to these entities (ibid.: 253). As students find connection between themselves and, for example, rivers, oceans, soil and whales, Galt's approach helps to create connection between different entities, and, potentially, between divergent places in a manner that brings to mind Heise's ecocritical exploding of 'an ethic of proximity'. Galt's exercise thus begins to resonate with Spahr's understanding of a global community proposed in 'Gentle Now', in which Spahr wrote of how 'we were a part of the stream and we were thus part of the rivers' (2011: 125). Creating an opportunity for her students to engage with a 'Native American' view of the world that accentuates equality with all beings, Galt suggests a practice of standing 'in good relation' to other cultures as well as to the environment. However, the ease and benign nature of identification that she fosters through her understanding of metaphor and connection goes no further. It is interesting to compare this with Joseph Cornell's exercise targeted for much younger audiences, which, while dependent upon a hierarchical sense of connection (he advocates use of the pyramid, rather than circle), demonstrates the extensive damage inflicted through the introduction of toxins, in this case pesticides. In contrast, Galt's exercise does not foster thought on how relations between humans and the environment or relations between entities might be more complex and potentially threatening. This awareness would seem useful for a more thorough understanding of why 'good relation' is important. Galt's exercise is, after all, included in *The Alphabet of the Trees* anthology, which aims to respond to how 'Our world today is in recognizable jeopardy' as editors Christian McEwen and Mark Statman state (2000: xviii). Galt fosters no awareness as to how, in the words of Spahr's poem 'Gentle Now', 'It was not all long lines of connections and utopia' (2011: 130).

Attending to the problems arising from connection not only enriches the subject of relation conveyed by Galt, but also the responsibility that previous educators intend to foster in their students. Spahr's writing shows some parallel to Galt's use of the Native American song of relation as Spahr intersects 'Things of Each' with her own version of a Hawaiian creation chant. Known as *The Kumulipo*, this chant conveys connection in terms of biological generation, as a short passage demonstrates: 'Born was the Grub, the parent / Out came its child the Grasshopper, and flew / Born was the Pinworm, the parent / Out came its child a Fly, and flew' (1972: 291–4). With the translating machine occasionally disrupting certain words, Spahr creates her own version:

> caterpillar of the moth
> ant of the dragonfly
> connection from connection
> pinworm of the fly
> connection of the connection
> egg of the bird
>
> (2011: 58)

While the connections she presents here are fairly straightforward, they become more complex as the poem develops:

> we are consequently
> we are consequently
> so we are
> alaaiha, `e`ea, alawi, crow, apapane, mudhen
> we are so
> bird, egg, fly, pinworm, grasshopper, grub
> we are thus
> fly-catcher, turnstone, a`u, a`o, plover, snipe
>
> (2011: 63)

Spahr's repeated use of 'we are' at first parallels Momaday's metaphorical use of 'I am'. Indeed, her statement 'we are alaaiha, `e`ea, alawi, crow' echoes her portrayal of a global community represented by 'we' in 'Gentle Now'. Yet, a closer look at the poem introduces a less benign connection. This becomes evident when we consider that the birds Spahr lists are all endangered or already extinct in Hawai'i due to the effects of Western settlers. In turn, her repeated use of 'consequently' takes on a more sinister tone. It is not simply that 'We are' the 'alawi' or 'crow' because 'we' represents a global community inclusive of these species, but 'we are' the 'alawi' or 'crow' because 'we' have taken the place of these species. The creatures that Spahr goes on to list may not all be threatened, but framing them within the context of these birds produces a looming sense that they will be lost too. Her mention of *The Kumulipo* in her prose text, *The Transformation* (2007), pursues this focus on imposition, interaction and loss. Noting that the creation chant 'pointed out the connectedness of life', Spahr proposes that 'to see the connection between land and sea is also to see how one nation's oil-use could cause the disappearance of another's land' (2007: 107–8). An awareness of connection generates an awareness of destructive environmental connections for Spahr. If we pursue this perspective we can develop Galt's exercise by encouraging reflection on what consequences the 'I' might have across spatial frames in terms of particular actions or behaviours: of what 'I am' in terms of what these behaviours ultimately replace in the environment. Spahr's careful consideration of causality becomes a way of extending pedagogical strategies to foster responsibility for place in their students. It speaks to other examples of imposition, interaction and change that defy a straightforward sense of place such as that between carbon emissions and glaciers, or a cosmetic product's plastic microbeads and marine life across the planet's oceans.

Rewriting place

Suggestions about how to reconsider place have guided this chapter, yet how might we go on to propose particular strategies that teachers can give to their students, or for students to pursue independently? How might these strategies speak of Heise's ecocritical argument to extend perception towards the global? In her connections to many different places, people and issues, Spahr's poetry provides a model with which to open up discussion of our myriad global connections and implement Heise's 'zooming techniques' on the page.

Reading the selection of poems above offers a playful, but nonetheless rigorous introduction to considering the ways in which one place is linked to another and another. Different natures of connection have been explored here: from the idea of a harmonious global community and a global community connected through the intimate medium of breath, to the chemical inheritance handed down to new generations and the chain of events resulting from colonial acts that will continue for years to come. With each unsettling of place identity, Spahr experiments with different forms: repetition, lists, journal entries, an online translation machine, creation myths and creation chants. Within these forms, Spahr's manipulation of literary styles and devices such as lyric, confessionalism and metaphor further demonstrate new ways of writing creatively about a sense of place in terms of a sense of planet. The suggestions I make aim to outline a way of ecocritically reimagining place, while also introducing a much-needed sense of creativity that counters some educators' concerns that an engagement with issues might only depress their students.

Spahr's repetitive 'Poem Written after September 11, 2001' in which she linked the space around the hands to the mesosphere, serves as a valuable bridge between current teaching on place and a revisioning of the local through the global. Asking students to follow Spahr's example and write from the perspective of their own body outwards, towards the mesosphere, prompts reflection on the boundaries they consider between the personal, the local and the global. Heise's key point concerning 'dispersed allegiances' is raised through this exercise as the defining nature of neighborhoods, nations and continents is brought into question. While Spahr's poem depends upon air to consider how each part of the world 'breathes the space in and out', reading 'Gentle Now' gives students the opportunity to explore other media that connect them to the rest of the world. The poem's focus on the life-giving stream which is described as 'a part of us and we were a part of the stream' might resonate, particularly if students are reminded that the human body is half, if not more than half, comprised of water.

More thought might be given to the titles of Spahr's work in *This Connection* that appear like journal entries. Suggestive of her interest in the confessional, this framing of her poems also parallels teachers' instructions for students to keep journals. As noted, students are often expected to visit particular sites in their local environments and write accounts of these visits in their journals as a way of documenting observations of species and recording change. As students revisit and closely attend to their place, educators hope to create an attachment to place and, taking this a step further, potentially foster feelings of environmental stewardship. To develop pedagogical strategy with ecocritical thought on 'eco-cosmopolitanism', the journal might be reimagined to take account of the connections between objects in our personal and local environments and the world. How is a paper or polystyrene cup that we hold in our hands, and the coffee inside that cup, connected to the rest of the world? A journal can be used to take account of this, just as it can take account of how a nearby farm's agricultural run-off might affect other fields and streams that are, in turn, connected to other places. Teachers of cultural geography, Ian Cook, Tim Angus and James Evans propose a strategy not unlike this one (2010). They explain how making a cup of coffee links them to reservoirs, miles of piping, a plastic kettle, a heating element connected to the national grid, wires, pylons, power stations and their fuels (ibid.). Evoking Val Plumwood's concept of 'shadow places' that reflect our footprint on the earth, this exercise on ethical consumerism is clearly relevant in developing pedagogical approaches to place. As well as identifying a 'towhee' through a series of careful notes as Wallace suggests, students writing these globally focused journals are given the chance to productively problematize the identification of anything they see by apprehending connections that blur contextual boundaries. This becomes a method to pursue the kinds of concerns highlighted by Spahr: in particular, the 747 poems that 'tended to show the beautiful bird and not the bulldozer off to the side'.

While these suggestions consider the form and framing that students might deploy in order to write toward the global, what other prompts might be explored to think about content, style and device? Associated with autobiography, a confessional style is not usually one that would seem immediately relevant for environmental writers. Yet, rather than being dominated by the personal 'I', Spahr's confessional style explores the connections between the 'I' and the world. As St Germain suggests, students might imagine their human relationships with people and animals as metaphors for their relationship with a certain place. Spahr's pronoun-distorting work in 'December 8, 2002' shows how a sensual human relationship can express a relationship with the world. Moreover, *That Winter the Wolf Came* reveals a disturbing maternal dynamic as representing significant environmental interactions. With questions concerning attachment, detachment and personal boundaries, students can be reminded of the variety of human relations to be considered: between siblings, adopted children/parents, separated or divorced couples. An exercise based on parallels between our human relationships and our different relationships to the world might, among other things, reflect on our literal physical relation (our genes), our ability to share, as well as our desires and disagreements both petty and profound. Synchronizing personal and global scales, this exercise might raise a range of emotions, but it also challenges students in the way it raises different understandings of respect and responsibility.

The distortive effect that arises from Spahr's use of the translation machine provides another angle that, this time, offers an opportunity to focus on cross-cultural relations with Heise's eco-cosmopolitan perspective. Though students might want to experiment with the translation machine, introducing their own interests between the local and the global, the traditional practice of translation provides more opportunities still. Albeit wary of Heise's dismissal of the local in place of the global, Terry Gifford's essay 'Towards a New Multi-Dimensional Ecopoetics of Place' (2016) recounts an exercise that reveals tensions between local and global perspectives through differing mother tongues. Pitting 'intimate bioregional experience' against globalism's belief in 'multilingual communication', Gifford asks bilingual students to write about one place in two different languages (2016: 216). As a Spanish student finds it easy to write about their Spanish place in Spanish, but far harder to express the same place in German, Gifford concludes that 'the very words individuals use about place are subjective bioregional constructions that are untranslatable into another language' (ibid.: 225). While his argument aims to trouble Heise's claims for a planetary perspective, it proves an interesting exercise that prompts students to begin considering the very cross-cultural relations and misunderstandings Heise believes are central to an eco-cosmopolitan approach. On the assumption that most students are not bilingual, introducing them to translations of landscape poems can provide a necessary first step in recognizing both likeness and difference in conceptions of place from other countries. Reading a few translations of one text (Tang dynasty haiku are useful given their numerous different translations into English), students might be given the task to create a version of their own. Such an activity demands research into the writer's homeland: how has a particular country's culture shaped this writer's articulation of place? How has religion and politics shaped an environmental ethic? The construction of a version places responsibility into the student-translator's hands: is this a faithful rendition? How does your familiarity with your native landscape risk compromising the process? What might be lost in translation and why?

Spahr's use of analogy and metaphor make for further, more specific prompts to reconsider the local. Using the intimacy of two lovers to consider the intimacy of herself to the world, Spahr's statement 'All I know is that I couldn't get out of bed anymore at all without yous in my life' is at once a romantic hyperbole and a literal statement. Likewise, given the way the human body absorbs and carries toxins over time, it is possible to read Spahr's description of 'a breast cup filled with sound insulation panels and imitation wood' not only metaphorically (the breast cup representing the environment given to the next generation), but literally as the milk from a mother's breast passed to a child. As discussed, Margot Fortunato Galt's exercise created a benign sense of connection by drawing upon N. Scott Momaday's poem – particularly his phrase 'I am' – and this was compared to Spahr's phrase 'we are consequently' that portrayed a darker, more violent sense of destructive assimilation through connection. Expanding on the journal exercise that I have described above, students can use their accounts of global connection to inform and structure other pieces of environmental writing. Echoing the refrain 'I am', self-portraits might be generated that zoom in and out from immediate, physical detail to complex, causal chains prompted by such items as the clothes and cosmetics they wear, or the foods and fuels they consume. While these written pieces might, like the journal exercise, be documentary in style, they might also take a riddle-like form, asking, for example, how the carbon footprint of a pink cotton dress made in China is connected to the unprecedented growth of bananas in Vancouver during one (unseasonably hot) summer. Metaphor might be used to convey the narrative involved in these causal chains to greater dizzying effect. Just as 'we' becomes inextricable from extinct species in Spahr's work, a cotton field in western India might be described through the entities involved in the dress's production and distribution. For example, the field growing cotton might be described in terms of the frothy sea that a cargo ship, carrying the dress, crosses. Such an exercise, necessitating metaphors which illustrate global systems, develops a perceptual practice that is ready to leap between the local and the global.[10]

With their emphasis upon responsibility for environmental crises the latter suggestions risk St Germain's concern that engaging with environmental issues will depress students and, presumably, turn them off writing about the environment altogether. Spahr's sense of humour that emerges from considering our connections is, therefore, an important feature to maintain in reconsidering place. Returning to 'December 2, 2002', we see Spahr sleeping through violent environmental and social events that occur on the other side of the world. Yet, also, 'While we turned sleeping uneasily Liam Gallagher brawled and irate fans complained that "Popstars: The Rivals" was fixed' (2005a: 24). Likewise, in 'March 11, 2003' Spahr interrogates a statement by President Bush suggesting he would go ahead with the Iraq campaign without international support.

> Bush keeps saying he will go it alone if he has to …
> When I speak of alone I speak of how there is no alone as Pakistan

claims it is moving in on bin Laden, as Iran's nuclear plant is nearing completion ...

I speak of David Letterman's shingles, which he got from someone else.

(2005a: 61-2)

Interconnection is figured on a range of scales at once trivial and serious as my example of banana growth in Canada sought to suggest. To make note of this playful juxtaposition in teaching about place and environmental issues is to ensure students remain receptive to different forms of connection and to offer some opportunity to counterbalance the gravitas of environmental issues explored. I hope that this analysis of Spahr will prompt teachers and students to take up her writing as a valuable introduction to place as both a local and a global concept. Indeed, through fostering new forms of environmental commitment with a global outlook and finding the complex interconnections integral to place, teachers might begin not by asking students to identify 'where they are', but by asking students 'where they aren't'.

2

The 'I-me-my voice': The first-person in environmental writing

'We commonly do not remember that it is, after all, always the first-person that is speaking', writes Henry David Thoreau in the opening pages to *Walden*, adding, 'I should not talk so much about myself if there were any body else I knew as well' ([1854] 2008: 5). Implicit or explicit, the 'I' is the only means with which to convey experience: the self sits behind everything we say and do. Yet, practicalities aside, first-person narration clearly provides much value in literature. If the events of a story seem dull and distant, the first-person 'I' is often understood as a solution, providing a personal, and thus more engaging quality. In a genre such as environmental writing that attempts to combine science and literature, the connective potential of the 'I' seems, at times, compulsory. John Elder, who recently retired from Middlebury College, Vermont, after almost thirty years of teaching, claims that encounters with environments through personal narration are 'guided by a sense of connectedness' and 'discovery' with the environment and as such cannot help but lead to 'the most vivid, stirring writing' (2014). In *The Sierra Club Nature Writing Handbook*, John A. Murray offers a similar argument: 'You need that personal "I" as often as possible to remind the reader that this is not scholarly discourse or impersonal journalism but is, rather, a personal or nature essay' (1995: 19). Showing the other side of the coin to Elder's argument, a piece of writing that lacks the personal 'I' risks becoming too academic or too report-like in its bearing of cold facts.

Yet, Murray's wording remains slightly peculiar. As if it was a slip of the pen, the uncertainty expressed within 'a personal *or* nature essay' indicates tension between the 'I' and the environment (emphasis added). In what is branded as a guide to nature writing, Murray's indecision between terms could suggest that such terms are synonymous with one another. On the other hand, it could suggest incompatibility between first-person narration and environmental writing: are you going to write an essay about nature or an essay about yourself? Exploring the connective value of personal narration that Elder describes, this chapter also addresses pedagogical concerns about the potential for the 'I' to impose and manipulate the environment. Rob Nixon's ecocritical concept of 'slow violence' affords an opportunity to reverse this power dynamic and explore how an environment might manipulate the kind of 'I' that a student decides to adopt in their writing. Adapting current instruction on personal narration, this chapter proposes new writing strategies that develop different understandings of the subjective viewpoint while raising awareness of profound environmental change.

'The writer is the narrator', David Petersen describes in his chapter on 'Tense and Person', 'and it's from his or her point of view – mind, eyes, voice, heart, fears and hopes – that the story is experienced and told' (2001: 99). Like Elder's, Petersen's advice regarding the first-person in his guide, *Writing Naturally*, focuses on its capacity for emotional connection between reader and writer. Indeed, Petersen takes this one step further as he suggests that the first-person should create writing that is 'conversational – like talking to a friend' (ibid.). But Petersen doesn't stop there. He goes on to make several more suggestions: the 'I-me-my' voice is 'the voice of choice for nature narration' as it allows the writer to be 'at once observer, participant, commentator, translator and, at the best of times, philosopher' (ibid). *Walden* by Henry David Thoreau might, of course, be considered a manifesto for the subjective viewpoint. After all, in essence, the book is an account of leaving society for solitude in the woods, and it celebrates the independence of the 'I'. Thoreau's subjective viewpoint hints at philosophical communion with the natural world as he writes in 'Solitude', 'I am no more lonely than a single mullein or dandelion in a pasture, or a bean leaf, or sorrel, or a horse-fly, or a humble-bee' ([1854] 2008: 125). When he states that God, too, is alone, Thoreau's sense of ecological interconnection takes on a spiritual tone. In place-based approaches to environmental writing, Thoreau's *Walden* and Annie Dillard's *Pilgrim at Tinker Creek* recur as significant models. Both texts work in a Transcendentalist tradition and take a leading role in Margaret McFadden's pedagogical essay on ' "The I in Nature": Nature Writing as Self Discovery' (1985). Presenting her students with 'Thoreau's pungent philosophizing about individualism, and … Annie Dillard's mystical mediations', she describes how going into nature is 'a quest for pilgrimage in self-awareness, exploring the relation … of human to divine' (1985: 102).

However, as McFadden argues that 'One of the more satisfying reasons for spending time in Nature is to learn something about ourselves, as individuals', what role does the environment play, if any, in such an approach? (ibid.). Her capitalization of 'Nature' (which later becomes lower-case) might suggest a metaphysical conceptualization of the environment as discussed in the Introduction to this book. Concluding her essay, McFadden admits to the ways in which her perspective might become problematic. Beneath a subheading, 'A pitfall to be avoided', she notes that 'the pedagogue may be tempted to dwell too fully within the implicit worldview of the literary materials' (ibid.: 106). Raising doubt over the kind of Transcendental union of self and environment the exercise promotes through writers such as Thoreau, she calls for a more 'provocative critical standpoint' that would examine the 'self-deception' of writers who believe they can become one with the environment, with the aim of recognizing that we can never break out from our own human subjectivities (ibid.: 107). Despite his insistence on the first-person as the best option when narrating the environment, Petersen also makes a cautionary note not dissimilar to McFadden's. 'To master personal writing is to master ego acrobatics', Petersen warns as he contrasts 'charismatic personality' with 'annoying solipsism' (2001: 80). The warning concludes with an exercise that aims for students to become conscious of what kind of 'I' appears in their work. Students are expected to write down a personal experience with the understanding that it will be read by no one else but themselves. Fostering carefree, 'emotionally naked' writing, Petersen then suggests that students edit the piece, deleting as many personal pronouns as possible (ibid.: 88).

The relatively uncertain position of personal narration that emerges from US approaches to environmental writing corresponds to debate in the United Kingdom. A subjective viewpoint is rarely absent from contemporary non-fiction texts that serve as popular pedagogical models. As Thoreau remains present across many UK environmental writing courses, so does a notable work of British 'new nature writing': Robert Macfarlane's *The Wild Places* (2007). Macfarlane's book documents his search of the wild in the British Isles. A passage on Scotland's Black Wood of Rannoch provides an example of Macfarlane's personal narration in action. He writes:

> I wandered in the Wood all that day … I leapt streams, passed over sponge-bogs of sodden peat, soft cushions of haircap mosses. There were big standing groves of green juniper, alders, rowans and the odd dark cherry. The pines, with their reptilian bark, gave off a spicy resinous smell, and their branches wore green and silver lichens of fantastical shapes: antlers, shells, seaweeds, bones, rags. Between the trees grew heather and bracken. I climbed a whippy rowan, scattering its orange berries in all directions, and a tall old birch that shivered under my weight near its summit.
>
> (2007: 89)

The 'I' might only feature three times, but the self is inextricably linked to the deeply sensual quality of the description. It is, after all, Macfarlane's nose that detects the spicy smell of the pine's resin, his eyes or perhaps his hands that identify the bark as 'reptilian'. Such detail creates an immediacy that allows the reader to share in the experience.

Yet, just as many UK teachers set their students *The Wild Places* as a successful example of recent developments in environmental writing, they also set Kathleen Jamie's scathing review of it.[1] Described as a 'new nature writer' herself, Jamie identifies an inherent paradox in Macfarlane's book as she claims 'If there is a lot of "I" (and there is, in *The Wild Places*) then it won't be the wild places we behold, but the author' (2013). Developing Petersen's concerns regarding an overbearing 'I', Jamie claims that the authorial 'I' appropriates the land; becoming an '"owner", or if not an owner, certainly a single mediator' (ibid.). This sense of appropriation is a cause for concern. The dangers involved in putting the self first and the environment second seem only a step away from the dangers associated with physical appropriations of environments: habitat losses, species extinctions and toxic degradation. Indeed, Macfarlane's boyish decision to climb (and seemingly damage) a rowan tree provides a case in point. Jamie's argument has further consequences still. Referring to the same passage from *The Wild Places* included above, that of Macfarlane's trip to the Black Wood, Jamie comments on the solitary nature of his journeys: the fact that no other voices are represented in the text despite these landscapes being inhabited. While such solitude preserves the notion that these places are wild, coming from Scotland herself, Jamie delves deeper into the power dynamics present in his work. In a moment of deliberate and somewhat smirk-inducing exclamation, Jamie identifies Macfarlane as 'A white, middle-class Englishman! A Lone Enraptured Male! From Cambridge!' (ibid.) This perceived incongruity between the wild landscapes and Macfarlane himself raises questions about the role of class, gender and ethnicity in environmental writing. *The Wild Places* begins to look less like an important work of environmental literature and more a travel guide that treats wild landscapes as sites for escapism.

As American teachers such as McFadden tussle with a Transcendental outlook that is seductive but potentially deceptive, so British approaches to the first-person 'I' seem concerned by its potential to represent an unethical (if not implausible) Romantic solipsism. We could say that there is a history of 'enraptured males'. In his poem 'Lines Composed a Few Miles above Tintern Abbey', William Wordsworth finds that the landscape conjures in him 'elevated thoughts; a sense sublime' that leads to his description of a 'deeply interfused' state between mind and nature ([1798] 2006: 95–6). While scholars such as Jonathan Bate have interpreted Wordsworth's poem as ecologically engaged (2000: 145), Scott Hess has drawn attention to the poem's narrator as a 'traveller' whose 'aesthetic detachment and seemingly disembodied vision reflect his class position' (2015: 210–11). As Jamie's vehement assessment of *The Wild Places* has become popular in environmental writing circles it is perhaps not surprising that British teachers often appear more prudent in their instruction for personal narration than those in the United States. Paul Evans, previously the director of the Bath Spa Master's course and now teaching at Manchester Metropolitan University, describes the way in which he will guide students into putting more of themselves into their work when their writing appears imprecise, or lacking a sufficient sense of story (2014). Compared to Petersen's seemingly unbreakable faith in the first-person, however, Evans rather sombrely states 'Well this is the nature of literature – it wouldn't work if nobody wrote about themselves' (ibid.).[2] Jon Gower, the convener of a module in environmental writing at Swansea University, also praises the potential for the 'I' to share details about an environmental encounter, yet his support for such personal narration is in conflict with his scepticism of it. 'I think that letting go of the ego is really important', Gower explains, 'We can talk about me and my relationship with nature but if you're writing a biography it's the subject first and not the *biographer* … stop being interested in yourself, and telling us how you feel' (2013).[3]

It is worth reiterating that the first-person can be an incredibly effective form of narration in environmental writing. Numerous examples might be pursued, such as Kathleen Jamie's poem 'Fragment I' in which the 'I' undergoes metamorphosis, referring both to the writer and to a roe deer, or, 'The Whales', which provides another provisional 'I', this time emphasizing its physical limits when compared to underwater creatures (2012: 1–3). As discussed later on, in his essay 'Burning the Shelter' (1998), Louis Owens critically reflects on his own actions that have damaged the environment in a way that shows how the 'I' might productively argue with itself. These are not imposing egos, but egos that are in necessary dialogue with the landscapes that they encounter. A now classic work of environmental writing, *Refuge* (1991) by Terry Tempest Williams provides an example in which the 'I' is integral to writing about a particular place. The book juxtaposes the rise of the Great Salt Lake in northern Utah that threatens a bird refuge, and her mother's ovarian cancer. The personal account works almost as a metaphor for the environmental account and vice versa, raising questions as to what is 'natural', 'unnatural' and the lengths to which we try to control change. With such examples, it comes as no surprise that first-person narration is highly recommended by teachers of environmental writing. And yet the fact that teachers express anxiety regarding the 'I' is worthy of consideration, especially as this anxiety reappears in different forms as I go on to show.

At the end of *Writing Naturally*, Petersen makes a bewildering swerve in which he explains that if writers can compose 'one provocative paragraph' about environmental issues this results in 'nature writing at its best and most useful – more useful in probable fact than a book-length extravaganza of eloquently transcendental musings' (2001: 191). As discussed in Chapter 1, in many cases teachers hope their students will become sensitized to environmental threats, perhaps even 'tomorrow's caretakers of the world' (Wallace 2012: 103). Outward-looking, selfless essays, stories and poems that convey the environment and the issues affecting it might, consequently, seem like a resolution to writing that is dominated by the 'I'. Compared to 'transcendental musings' and the phrase's air of introspection, Petersen's provocative paragraph is 'more useful' as, presumably, it makes explicit an environmental concern and interrogates problematic behaviours with a view to correcting them. However, in the process of composing a provocative paragraph, it is necessary that the writer engages with her own opinions, biases and emotions. If a road is planned to be built on preserved woodland, it is unlikely that a person pleased about the prospect of the road shortening their commute could write a paragraph protesting against its construction. In discussing 'The Art of Activism' in *Environmental and Nature Writing*, Prentiss and Wilkins remind students of Aristotle's rhetorical triangle. In order for an argument to be successful a writer must employ credibility, logic and emotion: the latter crucial in creating 'a bridge, connecting writer to reader' (2016: 109).

Provocative writing, which might be defined as polemic in this context, depends on an implicit, but nonetheless strong-minded 'I', and, in so doing, often provokes quite different responses than the writer might first intend. Instead of communicating a particular concern, the preachiness that is often associated with polemic repeatedly raises questions as to the self-righteousness of the author writing it. Pointing to a number of well-regarded ecopoems in the anthology, *Earth Shattering* (2007), Terry Gifford calls them 'patronizing sentimental guff' and 'reductive propaganda' ([1995] 2011: 11).[4] Chris Kinsey, a teacher of writing workshops in the United Kingdom, finds polemic a 'big turn off' (2014). Indicating that such an approach can alienate rather than convince, Kinsey refers to Jim Perrin's Country Diaries as examples of what to avoid. Writing for *The Guardian*, Perrin describes a landscape near Snowdonia (2014b). A lyric quality emerges through the 'Shapely little peaks of the Llyn peninsula [that] stretch west against a declining sun' (ibid.). Upon hearing the call of a golden plover, Perrin turns to the data of the bird's decline 'over 80% in 30 years' (ibid.). He refers to shooters of wildfowl in the area who understand themselves to be protecting the plover, and concludes in a rather more polemic tone 'Hypocrisy, or what?' (ibid.). As a teacher of environmental writing himself, Perrin was shown in the last chapter to warn his students that, when writing with a 'polemical slant', you risk 'losing your closeness to subject, losing your attentiveness' (2014a). In line with Kinsey, it is not difficult to see this lesson at least partly illustrated by Perrin's own Country Diary as his highly charged rhetoric risks overshadowing his detailed meditation.

At the same time, however, we might question whether Petersen's comparison between 'transcendental musings' and 'provocative' writing sets up an unhelpful binary. This binary is seen again when, in their guide to environmental writing, Prentiss and Wilkin set an exercise for students on 'activist writing' in which they are to represent an environmental concern 'with a very muted tone. Then rewrite it with a loud, belligerent tone' (2016:115). Is there another way to write an issue-driven essay, story or poem without polarizing lyric meditation and aggressive moralizing? Terry Tempest Williams's *Refuge* offers an example in which lyricism, elegy and provocation coexist. In the final chapter of the book, 'The Clan of One-Breasted Women', Williams argues that her mother's cancer (and cancers suffered by other women in her family) is a consequence of atomic bomb tests in the Nevada desert in the 1950s, a practice that was still in operation as Williams wrote and published her book. Likewise, we might look to the discussion of Juliana Spahr's poetry in Chapter 1. Indeed, this intimacy occurs quite literally as Spahr juxtaposes global political and social events with lovers touching one another in bed. To distinguish between environmental 'polemic' that suggests a strongly worded attack (polemic, after all, derives from the Greek *polemos* meaning 'war') and environmental 'argument' might be a useful first step in reconsidering not only the different forms 'provocative' writing can take, but also the relatively fraught role of the 'I' within such writing.

Recent studies in ecocriticism have focused upon the representational challenges posed by the environment. Timothy Morton has drawn attention to the gap between word and world, suggesting that any attempt to accurately reproduce an environment on the page cannot help but be a failure. In response to increasing globalization, critics such as Ursula Heise have called for the need to expand our perception from local to global scales. How might challenges such as these, which arise from environmental complexity, help to form a new angle on the role of the self in writing about the environment? In the introduction to *Writing the Environment* (Kerridge and Sammells 1998), Richard Kerridge acknowledges that literature is often thought to be 'reserved' for the first-person and such a narrative mode 'tends to exclude the large-scale perspectives, political generalities, narrative time-scales and scientific vocabularies used in environmental debate' (1998: 6). As shown by the discussion above, much concern is expressed about the 'I' dominating and potentially appropriating an environmental representation. How might these power dynamics be reversed? Could an environment, given the challenges it poses in terms of 'large scale perspectives', help to construct the 'I' that a writer adopts?

Rob Nixon's *Slow Violence* expands on Kerridge's argument in pursuing the principle that ecological violence is not always immediately visible. In contrast to violence as a sudden spectacle (essential to disaster and apocalyptic films), Nixon believes

> that we urgently need to rethink – politically, imaginatively, and theoretically – what I call 'slow violence.' By slow violence I mean a violence that occurs gradually and out of sight, a violence of delayed destruction that is dispersed across time and space, an attritional violence that is typically not viewed as violence at all.
>
> (2011: 2)

Applying his concept to the global South, Nixon focuses his study on the environmentalism of the poor. Representative of a larger ecocriticial movement concerning environmental justice movements and postcolonial studies, *Slow Violence* investigates transnational interests that, bound up in financial and political matters, severely damage underrepresented communities and their landscapes over time. Arguing for the ways in which contemporary writers help to bring slow violence to light, Nixon turns to Indra Sinha and Arundhati Roy who, among others, seek to represent chemical fallout and the consequences of megadams in their novels.

Nixon's inquiry into structural violence might not immediately speak to pedagogical concerns about the position of the self in environmental writing. Compared to the marginalized communities of Nixon's study, the kind of personal 'I' advocated by teachers appears constrained by a very local, and potentially privileged, sense of time and space. However, Nixon's acknowledgement of our perceptual limitations in the light of slow violence provides a prompt to begin considering new ways of imagining the 'I'. In order to visualize a violence 'dispersed across space and time', could a writer imaginatively share the perspective of another 'I': an 'I' inhabiting different temporal and spatial frames? Nixon's close readings document the slow violence involved in, for example, South Africa's neo-colonial tourism and the repercussions of the Bhopal disaster in India. Yet, beyond Nixon's focus on the environmentalism of the poor, the concept of slow violence can be understood in any setting in which plastics are thrown away daily, imported goods are purchased and car keys turn in ignitions. Likewise, although the first-person narrators encountered in Nixon's book witness real events and their consequences, slow violence is clearly relevant to our concerns about what the future might bring: the effect of discarded plastics and the impact of carbon released into an already carbon-rich atmosphere. In the first half of this chapter I show how the process of writing about the environment can be enriched by a self-reflexive engagement with the tensions inherent to the 'I'. In the second half, I consider the first-person's emotional, connective capacity and investigate how imagined perspectives provide new engagement with 'slow' environmental issues. Developing strategies that play with the 'I-me-my-voice', this argument also responds to the concerns I have summarized about polemic.

Conscious of the way in which the self appropriates the natural world, Jorie Graham helps to creatively extend discussion of personal narration, particularly through her early poems. Furthermore, with an increasing awareness of environmental change in later poetry collections, Graham begins to reimagine the first-person she employs. Currently the Bolyston Professor of Rhetoric and Oratory at Harvard University, Graham has also held a long-term teaching position at the Iowa Writers' Workshop. Referring to the latter in an interview with Mark Wunderlich, Graham acknowledged a trend in recent students who were 'more questioning of subjectivity in general, more self-conscious regarding the representation of subjective experience' ([1996] 2000). Graham speculates that this 'questioning' comes from 'the distrust not only of the validity of personal experience but of the very notion of an essential self who might claim to have such an experience' (ibid.). Influenced by Modernist poets such as T. S. Eliot and Wallace Stevens and their portrayal of fraught, fragmented relationships between self and world, Graham's approach shares in her students' distrust of the 'I'. The following pages serve to explain how tensions are inherent to perception as well as representation in her questioning of both eye and 'I'. The subject of time exaggerates these tensions in a manner that evokes Nixon's concept of 'slow violence' as, for example, Graham believes the seeming finality of representation inappropriate given that the world continues. As Graham pursues alternative narrative stances in her later collections, her poems become valuable models with which to illustrate new relationships between self, environment and environmental issues at stake.

'I can make it carry my fatigue': The appropriative 'I'

'Having picked one / I can start anywhere', Graham remarks in 'Drawing Wildflowers': a poem collected in her first volume entitled *Hybrids of Plants and of Ghosts* (1980: 8–9). That the wildflower is physically picked from the ground emphasizes the fact that the wildflower is possessed by the artist and predisposed to her decision as to how it will be represented. Referring to the wildflower Graham continues the line with 'and as it bends, weakening, // ignore that' (ibid.: 9–10). Dismissing what seems to be the wildflower's own action, Graham's speaker draws attention to the action of the 'I': 'I can chart the shading of the moment – tempting – though shading / changes hands so rapidly. / Yes should I draw it changing, making of the flower a kind of mind' (ibid.: 11–13). In the words Kathleen Jamie used to describe Robert Macfarlane, 'this begins to feel like an appropriation'. Graham's repetition of 'shading' and 'changing' demonstrates the possibilities of the self imposing upon the wildflowers. Undoubtedly, the wildflowers present a certain shade of their own and this can change depending upon the light. However, the artist's pencil can also shade the wildflower. This shading 'changes hands' (or shifts responsibility) once again as the artist's own character – perhaps their mood – can shade the wildflower. David Petersen's pedagogical prescription of environmental writing as 'necessarily first-person and profoundly invested with (colored by) the writer's personality' (2001: 3) makes it possible to see the wildflower as literally 'colored by' the 'I' as the artist considers 'making of the flower a kind of mind' and even more dramatically, 'I can make it carry *my* fatigue, / or make it dying' (1980: 13, 15–16).

The role of subjectivity in certain pedagogical exercises discussed previously, such as Margaret McFadden's 'The 'I' in Nature', suggested writing as a kind of ecotherapeutic experience. Graham's poem demonstrates a very different 'quest for pilgrimage in self-awareness' as she realizes the opportunities for the 'I' to impose and manipulate. This awareness occurs again in 'Thinking' in which, trying to represent a crow, the speaker in the poem makes 'a *version* of a crow' (1998: 3, emphasis added). 'Thinking' begins

> I can't really remember now. The soundless foamed.
> A crow hung like a cough to a wire above me. There was a chill.

It was a version of a crow, untitled as such, tightly feathered
in the chafing air. Rain was expected. All round him air
dilated, as if my steady glance on him, cindering at the glance-core where
it held him tightest, swelled and sucked

(ibid.: 1–6)

In such an excerpt it becomes difficult, if not impossible, to differentiate the crow from the seeing of the crow. Why does a 'version' of the crow and not the crow itself hang on the wire? Vision itself seems to create its own reality. The crow, described as 'tightly feathered' could simply be tightly feathered, but he could also be tightly feathered because of the 'glance' that 'held him tightest'. Later in the poem, Graham appears to reinforce this dynamic as she writes 'If I squint, he glints' (ibid.: 13). The opening of the poem that claims 'I can't really remember now' indicates yet another rendering of the real crow through memory. In turn, the crow becomes as intangible as the 'cough' to which he is first likened: a quality that is only emphasized by the title, which, rather than 'Crow' is 'Thinking'.

Although several teachers recognize the problems involved in employing a first-person perspective when writing about the environment, Petersen's term 'ego acrobatics' does not quite encompass the subtle, seemingly unconscious manipulations of Graham's 'I'. The question of how basic acts of perception might be implicated in an ethically dubious relationship between self and environment continues in her later volume, *Never*. Concentrating on the process of observation in 'Philosopher's Stone', Graham writes

– eyes open now – over
sky, blue, stonewall, vectoring grasses, three trees,
distance, close-up – all as if
being drawn-in without it affecting *how*.
If you open and close your eyes
there should be a difference, no, in the way
the thing seen *is* – in its weight? – and then
what the thinking has begun to make –

(2002: 21–8)

The latter part of the perceptual process Graham describes suggests that when the observer's eyes are open the environment appears to be viewed objectively. When the eyes are closed, however, the environment weighs differently in the mind because thinking has begun to remake the perception. In his guide to environmental writing, John A. Murray emphasizes the 'importance of eliminating self-deception and half-truths in thought and writing' (1995: 2). In a statement pertinent to Graham's concern over the act of perception that precedes language, Murray proposes the journal that, as an 'unflinching mirror', records the environment in situ without memory or 'thinking' manipulating the observation (ibid.). Central to many place-based pedagogical approaches, the journal, as understood by Murray, permits a kind of self-effacement within the writing practice – surprising, given his statement that 'You need that personal "I" as often as possible' (ibid.: 19). Albeit well-intended in its attempt to moderate the role of the self in a writer's account of the environment, Murray's belief in the journal as a mirror cannot help but look naïve in the light of Graham's study. It might be interpreted from 'Philosopher's Stone' that the manipulative 'I' can be turned on and off with a blink, but Graham's line concerning the external world 'as if / being drawn-in without it affecting *how*' adds further nuance. Graham's 'as if' draws attention to the obvious question of whether it is possible to receive the environment without some selectivity in the observation. The italicized '*how*' similarly undermines the idea that there is one objective way in which the stonewall and three trees can be perceived. As Graham declares in a later poem entitled 'Futures', 'Is there a skin of the I own which can be scoured from inside the glance / – no' (2002: 23–4).[5]

Advising his students to think about 'the differences between perception, interpretation and imagination', Laird Christensen provides a pedagogical approach that begins to correspond to Graham's scrupulous account of observer and environment (2014c). Teaching at Green Mountain College in America's greenest state, Vermont, Christensen asks his undergraduates the following questions: 'How does perceiving an environment differ from interpreting an environment?' and 'Is it possible to perceive an environment without interpreting it, to represent an environment in words without interpreting it?' (2014d). Christensen's careful approach throws doubt over Murray's advice that stresses the journal as an 'unflinching mirror' and begins to suggest that the self plays a role in mediating between the observation and the writing of the journal. Attempting to define the different stages of perception, interpretation and imagination, students begin to respond to Christensen's questions. One student claims that 'the ability to classify an oriole' is interpretation rather than perception of the natural world, raising matters of taxonomic classification. Another student suggests that the difference is 'a case of objectivity versus subjectivity and that the latter happens with filters'. A further student chimes in by questioning whether these 'filters' can be avoided: she suggests that our past is always going to 'influence us' and filter what would otherwise be objective perception (2014d).

The 'filters' of looking, naming and writing about the environment also become central to Randall Roorda's pedagogical account in *Dramas of Solitude* (1998). Focused on 'depopulated narratives of retreat' exemplified by writers such as Thoreau and Dillard (Macfarlane, too, would seem eligible), Roorda examines the ethics involved (1998: 12). He finds that the retreat narrative, often deemed a practice of self-effacement, may well attempt a dissolution of the self in an attempt to achieve unmediated perception of an environment. Yet, as he goes on to explore, in aiming for humility, these retreat narratives paradoxically present a kind of heroic quest (ibid.: 19, 115). Recounting a field-trip that was part of a writing class he taught, Roorda describes how his students 'Unprompted ... distribute themselves over the terrain, metamorphosing ... into single figures dispersing over the ledges and boulders' (ibid.: 143). He recognizes with a certain degree of unease that his students are 'versed in the cultural script of retreat and are moving to enact it', raising further ways in which the 'I' filters the environment (ibid.). Both Christensen and Roorda draw valuable attention to the ways in which the acts of writing and even of looking are subject to subconscious influences. Of course, cultural scripts go beyond just the retreat narrative, and beyond literature itself, influencing the very moment in which a writer steps outside.

Useful as these discussions might be, it is also possible that such attention to the processes of perception means that the object of such perception – the environment – is almost forgotten. It is important to be aware of how perceptual processes determine an understanding of the environment, but it is also important to explore how, as Nixon suggests, the environment challenges and determines our perceptual processes. Nixon's argument draws attention to a particular dynamic within the environment: that of an attritional violence that given its effect over space and time is beyond the bounds of our perception. In an interview with Thomas Gardner, Graham becomes similarly mindful of certain challenging dynamics as she asks 'how much of the world can we bear-in via sense perception and its rendering in language?' (2013). Graham is concerned by the very copiousness of materiality in the here and now. Speaking on this problem with Gardner, Graham explains that in *Never* she was interested in 'porting' the environment rather than 'reporting' it (ibid.). She describes her practice of writing '*en plein air*': 'In front of me – water and gulls on the beach in a certain moment of sunset, say – and I look up and describe the thing – then

I look up and it has changed, and I change the word' (ibid.). By changing the word, Graham offers 'an attempt to change the power ratio of witness to the world, to give the world – the subject – more power': aware of an environment's changeability, she wants to be '"corrected" by the given' (ibid.).

Graham's decision to write outside anticipates the greater temporal thrust of *Never*. As she explains in the collection's notes, the book is an 'attempt to enact the time in which it takes to see the thing, the time in which that seen thing is living and constantly changing' in terms of 'the rate of extinction [that] is estimated at one every nine minutes' (2002: 111). Although this alarming frequency of extinction might not seem in keeping with Nixon's understanding of 'slow violence', these extinctions take place all over the globe and are often the result of causal chains spread out over time, meaning that the loss of a particular species is, as Nixon indicates, 'out of sight'. Additionally, rather than an instant spectacle of catastrophe, an extinction is a loss: a kind of violence that is difficult, if not impossible, to see. By revising the power ratio of witness to world, Graham attempts to lessen the possibility of the 'I' changing the environment further. This revision affords appreciation of the changes occurring within the environment: for instance, the gulls on the beach arriving and departing. Demonstrating an alternative approach to those often taken in current pedagogy, Graham's process of 'porting' the environment rather than 'reporting' is no easy task. Although the process responds to the problem of how much materiality can be carried via perception, the changes she wishes to record are ongoing, making it impossible for the writer to keep up.

In 'Afterwards', Graham demonstrates the way perception is challenged by materiality as the observer struggles to focus upon a group of starlings that cannot be seen, only heard:

> Invisible in the pruned-back
> hawthorn, heard and heard again, and yet again
> differently heard, but silting
> the head with inwardness and making always a
> dispersing but still
> coalescing opening in the listener who
> cannot *look* at them exactly,
> since they are invisible inside the greens
>
> (2002: 11–18)

As the physical presence of the birds is lost, the observer experiences a synaesthetic reaction: the starlings are 'yellowest, / fine thought' (ibid.: 19–20).

Like the crow in 'Thinking' that is the product of the observer's perception, the starlings become made of thought 'finespun' (ibid.: 20). However, two of the birds do finally appear, seeming to bathe in a pool of water as Graham describes their 'thrash, dunk, rise, shake, rethrashing, reconfiguring through / reshufflings and resettlings' (ibid.: 25–6). There is a 'porting' of the event: verbs and adjectives replace one another in a way that is consistent with Graham's process of looking up, recognizing change and changing the word. The four instances of words prefixed with 're' (reconfiguring, reshuffling) imply that as the birds move and change position, the language reconfigures and reshuffles too. However, this process is still doubted by Graham as she ends her description with the question, 'How shall we say this *happened*?' (ibid.: 32). In the preceding ten lines Graham has attempted to explain what has happened, so why this uncertainty? Rather than *how* shall we say this happened, Graham has put the italicized stress on *happened* as if doubting the finality of the past tense. 'Afterwards' may attempt to negotiate the tensions involved with a narrative 'I' by 'porting' the starlings, but the starlings supposedly continue 'reconfiguring through / reshufflings' despite the poem coming to an end. Graham's understanding of the relentless changes in the environment interrogates the immediacy, and thus the validity, of her technique. As Graham playfully recognizes with a hesitant enjambment in 'Philosopher's Stone', 'there's on / goingness' (ibid.: 2).

'Casting my eye out / to see'

Graham's decision to 'change the power ratio of witness to the world, to give the world – the subject – more power' is compromised by her realization that the world continues to change once the writer stops writing. Consequently, in 'Woods', Graham is anxious about what she calls the 'swagger of dwelling in place, in voice' (2003: 12). She continues to explain:

Surely one of us understands the importance.
Understands? Shall I wave a "finished" copy at you
whispering do you wish to come for lunch.
Nor do I want to dwell on this.
I cannot, actually, dwell on this.
There is no home. One can stand out here
and gesture wildly, yes. One can say "finished"
and look *into* the woods, as I do now, here,

> but also casting my eye out
> to see
>
> (ibid.: 13–22)

The stability of the environmental representation is questioned in a similar way to that in 'Afterwards'. Comparable to Graham's italicized *'happened'*, Graham's scare quotes parody the notion of an environment being 'finished'. The writer cannot hold the environment in a singular time. After all, if one looks up one will find it has changed, that it is different and thus the writing becomes unrepresentative.

In 'Woods', Graham moves away from the question of 'How shall we say this *happened*?' and even 'How shall we say this *as it is happening*?' to 'How shall we say what *will happen*?' Apprehending the continuance of environmental change, Graham's response is in 'casting my eye out / to see' (ibid.). Her choice of vocabulary suggests an attempt to extend perception of the surroundings at hand, which is developed by the potential pun in the line. Reading 'casting my eye out / to see' as 'casting my eye out / to sea' invites a comparison with a captain on board a ship who inspects the horizon for danger. Government offices and environmental agencies have adopted such an act into a key strategy identified as 'horizon scanning' in which the future is scanned for emerging concerns. By conducting this process, these agencies hope to equip themselves to deliver preventative or adaptive procedures. With these associations in mind, it is possible to interpret Graham as expressing a desire to depart from the immediacy of the present tense in order to apprehend change in a way that responds to Nixon's call to imaginatively bring the unseen into view. The act of 'casting my eye out / to see' invites us to project observation into other temporal frames that are not limited to the 'now'. Yet this practice should not be restricted to the future tense only. Murray proposed that the journal, as an 'unflinching mirror', should be used to deter students from depending upon their memories when representing environments, but other teachers have argued that drawing from past experiences can assist perception. Murray's guidance shares in Graham's understanding that the act of remembering can prompt an individual 'I' to representationally change an environment in a potentially misleading manner. However, some teachers have made the case that comparing past and present perceptions can productively show how a collective 'I' – a society – has physically changed an environment.

John Elder supports the use of the first-person, but he is also aware of its potential for 'self-absorption'. As an 'escape' from 'the litany [of] "I think, I feel,

I remember"', Elder values a temporal shift of attention in which students might imagine 'a local setting when the Wisconsin glacier rose a mile above it' (2014). Developing this approach involving environmental history combined with an awareness of contemporary environmental issues, Mitchell Thomashow plots other exercises that draw on a more recent sense of the past. In *Ecological Identity* (1995), a book aiming to cultivate reflective environmentalists, Thomashow describes an exercise entitled 'Childhood Memories of Special Places' (1995: 8). He instructs students to think about what their home region 'looked like when you were a child, and what it looks like now' in order to appreciate environmental change (ibid.). As Thomashow foregrounds the importance of memory he embraces the same act that concerned Graham in 'Thinking'. However, rather than the act of remembering being unhelpfully manipulative, Thomashow demonstrates how it can be conducive: the memory produces contrast with the present day therefore allowing students to witness 'the transformation of those places ... to appreciate the magnitude of environmental change, to understand and feel the impact of the changes' (ibid.: 10). Admitting that the exercise introduces personal aspects of the 'I', Thomashow comes to the conclusion that 'traveling into your past is less a nostalgic exercise and more an opportunity to observe a global environmental change' (2002: 99). Readily adaptable for environmental writing pedagogy, the process of 'casting my eye out' to the past uses the self as a tool to engage with issues affecting the environment. This practice begins to extend towards the future as Thomashow explains that the places students 'currently live in may also fall prey to development or pollution' (1995: 12). He elaborates upon this brief reference to the future as he explains that 'returning to a place where you once lived allows you to move backward and forward in time. Your memories represent the past in contrast to what you observe in the present, allowing you to feel like you're observing the future' (2002: 99).

This entanglement of temporal frames that invites a new perception of the present is given in reverse by Graham. In an interview with Deidre Wengen, Graham explains that if we imagine 'where we are headed' then this will incur consideration of 'what it will feel like to look back at this juncture' and consequently 'maybe we will wake up in time' (2014). Looking back from the imagined future makes the present appear like the past, but, given it is still the present, such a process acts as a reminder that measures can still be taken to mitigate issues affecting the environment. In her 2008 collection, *Sea Change*, Graham considers 'where we are headed'. 'Root End' finds that this 'desire to imagine / the future' is analogous to 'walking in the dark through a house you know by / heart' (2008: 1–4). She describes this attempt to imagine the future as exhibiting both arrogance and ignorance in the way that, in this dark house, the human mind

> says in you: accelerate! – it is your
> place, you be-
> long, you know it by
> heart, place –
> not imaginable, nor under-
> stood, where death is still an in-
dividual thing, & in the dark outside only the garden, & in each plant at core a thing
> by
heart

(2008: 26–34)

Like other poems by Graham, 'Root End' features a sense of misplaced ownership. The way in which the future is likened to 'a [dark] house you know by / heart' reveals the self's tendency to presume the future to be a continuation of the present. Graham highlights this misunderstanding with the detail that the imagined future is one in which 'death is still an in- / dividual thing'. As the line is juxtaposed with the previous qualifier 'not imaginable', Graham suggests that death will, in fact, happen on a larger scale. Indeed, the misplaced assumption that death is 'is still an in- / dividual thing' brings to mind the mass animal extinction events of recent years which have been linked to changes in the climate.

The kind of projection involved in Graham's 'attempt to see where we are headed' becomes even more vivid in 'Futures' (2008). Early in the poem, attention is drawn to 'the imagined fragrance as one / bends, before the thing is close enough' (2008: 11–12). This 'thing' is the future and yet described as if it were a flower. However, the expectation and the reality of this future are less pleasant than the 'imagined fragrance' with its associations of spring and new growth:

> You know the trouble at the heart, blue, blue, what
pandemonium, blur of spears roots cries leaves master & slave, the crop destroyed,
> water everywhere not
> drinkable, & radioactive waste in it, & human bodily
waste

(ibid.: 16–20)

Although 'Futures' does not present the future as a place known 'by heart', but instead acknowledges that there is 'trouble at the heart', the disturbing future environment remains punctuated with instances of intimacy and familiarity:

> Your lower back
> started acting up again, & they pluck out the eyes at the end for
> food ...
> & you try to think of music and the blue of Giotto,
> & if they have to eat the arms he will feel no pain at least
>
> (ibid.: 35–7, 41–2)

The future environment described by Graham shows the continuation of certain domestic and cultural references – there are still such things as teacher–parent meetings and the paintings of Giotto continue as a reference point. This lulling familiarity then jars with the descriptions of meteorological catastrophe and cannibalistic activity, provoking a shocking recognition of change.

Contrast is generated on a more intimate level too. Graham's conclusion appears to draw upon the opening of the poem (in which the future was compared to a flower) when she writes from the perspective of this future 'I' who is

> remembering money, its dry touch, sweet strange
>   smell, it's a long time, the smell of it like lily of the valley
> sometimes, and pondwater, and how
>   one could bend down close to it
> and drink.
>
> (ibid.: 66–70)

This conclusion that concerns the smell of money disturbs the assumption in the analysis above; that the 'fragrance' belonged to spring flowers. Consequently, this inconsistency between the opening and closing of the poem challenges an expectation or appropriation of the future as Graham parodied in 'Root End'. In this way, Graham draws attention to a desire to identify and find consistency when it is necessary to acknowledge change and difference. Graham cultivates further uncertainty in what appears to be a zeugma: a literary device in which one word applies to two others, creating a different meaning from each. The sensorial juxtapositions Graham makes between money, lily of the valley and pond water means that money also becomes a source that 'one could bend down close to' and drink from. This act of remembering – of how one 'could' drink – provides an illustration of her earlier hope that looking into the future will prompt a 'look back at this juncture': the sight of such future destruction might prompt thought as to how current freshwater sources are treated, as well as reflection upon contemporary attitudes to money and economic growth.

In *Slow Violence*, Nixon makes the case that the challenge posed to perception by the environment and environmental dynamics can only be overcome by 'giving the unapparent a materiality upon which we can act' (2011: 16). By reading certain texts, Nixon provides insight into how writers can generate this materiality. It is interesting to compare his analysis with Graham's technique. For example, measuring the toxic legacy of the Chernobyl explosion to that of the Bhopal gas disaster, Nixon explores how Indra Sinha addresses the latter tragedy of 1984 in his novel, *Animal's People*. The story is told from the perspective of an 'indigent social outcast' whose spine is twisted as a result of the tragic gas leak that occurred just before his birth (ibid.: 46). This character is named Animal because he walks on all fours, and Nixon argues that the character's contorted body comes to represent the damage inflicted by otherwise unseen transnational powers and globalized economies. While Animal's deformed body affords perception of the slow violence caused by the Bhopal disaster, Graham's poems suggest other practices that, in the words of Nixon, 'give figurative shape to formless threats' (ibid.: 10). Rather than a physical body as such, Graham provides the sensory data that a body receives from the landscape it inhabits. Interestingly, this practice seems to share much in common with SueEllen Campbell's exercise entitled 'Layers of Place' (2006). Campbell, who recently retired from Colorado State University, understands place to be 'finely and intricately laminated, not only with the immediate and personal, but also with what we don't see that is present, with what is past and future' (2006: 179). She begins by asking her students to choose 'one place that you know well, maybe a place you love. Put yourself there in your imagination and memory' (ibid.: 180), before asking a long series of in-depth questions such as

> How does the air feel going into your lungs? Can you feel your heart beating? Touch something you've been looking at – with your finger tips, with your face. How does it feel against your body? Taste something. How does it taste? ... How much water is around you, in what forms, doing what? What's the temperature?
> (ibid.)

This kind of awareness is intended to make the perception of a place 'immeasurably richer – not necessarily more comforting, but certainly more thorough' (ibid.: 179).

The precision of Campbell's sensory prompts immerses the writer in place. Unlike Sinha's *Animal*, the body does not stand in as a symbol for the environment, but is a medium with which to encounter and communicate the environment. Though Campbell's questions mostly attend to place in the present tense, the future creeps into her exercise later on in two questions: 'What might it be like here fifty or a hundred years from now? What might happen as the planet continues warming?' (ibid.: 181–2). Yet the hesitant tone accompanying these prompts obstructs the intention to 'put yourself there': her 'what might' potentially draws attention to the distance between now and generations hence. In contrast, Graham connects with the future as if it were the present. In her work, imagined, immaterial landscapes belonging to a time to come are materialized through a confident and sustained engagement with sensory phenomena. In the pages that follow, I will explore the particular narrative style that communicates such phenomena. Mixing pronouns and developing an inventive practice of apostrophic address, Graham continues to reimagine the 'I' as she deepens the connection with what is out of sight.

'From where you are now': Interconnective apostrophe

Graham may be 'casting *my* eye out / to see' in 'Woods' (emphasis added), but to whom exactly does the perception belong in 'Futures'? After all, in 'Futures' Graham addresses 'you'. Her work presents a complex use of pronouns that I will examine further. There is an omniscient quality to Graham's description of the large-scale pandemonium in which there is 'water everywhere not / drinkable', a slightly more familiar tone to the 'you' in 'you know why we have come', as well as another, far more intimate 'you' who is suffering from 'lower back pain'. This question of address and addressee arises also in 'Root End': '*you* know it by heart', Graham states, and yet later Graham refers to a collective '*we*' and 'mind knows *our* place so / deeply well' (emphasis added). In an interview with Sharon Blackie, Graham explains that her most recent collection *PLACE* addresses the question of how to 'make the "deep future" – seven to ten generations hence – feel actually "connected" to us, right down to this … this choice we make to use this styrofoam cup, this plastic bag' (2012b). This is similar to her previous statement regarding *Sea Change* in which apprehending the future provokes reflection of the present. However, in speaking to Blackie, Graham accentuates the need to 'feel actually connected' to future generations as if such connection could boost the productive potential of reflecting upon our current actions (ibid.). Graham's interest in sensory phenomena and her use of pronouns enacts this hoped-for connection, as I will show in this final section.

In 'Futures', in which Graham imagines a damaged future environment, she appears to address a human inhabiting the future. She writes 'don't forget / the meeting at 6, your child's teacher / wishes to speak to you' (2008: 35–7). However, the degree of familiarity expressed through what seems to be an internal reminder – 'don't forget' – seems more representative of an inner-dialogue, which complicates the address. In an interview with Katia Grubisic, Graham admits the confusion she experienced in this process of addressing future generations. She explains, 'I felt I was trying to address them directly, though – it did not feel easy as I could not figure out who I was. The hard-to-squint-in nature of them goes hand in hand with a dissolving sense of the self-in-the-now' (2010). Graham acknowledges the perceptual challenge of envisioning these generations. After all, she fears in 'Untitled' that humans in the future may 'become unrecognizable' (2012a: 37). In trying to figure out who they are, Graham becomes uncertain of who she is and thus indicates that there is a transaction of identities at work between herself and this other 'you'.

Apostrophe, otherwise known as an address to an absent other, is etymologically sourced from 'apo' (from) and 'strephein' (to turn): a process enacted by Graham as she leaves 'the-self-in-the-now' to engage with the life of an 'I' in the future. Evoking parallel with Nixon's argument for materialization, Graham explains in her conversation with Grubisic that 'the human imagination – in art – has an amazing way of helping into reality things that will from that point on become real, feel real, be thought of as real' (2010). She gives the example, that 'once you meet Emma Bovary, or Mrs Dalloway – will they ever not be real to you again?' (ibid.). The 'vocative' of apostrophe asserts the presence of an addressee even if the addressee is absent thereby helping the as-yet-unborn into reality (Culler 2015: 240).[6] Graham takes this a stage further when she asserts that making future humans 'feel real' is only possible 'if we use our sensorial imagination (supplementing our conceptual intellect for a minute) to bring them to life' (2010). Bringing the 'sensorial imagination' to the fore, 'Although' plays further with apostrophe to engage imaginatively with future humans and apprehend futural change. The poem begins with

> The vase of cut flowers with which the real is (before us on this page)
>   permeated – is it a page – look hard (I try) – this bouquet
>   in its
> vase – tiger dahlias (red and white), orange freesia (three stalks) (floating
>   out), one

>   large blue-mauve hydrangea-head, still
>   wet (this
> bending falling heavy with
>   load)
>
> (2012: 1–9)

Observation of the bouquet is made difficult as the words on the page are found to be a poor substitute for the reality of their subject. Yet, there is another perceptual challenge at work here that is created by a temporal shift made clear as Graham asks later in the poem,

> Is there still day, one of the days, are there still 'ones' of
>   things – vases or days –
> you think it is wrong, perhaps, to play this game
>   when we are all
>   still here
>
> (2012: 69–73)

The effect is similar to that of 'Futures', with its 'memory of money'. In 'Although', the suggestion is that vases and bouquets may not exist in the future. As the poem participates in time travel it demands a re-reading of the scrupulously detailed representation of the bouquet with which it began. Is the bouquet so lavishly described because it acts as a record of sensuous phenomena – 'blue-mauve', 'holding drops of rain' – that will be lost to the future? The 'you' addressed in 'Although' is less intimately known than those in previously discussed poems. When Graham writes 'you think it is wrong, perhaps', the 'you' is attributed with their own sense of judgement of which we are uncertain. Graham proposes that the future human thinks it wrong, perhaps inappropriate or insensitive, for the present generation (referred to as 'we') to 'play this game' of imagining the future and speculating about what will remain.

Perhaps, however, there is no reason to jump to the assumption that the 'you' refers to a separate generation from the 'we'. Identifying the 'you' as part of a collective 'we' makes it possible to argue that Graham is singling out a present reader with her apostrophic 'you'. In other words, it is the present-day reader of Graham's poem who is projected into the future by Graham's questions ('are there still "ones" of things') and thus may regard this projection into the future as an uncomfortable experience and an unethical 'game'. Implied reader participation is not unusual in Graham's work: a direct address to readers is present in several of Graham's earlier volumes including *The End of Beauty* (1987) and *Materialism* (1993). In 'Room Tone', collected in the former volume, Graham writes, 'Dear reader, is it enough for you that I am thinking of you / in this generic sort of way' (1987: 7–8). This continues in 'Break of Day', in *Materialism,* when Graham asks the reader another question: 'Can we make this a *thinking*, here, this determination / between us to co- / exist' (1993: 147–9). Returning to 'Although', it is necessary to reinterpret those hesitant opening lines in which Graham wrote 'Try to look (I try)' as an expression of her desire to 'co- / exist' with the reader. As the reader is transported to a future time in which the bouquet no longer exists, the particular instruction – 'Try to look' – requires the reader to use their own sensorial imagination to appreciate the rich materiality we currently have and stand to lose. In turn, Graham's practice of address not only involves squinting into the future, but also squinting into the past (otherwise the present) from an imagined future.

This chapter's ecocritical questioning of the first-person has tested some typical current pedagogical instruction and, via its readings of Graham's poetry, indicated ways of developing particular strategies for environmental writing. Like many teachers, Jon Gower is aware of tensions concerning the narrative 'I', especially when he suggests that writers are often more interested in themselves than the environment. My readings of Graham have sought to expand on these tensions, showing how the self's manipulative tendencies run deep: involving the act of perception itself. Attempting to negotiate this power dynamic, Graham practices 'porting' rather than reporting of the landscape, only to recognize that the ongoingness of environments makes such porting impossible. Conscious of change – from the movements of a starling – to the backdrop of species extinction – she finds that the inflexibility of the written word is doomed to be unrepresentative. Yet, as she begins to imagine the kind of change relevant to future environments – dramatic weather and water shortages – she begins to enact Nixon's intention to bring what cannot be seen into view. With a series of techniques involving the sensorial imagination and apostrophe, Graham's work reveals that rather than abandoning the 'I' in environmental writing, we might reconsider that 'I' to productive effect. According to John Elder and other tutors, the first-person provides the opportunity for 'discovery' within the environment and leads to 'the most vivid stirring writing'. Although Graham engages with 'you' rather than 'I' in her work, her apostrophic practice shares many of the positive, connective qualities associated with this first-person narrator. Indeed, it is possible to suggest that through her use of the sensorial imagination, Elder's sense of discovery is enriched. The representation of smell, sight or the active remembrance of such provides immediacy despite the fact that the environment is imaginatively experienced as hundreds of years from now.

Graham's use of apostrophe, then, plays with the 'I-me-my-voice'. Importantly, the threat of authorial appropriation is still present. As she notes, perhaps it is 'wrong' to play the 'game' of imagining ourselves in correspondence with, or in the shoes of, someone in the future. Importantly, too, however, this movement between the 'I' and the imagined 'you' introduces an empathic practice that ultimately aims to realize environmental change. This has consequences when we consider the place of polemic in environmental writing. As discussed previously, Petersen believes that one 'provocative paragraph … is nature writing at its best and most useful' (2001: 191). Yet, provocative environmental writing often receives criticism not unlike Jamie's ridicule of Macfarlane's 'enraptured' narrator that raises issues concerning authorial privilege and egotism. Writing in 2015 for *The New Statesman*, the well-known 'new nature writer', Mark Cocker, takes issue with recent environmental writing for its reluctance to communicate current ecological issues affecting the United Kingdom. Like the distinction Petersen offers between 'transcendental musings' and provocation, Cocker is opposed to what he identifies as a recent trend of re-enchantment (marked by an engagement with literary antecedents of the 'new nature writing' and conveyed in lyrical prose). If writers continue in this vein, Cocker concludes, 'we are just fiddling while the agrochemicals burn' (2015). Polemic is not a word used by Cocker, but given the polemical style of his article it is difficult to imagine what else he might hope for from environmental writing. But, as suggested earlier, do we need to subscribe to a binary between lyric and polemic?

Robert Macfarlane writes in direct response and calls Cocker's 'noisily game-changing' proposition 'wrong' (2015a). He makes the case for a diversity of voices and a diversity of aesthetic strategies in environmental writing, listing, among others, Richard Skelton's 'experimental work' and China Miéville's 'thrillingly weird prose' (ibid.). Admirable in its big picture thinking, Macfarlane's embrace of different strategies is significant in considering how literature can convey environmental arguments without becoming polemical. As discussed in the previous chapter, Juliana Spahr engaged with issues as broad-ranging as the Israeli-Palestinian conflict and the existence of everyday pollutants through confessional lyric. Though not explicitly argued, negotiations of polemic punctuate Nixon's *Slow Violence*. In his discussion of *Animal's People*, he highlights how Sinha has successfully avoided the dangers of polemic by constructing a narrator who is thought-provokingly 'ambivalent toward the pursuit of justice' (2011: 52). Not side-tracked by anger, nor sanctimonious, Nixon comments on other authors who intersperse memoir, irreverence, lyricism with reprimand and rebuke.

Graham's fascination with perception extends the range of aesthetic strategies used to portray an environmental message. The genre of speculative fiction is brought to mind by her imagining of a future in which the 'rain is everywhere switching-on'. Simultaneously, Graham's strategy of capturing a present day from the future in all its luscious sensorial detail leads to a kind of praise poetry, reminiscent of Mary Oliver's work. In its time-travelling nature, Graham's poetry fits the category of elegy too, while the apostrophic form of the poems might also lead us to see them as a series of epistles. Graham looks: she meticulously records details, reflects on her own manipulative gaze, and Graham also looks out: imagining altered landscapes of the future. Portraying the disorienting interaction between self and other in conversation with Grubisic, Graham states of the future humans she addresses: 'You can find yourself in them and them in you. Then what will you do?' (2010). Although Graham's question conjures the tone of Jim Perrin's polemical conclusion to his Country Diary: 'Hypocrisy, or what?', this question is turned in on itself in the mode of self-questioning. Identifying with others in environments otherwise out of the sight provokes emotional responses in us as the consequences of our current behaviour are brought into closer proximity to us. Yet the 'do' of Graham's 'what will you do?' suggests another type of response prompted by an exchange between the first-person 'I' and another 'you': environmental action.

Writing with another 'I'

Graham's poetry collections record a journey. Through her 'attempt to change the power ratio of witness to world', she moves from projecting her emotions onto a flower in 'Drawing Wildflowers' – 'I can make it carry *my* fatigue' – to projecting into other temporal frames in order to comprehend the possible loss of a bouquet and the fragility of current environments. As I will now go on to show by articulating new pedagogical proposals, Graham's work emerges as a creative model that not only sets out a comprehensive interrogation of a first-person for students to follow, but also initiates thought on futures-thinking and empathy, which may be used to develop thought about polemic, environmental argument and the need to speak on behalf of the environment.

Across 'Drawing Wildflowers', 'Thinking' and 'Philosopher's Stone', the 'I' and, in particular, the eye, are quizzed in relation to environments and their entities. What personal, cultural and ideological baggage do we bring to an environment in our narration of it? As demonstrated in Laird Christensen's class at Green Mountain College, it might be valuable to frame the conversation in terms of 'filters' or lenses that unintentionally introduce a first-person. Asking students to reflect on a piece of environmental writing they have previously written provides a good starting point to develop this self-reflexive exercise. What do you think your eye was drawn towards and what did it neglect? Did you set out with a particular intention to write about the environment? What were your expectations? Which tradition do you think this piece is written in and why? These questions, especially the latter, recall Randall Roorda's realization that in generating retreat narratives of their own, his students were (seemingly subconsciously) enacting a 'cultural script'. A list of enquiries such as these can similarly serve to punctuate writing *en plein air*. In the act of writing about an environment, this exercise works to disrupt otherwise unquestioned relationships between self and environment, producing, as a result, a more sophisticated understanding of the tensions inherent to narration.

Given that many of the concerns regarding the first-person emerge from concerns about egotism, thought might be given to whether it is possible to adopt less imposing, manipulative versions of the 'I'. In speaking to Gardner and in her poem, 'Afterwards', Graham attempts a practice of self-effacement by enabling the environment to correct her representation of it. While such a process is of course a dramatization controlled by the author, it is, at the very least, a gesture towards disarming the first-person 'I'. What other practices might writers undertake? Students might reflect on whether they have any preconceived ideas about the 'I' in environmental writing. David Cooper, who lectures on place writing at Manchester Metropolitan University, explains that he is 'upfront' about 'the whiteness and maleness of nature writing' with his undergraduates (2018). In an exercise introduced at the beginning of his module, he asks his students to name writers they associate with the environment. As he predicts, students respond with the Romantics (partly owing to a module on Wordsworth the previous year). With this short exercise, Cooper facilitates reflection and discussion on presence and absence, privilege and representation in environmental writing. With the aim of challenging the responses given by students, Cooper's subsequent classes introduce reading that includes Zadie Smith's *NW*, Testament's play *Black Men Walking* and Zaffar Kunial's *Us*. Questions of class, sexuality and disability are also pertinent here. Addressing the latter, Polly Atkin's essay, 'Why Is It Always a Poem Is a Walk', is valuable in its discussion of 'ecocrip poetics' and ableism in writing workshops that take place outside and expect physical activity from participants (2019: 43).

Drawing on Kathleen Jamie's criticisms of Macfarlane, students might consider how the implications of their class, gender and ethnicity would alter if they were to write about different environments such as their local park, the wilds of Scotland, the Himalayas and the Falkland Islands. In response to Jamie's disapproval of the fact that Macfarlane failed to include voices other than his own in writing about inhabited landscapes unfamiliar to him, students could explore the effect of speaking to, and perhaps interviewing, local communities. Letting the environment speak, as it were, through the people who know it intimately helps to increase knowledge and accuracy in environmental writing while also diffusing authorial control. However, this practice also requires careful consideration. The writer initiating and portraying these conversations would need also to take into account another set of self-reflective questions. Whose voices are you representing and how? Is anyone neglected? How does your presence bias their response?

Graham's work might be considered self-conscious, but it can also be understood as self-critical. Her accusatory 'Then what will you do?', which comes after a prompt to identify with future humans in landscapes compromised by pollution and climate change, has the potential to trigger feelings of remorse as to our own environmentally unfriendly behaviour. Polemic, as discussed, raises pedagogical concern as it runs the risk of drawing attention to the first-person 'I' rather than the environmental concern. This effect, however, changes when the critical angle inherent to provocative writing is directed at oneself in the way hinted at by Graham. In *Ecological Identity*, Mitchell Thomashow facilitates what he calls an 'eco-confessional' in which he asks his students to share personal accounts of environmental irresponsibility (1995: 152). He describes his efforts to steer the exercise away from what might be interpreted as self-flagellation, and instead to establish 'collective responsibility for the ecological commons' (ibid.). This task becomes a kind of group therapy designed to productively work through feelings of frustration and depression concerning environmental issues, but writing an 'eco-confessional' of one's own also turns the dominant, seemingly powerful 'I' into an 'I' that is necessarily empathic towards the environment and others.[7] 'Burning the Shelter' (1998), an essay written by Louis Owens, complements study of Graham and advances the pedagogical potential of a self-critical 'I'.[8] Owens tells a carefully nuanced story of when he was a forest ranger in the Glacier Peak Wilderness in Washington State. Believing himself to be conserving a wild landscape, he dismantles a shelter only to find that his actions have dismantled part of a long-established relationship between an indigenous people and the landscape. Moving beyond the Transcendental, musing 'I', students can realize other ways of writing from their perspective as well as alternative modes to polemic. In the manner of Graham, the 'eco-confessional' is achievable through different forms. In each case, a short story, report, lyric essay, epistle or documentary poem requires a different type of 'I' and a different way of expressing argument and emotion.

While these exercises explore the self from different perspectives, the dynamics of a particular environment can also help to construct the narrator in a piece of writing. In her poems, Graham has shown how looking into the future necessitates an 'I' that is not entirely her own. Students might follow Graham's example closely: they might ask themselves what the short-term or long-term future will look, sound, smell, feel and taste like. Which foods might be more available than others? Which surviving bird species continue to sing? What are clothes made from in the future? Enacting Nixon's ecocritical argument and bringing the unapparent into view, students might play with their own sensorial imaginations as well as apostrophe: addressing a generation or a present-day reader in, say, 2150. Formal starting points to initiate this dialogue with another time frame include writing an interview with a future human in which the student occupies the role of interviewer or interviewee. Echoing the epistolary character of Graham's poems, students might similarly imagine themselves in correspondence with an 'I' of the future. Given that Nixon's argument focuses on bringing different times and places into view, students might want to experiment with addressing the past or a place distant from their own. Whether the aim is to bring into view the Industrial Revolution of the 1800s, current floods in Bangladesh or the likely flooding of London in decades to come, the necessary imaginative leap will require research. Discussing the tripartite structure of his course, that as discussed earlier comprises perception, interpretation and imagination, Christensen describes how the latter stage often features writing about what lies ahead (2014c). In contrast to dramatic projections given by films such as *The Day after Tomorrow*, Christensen asks his students for 'educated visualizations' (ibid.). While deterring any hasty, far-fetched representations, Christensen's rule is also helpful in securing the kind of connection between the present and the future that is fundamental to Graham's reimagining of the 'I'. Indeed, before students begin to conceive of which birds may survive a century from now, they need to study current trends and projections regarding, for example, climate change, invasive species and urban sprawl.

The sensorial imagination creates a kind of virtual reality in which the otherwise intangible seems tangible. In addition to Graham's chosen tools of connection, students might seek their own. Alongside the data we might receive from their senses, what language will a future human use to tell us about their environment? In an article entitled 'The Swiftness of Glaciers', Nixon reveals that the term 'glacial', often used figuratively to denote an extremely slow pace, is now nonsensical in the context of a climate-changed world in which glacier recession is rapid (2018). Similarly, 'we speak routinely of carbon footprints, of wiping species off the face of the Earth, and of greenhouse gases, but we no longer see the feet, the hands, the faces and the backyard sheds that were once vivid when those phrases were newly coined' (ibid.). One route into the exercise is to create possible phrases that could, in the future, come to replace those we have in the present. Slang words and endearments suggest another route. How might symbols such as fire and ice used since the Renaissance to describe the different stages of a love affair acquire different meanings as the climate warms? An appreciation of daily routine serves as another tool with which to connect with the future. Graham's reminder of the parent–teacher meeting suggests continuity, yet how might certain routines be altered? If temperatures are too high, would the 'you' of the future sleep at night? Which chores are made difficult, which easy?

To take this empathic experiment between the 'I' and 'you' a step further, it is possible to change the subject of study from a future human to a more-than-human entity: the landscape itself or an animal inhabiting the landscape. To address an animal or landscape as 'you', or begin to apprehend its perspective, demands a radically altered understanding of the 'sensorial imagination' alongside different connective tools and, in turn, has the potential to generate awareness of environmental issues at different scales. In her most recent collection, *FAST* (2017), Graham writes of topics as far ranging as artificial intelligence, social media and plastic surgery, but this does not mean she is finished with conversing with otherwise unseen or obscured environments. Depicting the damage inflicted by fishing trawls on species and habitats in 'Deep Water Trawling', she gradually introduces dialogue with the non-human into factual material: 'nets abandoned in the / sea they continue through the centuries to catch – mammals fish shellfish – we die / of exhaustion or suffocation – the synthetic materials last forever' (2017: 27–9). The pronouns continue to shift, though in a less certain manner when Graham writes 'Did you ever kill a fish. I was once but now I am / human. I have imagination. I want to love. I have self-interest' (ibid.: 33–4). The fragmentary, collage-like quality of the poem means it is difficult to ascertain who is speaking: the 'I' of the poem resembles the self-interested 'I' of the writer, yet apparently belongs to a marine species. Conversing imaginatively with environmental entities beyond the human, students can develop new versions of the 'I' while expressing different aspects of environmental concerns. However, as I will explore in the following chapter, anthropomorphism brings its own set of tensions.

3

'I am not a swift': Approaching non-humans

'The presumption is that the fox had a watch and a time-table about his person', writes John Burroughs in an essay that spurred the 'Nature Fakers' controversy at the turn of the twentieth century in America ([1903] 1998: 134). Burroughs draws attention to the ridiculousness of Ernest Thompson Seton's description of a fox deliberately leading a pack of bloodthirsty hounds onto the railway tracks with such precision and attention to time that they are immediately killed by a passing train. As 'Nature Fakers' suggests, the controversy concerned 'the line between fact and fiction' that Burroughs felt was utterly compromised by the anthropomorphic tales published under the guise of non-fiction (ibid.: 133). A well-regarded naturalist and writer, Burroughs criticized other authors too. Taking issue with the central principle of William J. Long's popular *School of the Woods*, Burroughs scoffs: 'The crows do not train their young. They have no fortresses, or schools, or colleges, or examining boards, or diplomas, or medals of honor, or hospitals, or churches, or telephones, or postal deliveries, or anything of the sort' (ibid.: 137). This criticism may not seem all that unusual in the light of this book's previous chapters, in which we have seen teachers of environmental writing advise students that their written descriptions should be 'unflinching mirror[s]' of the environment in question. But President Roosevelt's involvement in the controversy is somewhat surprising. Friends with Burroughs and a nature enthusiast himself, the president expressed private disapproval of the 'sham' nature writers, which later became public in a newspaper article. 'In one story a woodcock is described as making a kind of mud splint for its broken leg', Roosevelt writes of Long and adds, 'it seems a pity not to have added that it also made itself a crutch' ([1907] 1998: 195). Such 'deliberate perversion of fact' led Roosevelt to compare Long's depictions of animals 'exalted by humanitarianism' to the caricatures of medieval fables (ibid.: 196).

With today's proliferation of animal videos in which, for example, a cat adopts an abandoned monkey, a dog rides a Shetland pony and an orangutan saves a drowning coot chick, the anthropomorphic quality of Long's representations might seem more plausible. Whether or not Seton's death-dealing fox and Long's self-medicating woodcock merge animal and human behaviour in a preposterous manner, Long's response to Burroughs's dismissal of his work explains the reasons behind his approach:

> The nature-student ... must have not only sight but vision; not simply eyes and ears and a note-book; but insight, imagination, and, above all, an intense human sympathy, by which alone the inner life of an animal becomes luminous, and without which the living creatures are little better than stuffed specimens
> ([1903] 1998: 149)

Long proposes that the argument between fact and fiction pursued by Burroughs and Roosevelt is in fact a battle between imagination and science, sympathy and intellect, and, ultimately, animal life and death. This latter tension comes to the fore in Long's rebuttal to Roosevelt in which he argues against the President's role as naturalist by drawing attention to his passion for hunting ([1907] 1998: 174). Anthropomorphism might create works of complete fantasy, but, according to Long, its sympathetic potential challenges the perception of animals as objects for sport and display cases.

Anthropomorphism risks inventing – rather than responding to – the environment. Simultaneously, however, to rule out anthropomorphism risks viewing the human as separate from – or superior to the non-human and the environment more broadly. Such an argument returns again and again in contemporary thought. Articulating his concerns about anthropomorphism as a teacher of environmental writing at Middlebury College, John Elder asserts that 'anthropomorphism is to be avoided ... animals are interesting and we don't have to anthropomorphize them to make them interesting' (2014). Roosevelt's reference to fabular animals behaving and speaking like humans in order to give moral lessons and critique institutions is pursued by the idea that anthropomorphism makes no gesture towards how animals might be, in Elder's words, 'interesting' in themselves. Having made this point, however, Elder considers how the attitude he has just expressed might lead towards an unhelpful boundary being drawn between animal and human and, noting how 'biological orthodoxy' has guided us into 'saying that birds and other animals don't have feelings', concedes his position (ibid.). Maintaining that we should be careful 'not to automatically promote animals into human beings' (and qualifying this with 'if that were a promotion'), Elder ultimately decides that he would like his students 'to hold the question of where we might be similar' (ibid.). Though problematic, anthropomorphizing an animal through Long's 'human sympathy' seems like a better option than holding a Cartesian belief that animals are automata devoid of consciousness. A student on Laird Christensen's Environmental Writing Workshop at Green Mountain College exemplifies the kind of transformative potential of seeing the non-human as human when Christensen asks his class to describe a tree like a person. Exclaiming 'that's not something I would have thought', the student explains that 'before [the exercise] the tree was just a tree, it was just there for decoration' (2014d).

Despite its potential for good, many teachers remain distrustful of anthropomorphism. The environmental ethics that Long presents in his response to Burroughs and Roosevelt have grown more nuanced in today's environmental writing courses. Though sympathy with an environment's inhabitants might develop from anthropomorphic representation, anthropomorphism also encourages what teacher Chris Kinsey has described as 'appropriating' behaviours (2014). The previous chapter's study of the dominating and manipulative first-person 'I' reappears in discussions of anthropomorphism. 'I hate it. I absolutely hate it', asserts Andrew Motion when describing his feelings on the figurative device (2013). Having designed and taught on the 'Place, Environment, Writing' Master's course at Royal Holloway, University of London, Motion describes how writers 'divide into two kinds': those that, like Ted Hughes, 'think that if they crank up the energy levels and the volume then they can be like a swift, or an otter or a fox' and those

> people who want to register the difference between themselves and creatures. They feel that however sympathetic they are to whatever they're writing about, they are hopelessly trapped in their humanity, which is what I feel for what it's worth. I am *not* a swift, I am not. I sometimes wish I were, but I can't be. And the implications of that are quite potent I think.
>
> (2013)

Coming to the conclusion that anthropomorphism is 'soppy and wrong … it looks like sympathy but in its blasé way it is predatory', Motion expands on Elder's initial comment regarding the need to retain species' boundaries (ibid.). The 'implications' of accepting our human form and maintaining the line between humans and non-humans are 'a way of reminding yourself that in our intelligence and power as a species the responsibility lies with us' (ibid.).

Recent titles of British 'new nature writing', and their critical reception, serve to illustrate these concerns – and others. Helen MacDonald's *H is for Hawk* (2014) provides one such example. As an autobiographical story of grief in which MacDonald trains a northern goshawk in the year following her father's death, the book was seen by a few to be 'masquerading as nature writing' (Battersby 2014). Mark Cocker points out that although the goshawk in MacDonald's writing provides an 'aura of raw otherness … it is ultimately not a wild bird', as though tamed or domesticated animals are not suitable subjects for environmental literature (2015). Other reviews, meanwhile, praise the book's lack of anthropomorphism. Echoing Motion's concerns, MacDonald herself explains her decision not to attribute her feelings to the bird, saying that 'It's so important to recognise that the world is not full of things like you' (2014). There is perhaps no better example to cite in contrast to her work than *Being a Beast* (2016) in which Charles Foster spends six weeks underground trying to be a badger before describing the successes and failures of living as an otter, a fox and a swift in subsequent chapters. By living in a sett (dug with a JCB), eating worms (that he describes through a wine taster's vocabulary) and attempting to rely on his sense of smell rather than vision, Foster intends to cultivate a closer relationship to the badger with both humour and a reasonable amount of research into animal physiology. And yet, much of the book details the impossibilities of being a beast: 'Becoming a swift? I might as well try to be God' (2016: 187). In the rushed epilogue, Foster apologizes for his anthropomorphic perspective and suggests that his attempt to relate to non-human animals not only helps him to better relate to other humans, it also helps him become aware of his own identity as a human. These are thoughtful reflections and yet reviews of the book, which remain mostly positive, repeatedly describe Foster's project as 'eccentric' (Barkham 2016; Cave 2016; Croke 2016; Garner 2016), even 'bonkers' (Clare 2016). It may be that Foster's sense of humour distracts from more reflective readings of what could be radical animal representations. Although his book attempts to do more than use anthropomorphism for entertainment value, does it risk perpetuating reductive understandings of animals as objects for human pleasure?

What, then, are we to do about anthropomorphism? By its very definition, anthropomorphism is an 'attribution' of human characteristics to the non-human. As teachers of environmental writing, Elder, Kinsey and Motion are surely right to be wary of writing that imposes ourselves onto others, confusing ideas of responsibility in the process. Yet, as this chapter aims to explain, anthropomorphism does not have to reinforce anthropocentrism. Though Motion and Macdonald assert the opposite, this chapter establishes how anthropomorphism can be practiced 'to recognise that the world is not full of things like you' in an intimate and illuminating manner. As a cornerstone of the Western imagination, the Aesopian tradition of fables that finds tortoises early pioneers of the Slow Movement is understandably hard to shake. The Peter Rabbits and Peppa Pigs of children's literature are similarly difficult to ignore. Yet some attributions of what might be considered human characteristics can be employed to explore difference. This means moving beyond Elder's recognition that animals, like humans, have feelings to the question of how these feelings might differ from, or exceed, our emotional spectrum. Similarly, giving a voice to a bird might be an anthropomorphic gesture, but the voice does not have to describe human sensibilities – or activities such as running errands, meeting neighbours and shopping for groceries. Of course, the language of environmental writing is exclusively human and there is no way of avoiding this. Yet, as I will show, anthropomorphism has the potential to conceptualize difference rather than simply likeness.[1] Challenging pedagogical concerns, my reconsideration of anthropomorphism helps students to respectfully and responsibly reconceive of the 'difference between themselves and creatures' as Motion states, but without the risk of seeing themselves as outside or above the category of animal.

The term non-human, used in the title of this chapter, is often understood to be synonymous with the term animal. Consequently, questions might emerge regarding my decision to use 'animal' and 'human', especially considering the potential for such terminology to perpetuate a counterproductive binary. While the following pages outline other articulations of 'animal', my use of the term is guided by the need for clarity as the chapter goes on to explore alternative definitions of the non-human. Indeed, formed of two complementary halves, this chapter studies both animals and matter. The fabular tradition contains a few instances of anthropomorphic objects, such as Aesop's 'The Oak and the Reeds', and recent as well as contemporary children's literature and popular culture exhibit a wide array. Thomas the Tank Engine and Mrs Potts, the teapot, in Disney's *Beauty and the Beast*, provide immediate examples. Everyday language finds a ship to be 'she', a guest room in a hotel to be 'welcoming' and a city possessing a 'heart', even a 'soul'. Strictly speaking, however, these latter examples fall under personification rather than anthropomorphism given how human characteristics are lent to matter momentarily, rather than matter assuming human characteristics. Urban environments and human-made entities are often neglected subjects of study in current environmental writing pedagogy; they are seemingly incompatible with many teachers' focus on 'natural' environments. Inorganic materials, however, remain present whether we like it or not. A recent prediction states that by 2050, the oceans will contain more plastic than fish (World Economic Forum 2016). In an age of non-biodegradable, destructive matter, I will argue that anthropomorphism has the potential to narrate the animate quality or 'agency' belonging to plastics and nuclear waste in a way that engages with many of today's pressing environmental issues. Expanding thought on likeness, difference and responsibility, my study of matter both converges with and departs from my discussion on animals that follows.

Gill-pulse

In 'What Is It Like to Be a Bat?' ([1974] 2012), Thomas Nagel discusses the subjective nature of consciousness, but finds 'we are completely unequipped to think about the subjective character of experience without relying on the imagination' and sees this as a barrier to further study ([1974] 2012: 178). Gilles Deleuze and Félix Guattari propose a theory of 'becoming-animal' (more broadly, a theory on becoming-other) that differentiates 'becoming' from 'imitating' ([1980] 2003). Deleuze and Guattari want to leave behind stable and singular understandings of identity. The animal is not any one thing, nor can 'becoming-animal' be plotted with particular coordinates. 'When Hitchcock does birds, he does not reproduce bird calls, he produces an electronic sound like a field of intensities or a wave of vibrations, a continuous variation, like a terrible threat welling up inside us' (ibid.: 305). Becoming-animal does not rely on likeness between identities, but on suspension or destabilization of identities. In like manner, Jacques Derrida's approach in *The Animal That Therefore I Am* ([1997] 2008) foregrounds the ontological difference between humans and non-humans. Stepping from his bathroom shower one morning, Derrida finds himself gazed upon by his cat. This gaze makes him conscious of his own nudity and provokes feelings of uncertainty and shame as to what nudity is in the context of the human when compared to the animal. The cat's gaze and the questions it provokes leads Derrida to examine the response of the cat and what 'response' means in the case of an animal.

Recent ecocritical studies reflect on these landmark works and indicate approaches that we might use to develop current pedagogical perspectives. Donna Haraway, a feminist scholar focused on science, technology and the interactions of species, believes that Derrida identified a key question in asking not whether the animal can speak but how to conceptualize an animal's response. Crucially, however, he 'did not seriously consider an alternative form of engagement … one that risked knowing something more about cats' (2008: 20). Haraway approaches Derrida's cat as a 'companion species' and contemplates 'what the cat might actually be doing, feeling, thinking' (ibid.: 20). With this closer focus, she explores the interactions between humans and 'companion species' that range from domestic dogs and cats to 'rice, bees, tulips, and intestinal flora' to argue that species of all sorts are involved in 'coshaping' one another (ibid.: 15). In contrast to Deleuze and Guattari's 'becoming-animal', Haraway's interest in 'coshaping' leads to a practice of 'becoming-with'. This practice does not exclude a physical dimension (unsurprisingly, a pet owner's microbiome is altered by her pet), but 'becoming-with' more often suggests a conceptual framework in which an attentive, ethical state of mind can allow us to attune to otherness and recognize the different world an elephant or stick insect inhabits. Cultivating this capacity for 'becoming-with' can make us more 'response-able' in our relationships with the non-human (ibid.: 71).

Haraway's willingness to explore what she knows can never truly be defined in these relationships with otherness, and to do so with extraordinary intimacy corresponds to Timothy Morton's approach that challenges appropriation and assumptive understandings of environments by putting, as he describes, 'hesitation, uncertainty, irony, and thoughtfulness back into ecological thinking' (2010a: 16). 'Saying "Humans are animals" could get you in trouble', states Morton, but 'So could saying "Humans are not animals," for different reasons' (ibid.: 41). He comes to the conclusion that 'neither choice is satisfactory' (ibid.). Stressing species boundaries in the manner suggested by teachers such as Elder and Motion is, then, a form of identification that might be as problematic as identifying the non-human as human. Deploying the term 'strange stranger' instead of 'animal' helps Morton to acknowledge that 'we can never absolutely figure them out' (ibid.). After all, if it was possible to figure them out 'then all we would have is a ready-made box to put them in, and we would just be looking at the box, not the strange strangers' (ibid.). Although Morton does not discuss the figurative device, his assertion that 'The more we know them, the stranger they become. Intimacy itself is strange' corresponds to Haraway's punning concept of 'significant otherness' and so to the possibility that anthropomorphism's connective capacities can conceive of difference as well as likeness (ibid.).

Illustrating this aptitude of anthropomorphism, the poet Les Murray provides a series of valuable models. Citing a range of influences from Gerard Manley Hopkins who taught him 'how to melt language' to Elizabeth Bishop's attention to the dignity of animals (2009), Murray is also influenced by the indigenous culture of Australia, particularly Aboriginal song traditions and views on what we might call ecological kinship.[2] In *Translations from the Natural World* (1992), hereafter referred to as *Translations*, Murray gives voice to creatures. Discussing the collection in an interview with Barbara Williams, he explains his intention of 'getting to that other, absolutely timeless world in which the eagle's never heard of America' (1992: 126). Despite the eagle metonymically representing the United States, Murray acknowledges that this symbolism is confined to the human world. Consequently, in contrast to pedagogical principles that ask students to consider 'where we might be similar' with non-humans, Murray's statement immediately conjures difference. This mismatch between humans and animals continues when he explains that 'living things do all talk, I say, but they don't talk human language, or always speak with their mouth' (quoted in Fürstenberg 2004: 145). As Jorie Graham connects to future humans through the sensorial imagination and Juliana Spahr connects to life across the globe through breath, Murray connects to animals primarily through voice. Yet, in creating this connection, he uses it to convey radical contrast. Not only does he anticipate the linguistic difference of animal voices, but the content of their communication is bound by certain 'constraints: no hands, no colour vision if they're mammals' (ibid.).[3]

Reading Murray's *Translations* is not so dissimilar to being plunged into a dark forest or pitch-black cave. We grope our way through the words on the page, searching for some kind of landmark with which to orientate ourselves. In 'Shoal', we are plunged into the sea. The poem begins with a voice that speaks of self-identity: 'Eye-and-eye eye an eye / each. What blinks is I' (1992: 1–2). 'Eye-and-eye' shows Murray playing with 'I and I', a Rastafarian phrase used instead of 'we' to denote equality between people. Murray, however, subverts this human association by continuing to play with the 'eye'/I' in different ways. While one 'eye' refers to the visual organ, another 'eye' appears to be a verb. The attempt to find a stable connection between how a human and a shoal self-identifies becomes impossible as, 'again the eyes' I winks' (ibid.: 5). Here we might compare Murray's approach to Jorie Graham's use of the 'sensorial imagination'. Describing the shoal as 'tasting', he invites the human into the body of the non-human only to deviate from such familiarity when he describes each fish 'being a tongue' (ibid.: 10). Other bodily sensations are recorded by Murray in ways that introduce a shared sense of physical experience with a simultaneous undermining of such connection. The shoal's 'gill-pulse' posits similarity ('pulse') and difference ('gill') in the limited space of a kenning (ibid.: 7).

Beyond this sensory connection, however, Murray makes a connection to a conceptual dimension in 'Eagle Pair'. Here, a pair of eagles describe what appears to be their daily routine. The eagles sleep, they wake, they fly and they hunt, though none of these are depicted in such simple terms. As the eagles comprehend the transition from night to day and begin searching for their next meal, they reflect that 'Meat is light, it is power and Up, as we free it from load … But all the Down is heavy and tangled'. (ibid.: 8, 11). Throughout the short poem, the sky is represented as an animated and capitalized 'Up' and the sun pictured as an 'Egg' in a way that potentially evokes the 'cosmic egg' from which all life is said to hatch, according to a number of mythologies. With such representation, it appears that Murray is making some gesture towards the idea that eagles share a myth-making capacity with humans. In their influential work, *Metaphors We Live By* (1980), Lakoff and Johnson explain that 'up' and 'down' are often associated with Western approaches to mood, consciousness and ideas of progress. Murray, however, finds 'up' and 'down' occupying different conceptual domains. As he says, the eagles have 'never heard of America'. Instead, he imagines them as having their own figurative consciousness that reveals their particular conceptual geographies and priorities concerning prey.

The poems in *Translations* are, of course, still inescapably human: not only are they written in human language, but sometimes, as in 'Eagle Pair', they are also written in rhyming couplets. The content of the poems, however, continue to portray animal difference. Indeed, the experience Murray describes is difficult to identify: how are the eagles freeing the meat 'from load'? Do the eagles liberate otherwise ground-dwelling prey into the air? The representation of the 'Down' as 'heavy' seems to support this. Is it too simplistic to read 'tangled' as indicating the Australian bush, or might 'tangled' indicate a snare or even, resembling human conceptual metaphor, a more complex existence? It is this uncertainty which interrupts the potential figurative projection into a non-human body that is initiated by an otherwise intimate first-person voice. As one begins to take the perspective of a shoal, or eagle, one finds the non-human experience impossibly different and is forced back into humanness. 'The capacity to respond [to non-humans], and so to be responsible, should not be expected to take on symmetrical shapes and textures for all the parties', states Haraway, as she moves the discussion from 'becoming-with' to a theory of 'non-mimetic sharing' (2008: 71). An argument on animal experimentation leads her discussion. The instrumentality of non-human participants in laboratories is not a problem for Haraway; rather, the problem comes with how we *respond* to non-humans in that context. When we consider animal testing, mimicry is impossible: 'We do not need some New Age version of the facile and untrue claim "I feel your pain."' (ibid.: 75). Non-mimetic sharing, on the other hand, which, according to Haraway, attends to the asymmetry between non-humans and humans, becomes an ethical obligation. A willingness to imaginatively share in non-human experience, coupled with an appreciation for difference, means one is continuously involved in 'the epistemological, emotional, and technological work to respond practically in the face of the permanent complexity not resolved by taxonomic hierarchies' (ibid.).

Haraway's practice of 'non-mimetic sharing' does not intend to create an accurate portrayal of animal suffering, but rather to help us question instrumental relations with the animal and to prompt us into becoming more 'response-able' towards the animal's experience. (ibid.).[4] Beyond the provocative context of animal testing, Haraway's argument helps to challenge Andrew Motion's pedagogical concern regarding anthropomorphism. It is important, as he describes, to be reminded that 'in our intelligence and power as a species the responsibility lies with us', but his statement wrongly suggests that this process precludes imaginative participation with non-human experience: 'I am not a swift' declares Motion. As it happens, after reading Murray's poems I do not share mimetically in animal lives: I am not a fish, nor an eagle, but rather, I become intimately aware of the difference between their reality and my own. I share not physically, but imaginatively in their lives, and I do so non-mimetically.

Chris Kinsey, who designs and teaches short courses in environmental writing, discusses an exercise she frequently uses that corresponds in part to Murray's practice. Analysing her exercise prompts further thought towards a non-mimetic anthropomorphism and the 'response-ability' it might foster. Despite criticizing the 'appropriating' potential of anthropomorphism in animal representation as we saw earlier, Kinsey has no problem using anthropomorphic techniques to write about landscapes. Taking her students outdoors, she asks them to speak from the landscape in the first-person: 'Imagine being the island and speaking in the voice of the island' (2014). When asking her students to write, for example, 'about a feature – a forest, an outcrop', she gives the following prompts to help them adopt these non-human perspectives: 'How old are you? I nudge them not to give a numerical answer so they often answer in a kind of riddling form. What languages do you speak? What names are you known by?' (ibid.). Like Murray in *Translations*, Kinsey is clear that these anthropomorphic connections will go beyond human likeness and towards difference. In particular, her mention of a 'riddling form' is refreshing in its instruction for a figurative style that playfully offers both opportunity for, and withdrawal from, identification (ibid.).

There is a danger, however, that Kinsey's approach might come across as detached and impersonal. Her focus on age, language and name gives the exercise the air of a census form's opening questions. The environmental entities, which students are to speak from, are not active entities but passive collections of data and this limits the exploration of them. Kinsey's approach may well result from the topographical features that she draws attention to: a forest and an outcrop are physically more fixed in their environment and thus less animate than Murray's fish or eagle. Yet, as I will demonstrate in my discussion of non-human materials in the next section, an outcrop and a forest are active, collaborative and responsive entities in an environment. She gives few prompts that allow students to consider the experience of these entities: 'What do you dream of?', 'what are you afraid of? Or, what do you fear for this place?' (ibid.) When asked whether this focus on fear could invite more of an emphasis upon non-human experience in terms of environmental issues, she explains 'It hasn't particularly' (ibid.). This seems like an opportunity for further engagement, given that Kinsey responds to the question of whether she hopes her teaching will provoke or increase pro-environmental attitudes with 'I'd like to think that it did' (ibid.). Although verbally committed to raising students' environmental consciousness, she seems in practice reluctant to make this strategic move. Kinsey goes on to say how this issue-led angle 'might suit' the exercise and recalls her use of it on Bardsey Island in Wales where conflict exists between fishermen and marine conservation projects. With these marine conservation issues in mind, it is not difficult to see how students might take the perspective of a fish, a crab, the shoreline, a fishing net or even the water itself and respond to her question of 'what do you fear for this place' (ibid.).

In its approach of meat consumption and factory farming, Murray's poem 'Pigs' provides further nuance in our discussion of pedagogy, anthropomorphism and responsibility. Like the fish in 'Shoal', the pigs speak from a collective 'we'. However, unlike the immediacy of 'Shoal', Murray gives these pigs a long-distance viewpoint, from which they can reflect upon their ancestral past in contrast to their present lives. His use of the pronoun is comparable to Jorie Graham's deployment of it when she unites speaker and reader and projects our shared viewpoint into the future for the purpose of comprehending environmental change, as discussed in Chapter 2. 'Pigs' begins with an evocation of the modern farm environment: 'Us all on sore cement was we' (1992: 1). Continuing this collective viewpoint, the speaker (or speakers) contemplates their once wild existence: 'Us back in cool god-shit. We ate crisp' and 'Us all fuckers then. And Big, huh?' (ibid.: 5, 7). Despite Murray's *Translations* conveying what might be called non-mimetic anthropomorphism, his depiction plays into cultural stereotypes of the pig as a brute. Not only do the pigs speak in Anglo-Saxon as opposed to Latinate diction, they also swear!

Murray's imagining of the sensory capacity of the pigs, however, introduces more surprising detail that continues to portray the difference between human and non-human worlds. The pigs' food is 'mush' at the farm and 'crisp' in their previous lives in the wild. Likewise, Murray contrasts the 'sore cement' of industrial buildings to the 'soft cement' of the rivers. This contrast becomes more provocative towards the second half of the poem, as the sounds of the slaughterhouse jar with a lazy, rural scene. The pigs' hooves, described earlier as buried in mud, are similarly replaced by weightlessness and a sense of disembodiment as the animals' death entails 'our heads on upside down' (ibid.: 17). Eerily, we are prompted to come to the conclusion that the non-human voice in the poem speaks posthumously. Through the intimate and yet ultimately distant voice of 'Pigs' we are given a self-elegy of sorts that is, simultaneously, an ethical comment on the conditions and violence of factory farming and, more broadly, on meat consumption. In the next section, I will pursue Murray's inclusion of the human world in the form of the farm and the kind of environmental awareness this can provoke. In doing so my aim is to rethink pedagogical attitudes towards anthropomorphism by showing how the device approaches urban environments and their supposedly inert materials.

Material narratives

Murray approaches a range of familiar animals with his estranging anthropomorphic practice, but he also extends this practice to less animate entities within the environment: he gives voice to a tree in 'Great Bole' and grass in 'The Masses'. Engaging with the process of photosynthesis, Murray writes, 'We thicken by upper grazing', before recognizing a greater sense of agency in the grass that 'Tied in fasces, / dead, living, still we rule' (ibid.: 5, 11–12). While 'fasces' refers to the symbol used in ancient Rome to indicate power and jurisdiction, adopted in the twentieth century by Italian fascists, 'fasces' etymologically means 'bundle'. How can a bundle of dead grass 'rule'? If a bundle of dead grass is interpreted as a hay bale then the answer seems clear: grass not only feeds animals but also feeds animals in order for animals to feed humans. Grass as pasturage comes up again in the line 'No god is bowed to like grass is' (ibid.: 12). Lastly, given Murray's regular phonetic play elsewhere, it may even be possible that 'fasces' is a deliberate misspelling of 'faeces' given that manure (with a high grass content) performs a crucially active role in the environment.

Explaining his concept of the 'strange stranger', Timothy Morton suggests that as the non-human is found to be 'uncanny, uncertain, she, he or it gives us pause' (2010a: 81). Morton's pronouns also require pause and reconsideration as, by using 'it', Morton appears to apply the concept of the 'strange stranger' to non-life. Jane Bennett, a political theorist in New Materialism – a movement that reframes ecocritical argument through debates on material agency – provides in-depth examination of how a material object can be understood as a 'strange stranger'.[5] 'The image of dead or thoroughly instrumentalized matter' in contemporary society 'feeds human hubris and our earth-destroying fantasies of conquest and consumption' according to Bennett (2010: ix). Challenging the Cartesian view of agency and mastery as solely human qualities, she aims to 'dissipate' the borders between 'human/animal' and 'life/matter' by drawing attention to the life of matter (ibid.: x). To 'catalyse a sensibility' of matter as vibrant, Bennett makes the significant, though seemingly reluctant claim that what is needed is 'a touch of anthropomorphism' (ibid.: 99). Resonating with Morton's argument about the dangers of categorizing beings as either humans or animals, Bennett believes that anthropomorphism challenges the belief that the world is filled with either 'subjects or objects' (ibid.).

By focusing upon matter rather than animals, Bennett's theory, which I illustrate through Roy Fisher's poems, demonstrates that there is further opportunity for anthropomorphism in environmental writing than pedagogy has so far indicated from the examples we have seen. Pedagogical exercises frequently focus upon, or take place within, 'pristine' natural environments inhabited by wildlife. Yet this is not consistently paralleled by published works of environmental writing. Cocker may ask whether a tamed hawk is suitable subject matter, but a distinctive feature of British 'new nature writing' is its attentiveness to where city and countryside converge in places such as wastelands, sewage plants and retail parks as I outlined in Chapter 1 with reference to Mabey as well as Farley and Symmons Roberts. This urban focus plays an important role in John Tallmadge's pedagogical exercise 'Giving Voice to the Voiceless', collected under a series of exercises entitled 'A Matter of Scale: Searching for Wildness in the City' (2000). His practice here is unlike the exercises on place-writing we saw in Chapter 1 that predominantly sought observation of local birds and trees. He asks his students to go out into their city – and, moreover, practice anthropomorphism. Drawing attention to pavements and car parks, he asks students to take the voice of an 'object or creature' especially a 'creature more distant from the human scale, such as insects, protozoa, lichens, fungi' (ibid.: 65). As Morton realizes that the category of 'strange stranger' could include a virus, Tallmadge's understanding of what a 'creature' is embraces the invisible, the almost invisible or seemingly invisible because of the creature's relative inertia (2010b: 271).

Tallmadge implicitly connects the practice of exploring the experiential worlds of non-humans with respecting these worlds. Rather than an extensive attribution of human characteristics to these lives, Tallmadge hopes that attributing a human voice to the non-human will allow students to 'speak to the group as if he or she were that object or creature witnessing to its life, experience, reality' (2000: 64). He explains how this exercise can develop. The next step is to ask each student to create an 'autobiography' for a local creature or plant and respond to questions from the audience 'in character' (ibid.: 65). This open-ended exercise highlights the consciousness of other beings and may well engage with environmental issues affecting them: it is possible to imagine a question and answer session with a bee on the subject of habitat loss and domestic pesticides. Tallmadge's choice of location helps him to challenge the dualisms between 'culture and nature, home and adventure, wildness and civilization' (ibid.: 61). However, his focus upon living organisms comes at the expense of seemingly lifeless objects such as brick, metal or litter that are also found in the city. Consequently, he continues the dualism between object and subject identified by Bennett and demonstrates a disposition to the wild in terms of the organic, not the inorganic (ibid.: 61).

Tallmadge considers protozoa. Morton considers a virus. Morton then goes a step further in recognizing that the 'strange stranger' might also be a computer virus (2010b: 271). This ecocritical departure from nature into the realm of (supposedly antithetical) technology suggests associated human-made entities also possess what Tallmadge calls 'life, experience, reality'. Bennett's work exemplifies such a perspective upon supposedly inert human-made materials in the opening pages of *Vibrant Matter*, where she makes the short but significant claim that a pile of rubbish is not 'dead' matter, but 'a pile of lively and potentially dangerous matter' (2010: viii). Her claim prompts us to reconsider the concept of 'wildness'. In this way, Bennett advances the aim of uniting 'wildness and civilization' that Tallmadge pursues when he asks his students to go out into their local, urban environment and consider 'insects, protozoa, lichens' (2000: 61). Contributing to my argument that anthropomorphism does not have to be anthropocentric, Bennett claims that anthropomorphizing matter can 'chasten my fantasies of human mastery' and 'expose a wider distribution of agency' thereby generating attention and respect for such matter (2010: 122). And yet what exactly does Bennett mean by 'agency', a term we might associate with conscious, deliberate behaviour? Perhaps the most important distinction she makes is that between agency and intentionality. She argues that matter has the capacity to 'impede or block the will and designs of humans but also to act as quasi agents or forces with trajectories, propensities, or tendencies of their own', but does so without 'purposive behaviour' (ibid.: viii, 29). This perspective is supported by the fact that she understands such agency to be 'distributive'. Instead of one thing having agency, she argues that agency depends on the interaction between things.[6] In what follows, I engage with Bennett's argument while remaining cautious of how language used to discuss lively matter is inseparable from a human perspective.

The avant-garde poet Roy Fisher once said that 'Birmingham's what I think with' ('Texts for a Film', [1991] 2012: 1). His focus on the urban environment, coupled with his subtle animist approach, establishes a creative model with which to revise current pedagogical advice and extend strategies concerning environmental representation. Jazz music, the open form poetics of William Carlos Williams and Romantic nature-mysticism are all identifiable influences in his work. In an interview, John Kerrigan asks Fisher 'why there's been no move to something like nature poetry' in his writing, given his relocation to rural Derbyshire after living in Birmingham for forty years (2008). Fisher responds that, although he sees 'there are many obvious poem-opportunities' of a 'celebratory' nature, these 'don't seem to me obvious at all' (ibid.). 'As for the animals', Fisher continues, 'I get on with them fine, but don't project, or mix identities with them' (ibid.) Though he may not 'mix identities' with animals, Fisher's approach to the city in *A Furnace* (1986) demonstrates an anthropomorphic approach to industrial materials. Frequently described as influenced by the late Romantic novelist, John Cowper Powys whose writing suggests a pantheistic perspective, Fisher explores an urban environment in which there are 'voices, / animist, polytheist, metaphoric, / coming through' (1986: 61).[7] This receptive stance of Fisher's is symptomatic of his impulse to engage with 'what is outside the range of vision, to try to break or catch time or the limits of the perceptive field at its tricks in limiting consciousness of the world' (1975: 21).

In his 'preface' to *A Furnace*, Fisher clarifies: 'A Furnace is an engine devised, like a cauldron, or a still, or a blast-furnace, to invoke and assist natural processes of change; to persuade obstinate substances to alter their condition and show relativities which would otherwise remain hidden by their concreteness' (1986: vii). The industrial tone suits Fisher's particular topic of Birmingham's development and his attention to corresponding materials such as iron, brick and glass. He explains that 'some of the substances fed in are very solid indeed' (ibid.). A literal furnace clearly has a role to play in altering the conditions of substances such as brick and iron, but there is also the sense that the poem itself is working as a furnace to alter perceptions of substances. After all, while the substances themselves are obstinate, so is the assumption that they consist of lifeless matter. Drawing attention to this furnace-like role of the poem, Fisher states that the cosmos is involved in 'the making of all kinds of identities' and that 'those identities and that impulse can be acknowledged only by some form or other of poetic imagination' (ibid.).

Human-made materials are usually subjected to actions, as in the 'Iron walls / tarred black' (ibid.: 8). Yet, Fisher frequently 'activates' these materials through his use of verbs. The opening of the poem finds 'the catenaries / stretching' and later 'the road … beating in' and the 'ironworks, / reared up' (ibid.: 2, 4). While Murray's poems recognize a range of activity in animal behaviour, Fisher's verbs more inconspicuously identify life in inorganic matter. He attends to the 'face-fragments of holy saints / in fused glass' in a 'small / new window' of a church beside the River Dee (ibid.: 5). In contrast to the typically dignified quietness of the church, these face-fragments 'scream and stare and whistle' (ibid.). Fisher's choice of verbs is unsettling. The glass has been broken and fused back together, a process that may well mean that the wind screams and whistles through these faces. Interactions between materialities continue as Fisher writes of the faces: 'Trapped and raving / they pierce the church wall / with acids, glances of fire and lenses out of the light' (ibid.). The screaming of the previous description becomes associated with the brightness of the light that the windows shed, which in turn is indistinguishable from the processes the materials of the window have undergone, involving a furnace and acids.

'A pick-handle or a boot / long ago freed them / to do these things', writes Fisher, explaining the history behind the repaired window (ibid.). Yet a greater narrative dimension arrives in 'or what was / flung as a stone / having come slowly on / out of a cloudiness in the sea' (ibid.). Is this an allusion to the material processes inherent to stone becoming sand and sand becoming glass? Fisher provides us with a kind of material narrative for the window. However, like 'agency', 'narrative' requires explanation in the context of non-human matter. Taking Bennett's argument a stage further, Serpil Oppermann argues that the concept of narrative helps to account for the actions exercised by material agencies (2018). Narrative in this case is not written or spoken but embodied by matter itself. 'Storied matter' has become a phrase frequently used by material ecocritics to represent how matter, whether stone, plastic, bacteria or tree trunk 'yields terrestrial tales of resilience, creativities, uncertainties, evolution, and dissolution' (ibid.: 412). Fisher's focus on the window provides us with a kind of vignette of storied matter set against a backdrop of other stories in progress, in which 'Whatever breaks / from stasis' is often subject to 'a single / glance of another force touching it or / bursting out of it sidelong' (1986: 11). Far from being under our control, materiality in Fisher's work appears to have a life of its own. When the poet declares that 'Something's decided / to narrate / in more dimensions than I can know', he seems to reiterate Murray's statement that 'living things do all talk ... but they don't talk human language, or always speak with their mouth' (ibid.: 3). Material narratives are difficult, if not impossible to follow with our human senses. Illustrated by the festive bulbs Fisher finds no longer festive as they 'buck and fail' in the night, matter physically 'rides over intention, something / let through in error' (ibid.: 7, 8).

A Furnace focuses chiefly upon materials involved with industrial development in the eighteenth and nineteenth centuries. Yet, Fisher's awareness of the unpredictable narratives of this materiality speaks strongly to contemporary industry. Oil, coal and nuclear energy serve as a few examples where materials are active not only in powering homes, transport and businesses, but also in polluting the atmosphere and warming the climate. Establishing this active capacity of what is commonly understood to be inanimate or inert matter helps to develop Tallmadge's pedagogical exercise. Furthermore, this strategy becomes a way of engaging with environmental issues. Bennett argues that matter 'can aid or destroy, enrich or disable, ennoble or degrade us, in any case call for our attentiveness, or even "respect"' (2010: ix). As noted earlier, Bennett's hope is that encounters with 'lively' matter will challenge anthropocentric understandings of mastery and agency. As Fisher delves into the life of industrial matter that 'rides over intention', we can see parallels with her argument. Yet her dismissive use of 'in any case' to usher in the claim on the relationship between material agency and respect needs to be questioned, and her previous claim about matter that 'destroys' and 'disables' examined. Clearly, materials such as oil and plastic might not only destroy or disable us, but also destroy and disable ecological systems. Consequently, these materials not only call for our attentiveness and respect, but also call for our responsibility. Bennett claims that considering active matter might provoke questions towards societal 'patterns of consumption', yet this remains something that she does not fully explore in terms of environmental issues (ibid.: viii). To investigate this possibility I go on to study the relationship between active matter and the human provocation of matter's particular actions. After all, like the processes which turn sand into glass, oil would not contribute to climate change if it were not extracted, refined and ignited first.

'Inseparable from all other things'

The person whose pick-handle or boot broke the stained-glass window is nowhere to be seen and yet their action is recorded by the window. The generations of people that were part of Birmingham's industrial development are long dead, yet their influence lives on in the materials of the city. Human identities are inextricably linked to material identities. Society is 'trapped into water-drops / windows they glanced through' (1986: 12). In an appropriately indirect manner, Fisher's former description implicates domestic and industrial chemical products and, of course, sewage, whereas the latter description is a little more complex. This particular window may afford a momentary reflection of society when interpreted literally as someone glancing through the glass, but given Fisher's engagement with the way in which Birmingham's landscape was transformed by housing development, perhaps this window works as a synecdoche for more tangible proof of society. After all, the terraces that Fisher associates with urban renewal 'reflect' the society which built and inhabited them to this day. Writing on *A Furnace*, Clair Wills comments on the poem's blurring of boundaries between the living and the dead: she explains that 'Fisher's aim is to restore a sense of the dignity of buried, occluded, everyday lives that swarm around us' (2000: 259). Yet rather than these lives being 'overshadowed by the immense material presence of the city' as Wills states, it is the city's materiality that allows their existence to continue (ibid.).

In 'White Clouds and the BQE' (2000), Susan Karwoska describes an environmental writing exercise for elementary (or primary) school children. Born out of the customary split between nature and city, Karwoska's focus lends itself to thinking about 'how these two worlds come together' in the context of a modern metropolis, symbolized by the BQE or Brooklyn-Queens Expressway (2000: 17). The exercise's aim, she explains, is 'to explore my students' understandings of how such a magnificently complex place as New York City arose from the primordial ooze, how the natural world begot skyscrapers and steel bridges and the world with which they are familiar' (ibid.: 26). Unlike Tallmadge, who attributed 'life, experience, reality' only to creatures and asked students to create their autobiographies, Karwoska blurs the boundaries between life and matter as she asks students 'to tell the story' of 'the buildings ... the cars' as well as 'the trees, the animals' (ibid.). A children's book, *Marduk the Mighty and Other Stories of Creation*, showcases a range of creation myths from different cultures that she uses to focus on how 'all the things of the world came to be' (ibid.). She emphasizes the 'dreams, lies, [and] made-up things' she sees at the heart of creation myths, including 'the rainbow snake' in Aboriginal mythology that holds the world together (20). Although it is likely that this emphasis causes the students' resulting work (which she includes) to lose sight of the material processes inherent to urban development – the very processes that instigated the exercise – the mythological remains a valuable approach. Fisher's work holds on to a material focus: the lives of industry and the lives of society are entangled as 'Ann Mason' conjures 'the masons … quarrying for Christminster' (1986: 15), but the mythic is present too. When Fisher writes of identities that are long 'like the one they called Achilles, / or short, like William Fisher' (Fisher's great great uncle who is identified as a jeweller), the Homeric rubs shoulders with the everyday (ibid.).

The lives of individuals within society and the lives we can attribute to industrial materials are interdependent. Fisher goes on to consider this relationship as part of a larger system that echoes Romantic notions of nature-mysticism. Evoking cyclical concepts of endurance, change and renewal, Fisher describes how this merging of human and material is a practice 'of encoding / something perennial / and entering Nature thereby' (ibid.: 12). Subtly reversing the oft-used metaphor that describes nature as a machine (and potentially playing with the botanical associations of 'perennial'), Fisher likens the generative force of industry to the generative force of nature. In doing so, the poem offers us a way of thinking that can be used to develop Karwoska's exercise that intended to cultivate 'a larger view of nature as a generative force' in her students' perceptions of the city (2000: 26). Fisher's capitalized use of 'Nature', however, extends meaning here. Rather than referring to an immediate physical environment, the term conjures associations with wider laws and forces regulating earthly phenomena, as well as more Romantic ideas of a union between self and nature. There is a metaphysical quality in Fisher's 'Nature' and yet this is supported by *physical* transformation as he extends his exploration of the relationship between human and materiality. Illustrating 'the entry into Nature' is a stately gentleman

> he having lately walked
> through a door in the air
> among the tall
> buildings of the Northern Aluminium Company
> and become inseparable
> from all other things, no longer
> capable of being imagined
> apart from them, nor yet of being
> forgotten in his identity.
>
> (1986: 13)

We might see Timothy Morton's attention to 'the paradoxes and fissures of identity within "human" and "animal"' that anticipates his concept of the 'strange stranger' echoed in Fisher's blending of society, industry and Nature that refuses one, fixed identification (2010a: 41). Like the inhabitant of one of Birmingham's built terraces who lives on through its window, so the man that walks, like a phantom, through the door of the newly erected company building becomes identified with the company, that in turn is identified with other entities, until he becomes 'inseparable / from all other things'. To borrow Haraway's language associated with companion species, we could say that the poem is a record of 'becoming-with'. Human identity is 'encoded' in a material identity that is ultimately 'encoded' into Nature's system of perpetual continuance and change.

Fisher's perception of the entanglement between human and material identities has significant repercussions when we consider an anthropomorphic literary style with which to rethink pedagogical instruction. The possibility of speaking in the first-person from the perspective of matter arose in my discussion of Chris Kinsey's pedagogical exercise, yet the intimacy Fisher perceives between people and matter suggests that matter involuntarily speaks of the society associated with it. Andrew Motion may praise writers who take a stand against anthropomorphism in order to productively realize that 'they are hopelessly trapped in their humanity', but Fisher's writing suggests that humans are anything but trapped in their humanity given their inevitable shaping role in matter. Motion equates liberation from our human form with an escapist tendency that neglects recognition of human power and responsibility, yet Fisher's view of materiality in *A Furnace* leads to the formation of an anthropomorphic style that contests Motion as it identifies the influence of society on matter. Fisher's approach creates a new model with which to think about the relationship between contemporary society and matter. Like the humans that are 'trapped into water-drops, / windows they glanced through', humans today may well be considered as 'encoded' in the carbon released from cars, planes, and power stations as well as in the Great Pacific garbage patch. After all, to be 'encoded' – to be inextricably entangled in matter – resembles the very definition of the Anthropocene: a term used for the current geological epoch that is marked by human activity. An anthropomorphic style affords a strategy to conceive of the life of matter, apprehend its threatening potential and, crucially, realize that society is frequently accountable for environmental damage. Indeed, anthropomorphism in the light of the Anthropocene becomes a practice of reidentification with the matter we have created or, at the very least, influenced.

Ethical anthropomorphisms?

What sensory capacity might a brick possess? How would you imagine the conceptual understanding of a crisp packet? Although it might prove an interesting experiment, applying Les Murray's techniques to Fisher's human-made materials demonstrates that there is no one anthropomorphic strategy that can be applied to different understandings of the non-human. Animals and materials require different techniques in order for their different identities to be appreciated and explored. While distinct, these techniques modelled by Murray and Fisher unite in illustrating how ecocritical theory can be introduced to environmental writing pedagogy in order to expand creative possibility in a self-reflexive, ethical manner. In *Translations*, Murray's depiction of animals is strange and estranging. Although the first-person 'I' might invite us to adopt, say, an eagle's perspective, the world that the eagle supposedly inhabits is so startlingly other to our own that this anthropomorphic technique speaks of the difference between the human and the non-human far more than likeness. To attempt, however falteringly, to intimately imagine the experience of an animal whose organs of perception are so challengingly different to ours is to begin to acknowledge and appreciate the sheer otherness of that animal's perspective. My argument takes a contrasting form when it comes to non-human materials in Fisher's work. After all, there is a literal quality to the way in which the identities belonging to humans and to inorganic matter merge in *A Furnace*. The human is found to be irrevocably entangled in matter itself as well as the interactions and consequences resulting from such matter. While seeking to see ourselves in animals becomes an ethically questionable activity, seeing ourselves in matter seems appropriately accountable, especially in the light of contemporary environmental issues.

I hope that these analyses of Murray and Fisher will provide a basis for a new pedagogical perspective towards the non-human in environmental writing courses. What are the practical classroom exercises that might follow? An initial step could be to acquaint students with the debates about anthropomorphic representation that are to be found in environmental literature, old and new. It might be helpful to ask students to choose a familiar animal (one that they come across frequently such as a blackbird, a squirrel or even a pet) and represent it through four lenses. Through the first lens, students write about the animal as if it featured in a fable. How might this animal communicate a particular moral or stance towards an institution or politician? Students then describe the same animal as if it were a character in a children's book or Disney film. What does the animal wear? How does she speak? Who are her friends? In the third lens, students might imitate Murray's technique by considering that animal's sensory or conceptual capacity and its difference from our own. The fourth and final lens then asks students to write about the animal with no anthropomorphic language whatsoever. This exercise calls for research into the animal chosen. Although students should not be expected to live in a badger sett for six weeks in the manner of Charles Foster's experiential *Being a Beast*, they should be able to explore the habitat and behaviour of the animal first-hand. Comparing and contrasting the results of these four lenses should allow students the opportunity to identify where they stand in the argument. How do the effects of the description written in the first lens compare to the fourth? What advantage does one have over another in the context of, say, animal rights?

Students could explore the third, Murray-esque lens alongside Haraway's idea of 'non-mimetic sharing' in terms of creative practice. What would result from these explorations? As we saw at the very beginning of this chapter, we might construct a voice that speaks for a bird, but this voice does not have to describe an experience we recognize. Sympathy may arise from mimetic sharing between human and non-human (as when William J. Long's woodcock makes a splint for its broken leg) but a more scrupulous and ethical responsibility becomes possible through non-mimetic sharing: the appreciation that non-humans are distinct beings with distinct experiences. Ian Bogost's work that combines elements of New Materialism with Object-Oriented Ontology is useful here. Considering both animals and inorganic matter, Bogost forms a theory of 'alien phenomenology' or, put more simply, 'what it is like to be a thing' (2012). He acknowledges that all things experience the world in one form or another. The only condition is that 'the subjective character of [these] experiences cannot be fully recuperated objectively' (2012: 64). Like Murray, then, Bogost's approach to the non-human is imagined, provisional or, as he describes it, 'speculative' (ibid.: 78). Playing with Nagel's 'What Is It Like to Be a Bat?', Bogost writes: 'In a literal sense, *the only way to perform alien phenomenology is by analogy*: the bat, for example, operates like a submarine. The redness hues like fire' (ibid.) Rather than reinforcing *anthropo*-centrism, such a creative practice aims to imagine, at least in the context of the bat, *bat*-centrism.

With 'Shoal', 'Eagle Pair' or 'Pigs' in mind, students might explore literary synaesthesia with the animal they have chosen. What do we know about the pigeon's sense organs? Can we understand them better by engaging with another sense? Likewise, inspired by Murray's interest in non-human conceptual systems, students can be prompted to play with and rewrite the metaphors explored in

Lakoff and Johnson's *Metaphors We Live By*. How might we re-evaluate the phrase 'life is a rollercoaster' from the perspective of a caterpillar's metamorphosis? Analogy is important to Bogost's argument: his comparison of a bat to a submarine emerges from a more general comparison between echolocation and sonar technology. Which analogies, then, might help to draw out the experience of a rhino, or a rabbit? Analogy, Bogost explains, is 'a move that solves Nagel's puzzle: we never understand the alien experience, we only ever reach for it metaphorically' (2012: 66). Like human and non-human animals, things 'try to make sense of each other through the qualities and logics they possess' (ibid.). Anthropomorphism is frequently regarded as 'soppy', 'wrong' or 'appropriative' because of its potential to create unrealistic, distorted representations of the non-human. Yet, as Bogost argues, the 'mechanism that facilitates this sort of alien phenomenology is not … one that clarifies foreign perception by removing distortion – but instead a mechanism that *welcomes* such distortion' (ibid.). Supported by research into animal physiology and psychology, playfulness and experimentation in writing about the non-human are qualities that can guide, rather than compromise, a conscientious, ethical literary practice.

These exercises could guide students into writing poems – perhaps even a sequence. They could also be used more broadly as an introduction to non-mimetic anthropomorphism. Indeed, Bogost's viewpoint might be a springboard to thinking about distortion on larger scales that might suit the short story form or creative non-fiction essay. One productive method is to start with an existing text. How might we respond to Keats's 'Ode to a Nightingale' or Poe's 'The Raven' through a more animal-centric perspective? How might the raven, for example, contest the tale narrated by Poe? Attending to the background in literary works is also valuable in shifting emphasis from human to non-human. In Gabriel García Márquez's 'magical realist' short story 'The Very Old Man with Enormous Wings', an angel lives inside a chicken coup. A prompt-question for students: do the chickens experience anything unusual? In response, students might write a third-person narrative, but with 'non-mimetic sharing' and 'distortion' in mind, would it be more challenging to consider how the animal would narrate the tale? Or students might consider techniques and styles such as non-linear narrative and unreliable narrators, and sensitively adapt them to non-human representation.

Similar possibilities arise in relation to film and television. Inspired by a short story by Elizabeth Gaskell, 'The Half-Brothers', and later, a full-length novel by Eric Knight, *Lassie Come-Home*, the canine, Lassie, became a popular character in cinema and television from the 1940s to the 1960s. In the films, the

Rough Collie dog is anthropomorphically rendered a brave hero. How might an alternative anthropomorphic strategy reframe her? What difference does it make if we know, for example, that Lassie was really running towards an edible reward rather than a boy stuck in the ice? How might we explore the paradox of Lassie's sex? The dog was consistently portrayed as female, even though many of the animal actors playing her were male. Such inconsistencies and bizarre interventions occurred also in the similarly popular TV series, *Flipper*. Having studied Murray's attention to voice in *Translations,* how might we respond to and represent the fact that Flipper the dolphin was dubbed by a kookaburra (Arthur 2003)?

The four 'lenses' that I suggested earlier can help shift the focus from animals to materials. Sparked by Murray's 'Pigs', students can select an animal compromised by human activity. They might consider the effects of climate change on bird migration, for example, or the consequences of an oil spill in the Pacific Ocean on marine life. First, students would take the animal's perspective, then that of the threatening material. These steps would help students to draw out the nuances, limitations and potential of anthropomorphism in the light of the animate/inanimate boundary challenged by Jane Bennett's theory of 'vibrant matter'. How do we envisage oil being animate in comparison to a more obviously animate seabird? Such questions would prompt research into the inherent qualities belonging to different materials. What sort of agency can these materials be said to have in these distressing contexts? The chemical disposition of oil, for example, means that it burns the mucous membranes of the seabird's eyes and mouth. If ingested by the bird, and the bird survives, the oil leads to thinner egg shells. The idea of 'storied matter', touched on earlier with regard to Fisher, may prove valuable here not only as a theoretical concept, but also as a prompt for creative practice. In her contribution to the recent collection *Teaching Climate Change in the Humanities,* Stephanie Foote appears to pursue this opportunity as she argues that in order to generate narratives from a culture of waste, it is necessary to think of a discarded object as one might think of 'a character in a novel' (2017: 195).

Another valuable resource here is Ramin Bahrani's fifteen-minute film, 'Future States: Plastic Bag' (2015), in which a bag, voiced by Werner Herzog, tells of its journey from supermarket to ocean. When a customer fills the bag with her purchased groceries, it comes to life and tells its story. Once discarded, the bag is presented as a victim romantically longing for its 'maker' as it drifts purposelessly through the world, unable to die. From the viewpoint of the student assessing non-human representation, is the bag's story excessively emotional?

What effect does this have? Is this emotion a way of challenging Bennett's subject–object dualism by presenting it as an entity that thinks and feels? Does the voice assist the environmental message? As this summary suggests, Bahrani's plastic bag provides a more anthropocentric understanding of 'narrative' than that explored by scholars in material ecocriticism. This contrasting example can help students to ask themselves how far we are able to attribute life to materiality and where this can become problematic. Terms such as 'agency' and 'narrative' are defined by theorists so that we can understand their meaning in a non-human context, but even these definitions can often feel strained. Consequently, what, if anything, can we make of 'experience' with regard to materiality? At the beginning of this section, I made fun of the idea that a brick could possess a sensory capacity, but perhaps this should be phrased as a question for students to explore and interpret themselves. Jakob von Uexküll's concept of 'umwelt' that he uses to describe the world as it is experienced by a particular organism can help support further study here ([1934] 2010). Both ecocritical approaches to biosemiotics (Wheeler 2016) and Ian Bogost's argument on how a camera experiences the world (extending from his discussions on 'what it is like to be a thing' in *Alien Phenomenology*) might be used to help students question whether it is possible for an entity comprised of inorganic matter to possess an 'umwelt'. The exercise of rewriting the bag's story in the form of a poem, short story or essay can highlight these distinctions.

Bahrani's representation of the plastic bag prompts other lines of enquiry too. The bag possesses life, given that it has voice and experience, but the bag is otherwise passive in its lack of agency. Do we agree with this representation, when thinking about how plastics ingested by marine species release toxins that accumulate as they pass through the food chain? Following an entity's journey through another entity has interesting repercussions when thinking about anthropomorphism. For example, if we pursue the first-person voice of Bahrani's plastic bag, how do we imagine it narrating through the body of a fish? Thinking also of Haraway's theory of 'becoming-with' and Bennett's theory of 'vibrant matter', how can we represent the way in which one entity becomes entangled with another? Fisher's speaker says: 'Something's decided / to narrate / in more dimensions than I can know'. Students might respond to this challenge by telling, in different ways, the stories of everyday non-human materials. How can we conceive of the life of a fossil fuel? Fisher creates a literary collage to convey, in third-person, the shifting human–non-human lives of *A Furnace*. He also employs a mythic vocabulary that challenges temporal boundaries. These techniques provide pathways into narrating the uncontainable, intertwined nature of beings. To push the otherworldly quality of the exercise further, students might seek other genres and hybrid-genres relevant to depicting this 'trans-corporeality': the ghost story, zombie fiction or epic fantasy, for example. In her most recent work, *Staying with the Trouble* (2016), Haraway identifies science fiction as a guiding force behind her belief that we need 'tentacular thinking' in order to perceive biological and cultural entanglement.

Fisher's account of animate matter embraces different scales: from the stained-glass window that screams, to the terraces that reflect the human lives inhabiting them. Representing the city of Birmingham and its past, *A Furnace* invites interpretation as a poetic work of psychogeography, a school of study and practice that, defined by Guy Debord in 1955, has found literary expression in the last two decades in the work of writers such as Iain Sinclair, Will Self and Rebecca Solnit. Psychogeography encourages transgressive wandering in the city, exploration of urban histories otherwise obscured, and, as its interdisciplinary title suggests, investigation of the influence of environments on psychology. These concerns establish the city as active matter that works upon emotions and behaviours. This is certainly the case when Fisher writes, 'Whatever / approaches my passive taking-in … will have itself understood only / phase upon phase / by separate involuntary / strokes of my mind … made up from long / discrete moments / of the stages of the street (1986: 2–3). Yet, the streets similarly influence other streets: 'Because / of the brick theatre struck to the roadside / the shops in the next run in a curve' (ibid.: 3). With their repetition of 'because', these lines and the ones that follow illustrate the often unpredictable cause and effect of material presences on one another.

At Manchester Metropolitan University, David Cooper and his colleagues who teach undergraduate and postgraduate modules on place writing emphasize the cultural geographies of the city often through psychogeographic exercises (2018). Introducing one such exercise, Cooper recalls the Situationalists of the 1950s who walked around Paris with a map of Berlin in their hands. Heading into Manchester armed with a map of central London, Cooper's students repeat the Surrealist game, and in so doing discover something profound. As they find their route to a park blocked by, say, a brick wall or no entry sign, they encounter questions of spatial politics. 'How is space managed? How [are] desire paths prohibited? … your bodily movements are being pushed' (ibid.). Using Cooper's exercise alongside Fisher's poetry might give us a new way of thinking and writing about urban landscapes as containing divergent agential forces. By following an incorrect map, students allow themselves to be 'pushed' by their environment. Questions arise as to which forces shape a path or direction.

Apropos Fisher: how does the layout of one street impact upon another? Which industries and authorities have shaped the city? Whose identities are entangled in these forces? What other forces or agencies have combined to shape the city and your place within it?

By using a range of anthropomorphic techniques, students develop their understanding of what defines the non-human while more broadly expanding their definition of environment. However, anthropomorphism remains a sensitive device. It requires attention and care. This chapter has shown ways in which ethical, ecocritical anthropomorphisms can be tailored to the subjects the writer aims to represent. Human language can be used to give dramatic voice to an animal's experience, while at the same time working non-mimetically to convey the difference and unreachability of that experience. Voices given to inorganic materials take on a broader meaning. Fisher's city, for example, speaks of the society that shaped it. When we attempt to develop pedagogical techniques that will foster respectful and responsible attention to these creatures and materials, the two approaches complement one another. Non-mimetic anthropomorphism helps to underline our differences with animals in an intimate manner, whereas an anthropomorphic view of matter does quite the opposite in helping us to recognize our role in materials as familiar as a crisp packet or abandoned warehouse, or as seemingly intangible as a tonne of carbon dioxide. For its role in aiding us to appreciate these relationships and our position within them, anthropomorphism should be valued.

4

Writing 'more in the world': Fact and figuration

In the garden, I spy a bird. In the garden, I spy a male blackbird. In the garden, I spy 'a small mad puritan with a banana in his mouth' (Baker [1967] 2015: 105). Which description is better at representing the bird in question? Why? In their guide to environmental writing, Prentiss and Wilkins ask students to 'think about a place you visit often … describe the place as well as you can. Identify the trees' (2016: 118). Once students have exhausted their knowledge, Prentiss urges, 'break out a tree and flower guide' (ibid.). As discussed in Chapter 1, the first step to writing about the environment is often to focus on a particular place. Embedded within such broad instruction, however, is another instruction: to identify the environment's particulars through a field guide's classifications. Emphasizing factual accuracy, plain speech and a scientific ambition, many teachers cultivate this naturalist's approach in their students. Elder, whose teaching I have discussed in Chapters 2 and 3, suggests that learning the names of the trees growing in Vermont means 'your writing will not be so solipsistic, it will be more in the world' (2014). Though Elder's phrase 'more in the world' is hard to define, as the practice of identifying species turns an undifferentiated forest of trees and birds into a forest of Scots pine, junipers, jays and nuthatches, it is understood to represent a deeper engagement with the physicality of the environment at hand. There appears to be a tacit understanding that if writing takes on the character of popular science it will be 'more in the world' in the sense that it will be more objective; it will be more trustworthy. Writing without this framework, as Elder suggests, runs the risk of solipsism – of relying on subjective perception.

 As this chapter goes on to explore, underlying much pedagogical advice appears to be an argument that pits literal, scientific language against metaphor and simile: the latter supposedly symptomatic not only of the self, but of the ego. Drawing on ecocritical arguments by David Abram concerning language, materiality and sensuality, I want to rethink the ethics which arise from the influence of natural history on pedagogical thought. I will propose a new perspective that aims to show how metaphor is not only valuable in conveying facts about the environment, but that the figurative device also conceives of environmental diversity. My intention here is not to suggest that we should dismiss scientific or factual languages altogether, although I do suggest that such languages can have unintended and problematic consequences. Rather, my intention is to question the binary that often emerges between fact and metaphor when writing about the environment and to demonstrate how metaphor can enrich the relationship we have between language and materiality. I will now discuss the instructions often given to students with regard to factual language and outline how the binary I have identified is often expressed in pedagogy and in the wider culture of environmental writing.

'A student who goes from saying "bird" to "starling" or "towhee" within a few weeks is already a more attentive, more *placed* student than she was at the start of the course', writes Allison B. Wallace (2012: 102). Often a necessary prerequisite for such identification is the field journal in which such observations are recorded. More often than not, students are expected to write their journals in situ – either as a one-off occurrence or as part of an ongoing record – bringing the experiential quality of the engagement to the fore. David Petersen advises his students to keep a 'detailed daily phenology for a full calendar month' as this will generate 'not only the natural history information recorded therein, but lucrative practice in observation, identification, recording, interpreting, ordering, ruminating and *feeling* the natural world' (2001: 50). Although Petersen includes some personal approaches to this phenology, the main thrust lies in fostering a catalogue-like accuracy ('identification', 'ordering'). Similarly valuing an empirical style of observation, Laird Christensen writes that the student is 'especially reliant on his [field] journal to keep him honest' (2011). Indeed, honesty is disputed by Christensen in the first month of the Environmental Writing Workshop at Green Mountain College as he finds his students' writing too 'artistic' and states, with some conciliatory humour, that he wants to 'squelch' this creativity (2014a). What Christensen wants is 'direct perception' which is 'not creative, but precise' (ibid.). He specifically warns his students, 'I don't want to see a metaphor or anything like that' (ibid.) The suggestion that metaphor is linked to creativity, and is therefore inappropriate when representing environments, is taken to an extreme in Petersen's guide when he endorses a quotation from *Men's Journal* that claims, 'The trouble with nature writing is that it's always reaching, trying to tease great thoughts, great metaphors, out of the world. It's a kind of narcissism, an ego on parade: "Look how well I can write, Mom!"' (2001: 8).

By responding to an environment with Petersen's phenology or Christensen's 'direct perception', students are engaged with a process of perceptual and representational immediacy. This process is often pitted against so-called 'armchair nature writing' in which the writer sits at home imagining such observations or elaborating upon the experiences they had in the field. The encouragement given by Christensen in particular responds to this topic as it informs the first part of his workshop's tripartite structure that moves from perception, to interpretation and, lastly, to imagination. Such a staged process is admirable in allowing students to reflect on their creative engagement with the environment. Rather than rushing into writing a piece of dystopic environmental fiction, as he anecdotally suggests many do, Christensen wants his students to closely observe their environs first. In many cases, the way in which popular science influences environmental writing parallels best practice in creative writing pedagogy more broadly. Teaching at Newman University in Birmingham, Elizabeth-Jane Burnett explains that she introduces her students to tree guides in order for their writing to be more specific, 'which is a good principle of writing' (2018). Similar guidance applies to metaphor: while Mark Cocker understands the device to be 'enriching' and thus 'essential' to all writing (2014), no one wants a far-fetched simile or too many metaphors that might result in 'purple prose': a disparaging term for a text that is written in an overly decorative or ornate style.

However, it can often be difficult to tell apart what might be described as a kind of literary 'common sense' and a veiled ethical coda. Useful as a naturalist's stance might be in helping students differentiate what they see, asking students to adopt it in their writing has the potential to perpetuate what ecocritic Patrick D. Murphy has identified as a reductive formula in which 'nature writing = nonfiction = fact = truth' (2009: 33). More problematically still, this formula sets the scene for its counterpart in which creativity is linked with the imagination and the ego, supposedly resulting in imprecise and dishonest writing – and, of course, showing-off to one's mother. The dichotomy between the plain and humble versus the decorative and egotistical, and the valuing of the former at the dismissal of the latter, suggests a kind of Puritan moralism. As Elder's advice and Murphy's formula help to suggest, an ascetic, self-denying approach to writing about the environment is considered virtuous. It is pertinent that the image of a blackbird as 'a small mad puritan with a banana in his mouth', written by J. A. Baker who I discuss in more depth presently, communicates something of this tension between the plain and the elaborate. Indeed, if anything, the playful metaphor appears to smuggle in an attack on Puritanism.

Natural history, a tradition often associated with amateur science, remains a key influence in many of these discussions having stimulated a genre of natural history writing that ranges from popular science to personal memoir. Set as reading on a number of current courses, *The Natural History of Selborne* ([1789] 1996) by Gilbert White records the physical phenomena of his Hampshire village with scientific precision and so exemplifies the 'daily phenology' Petersen intends his students to write. 'A few house-martins begin to appear about the 16th of April; usually some few days later than the swallow', writes White among letters to Thomas Pennant (and other naturalists) that similarly observe insect behaviour, trees, seasonal change and weather conditions ([1789] 1996: 184–5). White was an influence upon many later British writers such as the nineteenth-century rural writer, Richard Jefferies, the post-war naturalist, James Fisher, and, indeed, many contemporary authors of *The Guardian*'s country diary column initiated in 1906. His influence also extended to America in the writing of John Burroughs. As discussed in Chapter 3, Burroughs was relieved to find writing that was not compromised by fictional anthropomorphisms. He admired White for telling 'the thing for what it is' ([1903] 1998: 130).

A sense of authority arises from the understanding that a naturalist can make objective observations. 'Contemporary natural history writers speak for the earth', claims US naturalist and writer Stephen Trimble (1995: 2). He later quotes John Hay, writer and environmentalist, who admits 'I was quite flattered when I was first called a naturalist' (ibid.: 5). This attitude finds its way, across the Atlantic, into Burnett's teaching, when she points out that, given students are not scientists, the authoritative stance of the natural historian seems inaccessible. But, Burnett continues, students can be 'engaged amateurs' (2018). There is no doubt that the knowledge gathered by a naturalist over many years of study enables a deeply insightful mode of perception. However, associating this mode of perception with authority would seem problematic. Not only does such an association suggest that none other than the naturalist's scientific style of language 'tells the thing for what it is' – that authority depends upon the ability to convey impersonal evidence. Besides, the very idea of becoming an authority surely risks courting the ego.

The opening description of a blackbird as a 'small mad puritan' belongs to British writer, J. A. Baker and his 1967 work, *The Peregrine* ([1967] 2015: 105). Set against the damage inflicted by pesticide use, the book condenses ten years of peregrine observation in East Anglia into a year's worth of diary entries. The book often appears on set reading lists alongside White's, though the two are noticeably distinct. Where White's observations of Selborne are often dense with factual terms, Baker's writing is dense with metaphor, simile, adjectives and, in some cases, neologisms. Describing a male peregrine, Baker writes, 'He is the colour of yellow ochre sand and reddish-brown gravel. His big, brown, spaniel eyes shine wet in the sunlight, like circles of raw liver, embedded in the darker matt brown of the moustachial mask' (ibid.: 47). Later, another male in the air is 'speckled with brown like the scales of a trout ... He rocked and drifted like a boat at anchor ... He stooped ... revolving down in tigerish spirals' (ibid.: 61). *The Peregrine* has been heralded as a lyric masterpiece by many writers in the United Kingdom and United States. However, the problematic association between metaphor and ego quietly persists in some instances of the text's reception. In his article in the *Times Literary Supplement*, Richard Smyth opens with a quotation from the biologist L. C. Miall: '[Gilbert] White is interesting because nature is interesting' (2017). Later on, focusing on Baker, Smyth borrows the suggestion made by the British new nature writer, Robert Macfarlane, that 'in order to keep the reader reading through the same cycle of events, he [Baker] had to forge a new language of description' (ibid.). In turn, Smyth comes to the conclusion that 'Nature is interesting because Baker is interesting' (ibid.). Resonating with the argument in Chapter 2 on the dichotomy between self and environment that is prevalent in discussions of literary representation, Smyth's comparison between White and Baker asks the question as to whether Baker prioritizes himself before the landscape. Yet, is it simply a case of prioritizing one over the other?

Much of the 'new nature writing' pursues the kind of imaginative and exuberant linguistic eccentricity that might be described as 'Bakeresque', and, notably, is often subject to similar critiques. Cocker's *Crow Country*, for example, begins with the description of a flock of rooks and jackdaws which reminds him of 'a thousand small multi-coloured kites all at play in the hot desert gusts on that Rajasthani afternoon' (2008: 2). Discussing this opening on the module titled 'New Nature Writing' on the 'Wild Writing' Master's course at the University of Essex with students and Cocker himself, James Canton asks whether the simile, which introduces Cocker's experience of Jaipur, India, is 'too exotic' given that the observation of the birds takes place in the Yare Valley, Norfolk (2013). William Atkins's *The Moor*, a non-fiction work about the moorlands of England, finds an even more startling use of metaphor when he likens a lapwing taking off to 'a paperback blasted from a cannon' (2014: 7). Yet, as writer, critic and teacher Jim Perrin sees it, such images by Atkins are 'forced images' and represent 'an exhibitionist choice of lexis' (2014a).[1] Dismissing its accuracy, Perrin believes such language is 'simply for show' (ibid.). Perrin's view recalls the earlier idea that metaphor is 'a kind of narcissism, an ego on parade' as Petersen described. But, as I go on to explain, such views of metaphor are misleading and unhelpfully reductive.

In order to dissolve the tensions regarding metaphor, we might want to think about how structuralist arguments propose that all language is metaphor. 'Tree' is only a term we give to a physical entity. The word is never the thing itself. We might, however, simply look at the names of species in field guides to question the dualism between fact and figurative language. If a teacher asks her students to identify a selection of birds, and one, for example, is a hooded crow, then is it accurate to say that the student is engaged with fact or metaphor? Metaphor threads through natural history, just as it turns out to be a familiar feature of much science communication, as I will discuss later. The issue comes, then, with the insistence that fact is the preferred – or in some cases, the only – ethical mode and that conversely, metaphor speaks of solipsism. It is important to challenge Perrin's view and argue that Atkins's simile of a lapwing taking off 'like a paperback blasted from a cannon' might valuably convey the mixture of speed and fluttering specific to the bird's flight, even if we have not observed a book bursting from heavy artillery. Rather than literary self-indulgence or exhibitionism, this touch of surrealism helps to express details of the bird's physicality.

This question of metaphor's role in writing about the environment has prompted a range of contributions from ecocriticism over the years. David W. Gilcrest's *Greening the Lyre* follows the premise, and quotes William Bevis, that while 'metaphoric perception makes a virtue out of the active imagination, meditative perception relies on a more "passive" engagement with the world' (2002: 127).[2] According to Gilcrest, 'Such passivity is traditionally seen as corresponding to a diminishment of the self or ego' (ibid.). In turn, Gilcrest praises the concept of an 'unmediated perception' that might be represented through a poetics of 'direct treatment' and an 'economy of words', but ultimately realizes that any language creates mediation of environments (ibid.: 130). His discussion leads him to call for 'rhetorical abstinence' as a gesture of respect that acknowledges that 'the non-human world exists independently of human desire, including the desire for representation' (ibid.: 131). Gilcrest's argument might return discussion to how the ethics associated with writing about the environment often resemble Puritan ascetic ways, yet it is interesting to note that there are other religious dimensions to be considered here too. His instruction for 'rhetorical abstinence', for example, is influenced by Islamic prohibition of images representing God which 'shies away from mimesis toward (something like) representational austerity' (ibid.: 133).

The pedagogical exercises and approaches discussed so far would seem to share at least some of Gilcrest's principles. However, more recent, ecocritical arguments suggest alternative ways of thinking about the binary between the plain and pared-back, and the decorative. David Abram challenges the identification of unelaborate, factual expression with ethical environmental representation as he addresses the destructively reductive nature of scientific language and, conversely, argues for the unique value of metaphor in acknowledging and appreciating the material diversity of environments. Building upon his eco-phenomenological approach in *Spell of the Sensuous* (1996), in *Becoming Animal* (2010), Abram makes the case that scientific ways of speaking and referring to the world generate theoretical understandings, which are taken as 'more fundamental, more real than this palpable world that we experience with our breathing bodies' (2010: 75). Critical of the language or 'code' used to refer to DNA and black holes, his argument also encompasses the practice of naming:

> When I talk of the aspen or the granite outcrop as a determinate object, I push into unconsciousness my direct experience of trees and rock ledges, contradicting my carnal awareness of them as ambiguous beings with their own enigmatic ways of influencing the space around them, and of influencing me.
> (ibid.: 63–4)

Abram finds the materiality of environments to be sensuous, expressive and animate: a perspective that can be compared to those coming from New Materialism and arguments concerning 'lively matter', discussed in Chapter 3. In adopting the language of science, we lose sight of these qualities: we 'refer to nature only as a set of determinate objects', which isolates us from our senses and our surroundings (ibid.: 70). His perspective prompts thought as to whether some of the pedagogical strategies discussed so far that adopt scientific tropes might incur a mechanistic view that many environmentalist thinkers believe has led to the serious ecological issues faced today. Could the exercises in which students match their perception of a bird to a field guide's entry hinder the very experiential quality that they aim towards? As Abram seeks to 'free the things from their conceptual straightjackets' and establish 'a style of speech that opens our senses to the sensuous in all its multiform strangeness', it is time for a new approach (ibid.: 9, 3).

Abram's intensely descriptive passages initially resemble creative non-fiction rather than ecocriticism in their account of, for instance, the lively dynamics of rock and the sentience of birds. By way of these accounts, Abram seeks an approach with which to respond to 'an animate, expressive world' (ibid.: 4) Throughout his study, he finds the answer in the oral cultures belonging to indigenous peoples, arguing that it deploys a language closer to immediate experience. Much of Abram's thesis encompasses metaphor. 'We regularly talk of howling winds, and of chattering brooks', he states, 'Yet these are more than mere metaphors … language is not a purely mental phenomenon but a sensuous, bodily activity born of carnal reciprocity and participation' (1996: 82). To talk of howling winds is comparable to talking of water as splashing, gushing and rushing: it acknowledges how language has been influenced by the dynamics of environmental phenomena. Abram's argument emerges from setting scientific modes of thinking against 'primitive' modes. It has roots in the Romantic challenge to science via the imagination and, more specifically, the Romantic privileging of the 'primitive'. Giambattista Vico, for example, argued that 'metaphor originated in primitive men who, without language, expressed themselves by using bodies that were naturally related to the ideas they wished to signify' ([1744] 1999: 161). Pursuing this line of thinking, Abram focuses on how stories created and told by such peoples used metaphor to 'convey practical information regarding the tangible cosmos' (2010: 296). Metaphor is, according to Abram, a sensitive response to a diverse world 'in continual metamorphosis' (ibid.).

Does it follow, then, that an ecocritical pedagogy for environmental writing should guide students into oral storytelling, song and spoken word in order to follow Abram's argument? Though this is likely to produce some interesting results, Abram is clear to point out that his focus on oral culture does not exclude the written word: 'Our task, rather, is that of taking up the written word, with all of its potency, and patiently, carefully, writing language back into the land' (1999: 273). This qualification seems to be missed by Scott Knickerbocker who, delivering a similar argument with regard to the sensuous relationship between materiality and language in *Ecopoetics* (2012), remains alienated by Abram's emphasis on oral culture (Knickerbocker's emphasis lies in the work of a group of twentieth-century poets) and explicitly distances himself from Abram's work (2012: 3). Interested in how 'poetic artifice' – a term that includes a range of devices such as rhyme, alliteration and metaphor – 'rematerializes language', Knickerbocker studies the work of Elizabeth Bishop and Richard Wilbur among others (ibid.: 2). Rejecting the belief that 'a healthy dose of realism … serves as a cure for solipsism', Knickerbocker makes the case that poets do not embrace artifice 'for its own sake, but as a way to relate meaningfully to the natural world. Indeed for them, artifice is natural' (ibid.: 9, 159). In a gesture that might seem to necessitate far more acknowledgement of Abram, Knickerbocker describes such writing as 'sensuous poeisis' (ibid.). Such an argument challenges previous ecocritics such as Gilcrest who believe metaphor to be egocentric rather than ecocentric. The central tenet shared by Abram and Knickerbocker – that metaphor (far from being solipsistic) engages with material sensuousness – makes a valuable contribution to rethinking pedagogical guidance. By studying metaphor more closely it becomes possible to develop and enrich experiential engagements with environments.

To introduce contemporary ecocritical arguments to the environmental writing classroom, it is necessary to use a creative model which exhibits the argument regarding fact and figuration pursued so far. Consistently self-reflexive in his writing, the British poet Charles Tomlinson becomes a valuable poetic model as he moves from his belief in the efficacy of a plain, factual style to questioning these qualities in view of materiality itself. Tomlinson's questioning of fact leads him to recognize how metaphorical language can serve to represent the particularities of, for example, a sunset, or the colour of a lichen. Influenced by John Ruskin, Tomlinson's role as an artist informs his poetic inquiry into questions of the perception and representation of the physical world. Though his writing does not directly approach the environment or environmental themes, in his article 'The Poet as Painter', he articulates his concern about the self's ability to impose in a manner that we might compare to the poetics of Jorie Graham discussed in Chapter 2. 'You cease to impose and you discover, to rephrase another aphorism of [Wallace] Stevens' (1985: 210), explains Tomlinson before going on to suggest, in an interview with Bruce Meyer, that a suitably ethical 'lesson' is

> to make yourself a servant, as Adrian Stokes said of Cezanne, of 'the outwardness of the external world.' At one level, the issue is an ecological one and Ruskin was one of the earliest critics of industrial pollution. At another level, it means chastening yourself by realizing your relationship to all that surrounds you.
> (1990: 441)

Tomlinson's proposal contains some interesting metaphors itself. What does he mean by 'servant'? What master might the servant attend? Does the act of chastening oneself return us to the subject of Puritanism? It appears that Tomlinson wishes to reverse the power dynamic in which the human is master and the environment is servant by ensuring that his own writing attends to, rather than imposes upon, the world around him. He hopes for 'a less predatory relationship between the inner and outer – between our egos and all they threaten to aggrandize' (ibid.). As this chapter goes on to demonstrate with regard to his first two collections of poems, Tomlinson becomes a linguistic 'servant' to materiality, but not by using a plain literary style. On the contrary, metaphor is key to his practice. In analysing Tomlinson, I will pursue Abram's ecocritical argument that figurative language embodies material sensuousness to show how an alternative ethics of representation can enrich the relationship we have between language and materiality.

'Facts. And what are they?'

Three statements begin Tomlinson's 'Observation of Facts', published in his first collection *The Necklace*, 'The tree stands / The house encloses. / The room flowers' (1966: 5–7). The title declares each statement to be a fact rather than imagination, and while the first two examples seem accurate enough, the third – 'the room flowers' – suggests creative departure. How exactly can a room be said to flower? Surely the imagination has not been stripped away in this case? Tomlinson plays with our expectations as he later explains that such language is based upon the reality of pot plants inside the room. Playful as the poem seems, Tomlinson appears to be 'chastening' himself in a manner that recalls his discussion of servitude to 'the outwardness of the external world'. As the pot plants are said to compensate for the 'frippery' contained in the room's interior decoration, the domestic setting described in the poem functions ever more obviously as analogous to literary style (ibid.: 20). Unnecessary decoration stands in contrast to plainness, and the latter is clearly favoured. When Tomlinson asserts 'Style speaks what was seen, / Or it conceals the observation / Behind the observer' (ibid.: 22–4), an *ars poetica* comes to the fore. As certain teachers are concerned by what they take to be solipsistic or narcissistic approaches, so Tomlinson is concerned about those which are flamboyantly subjective.[3] Anxiety regarding the ego presents itself in the poem's conclusion that uses enjambment to tinker with the notion of authorial manipulation of materiality: 'Those facets of copiousness which I proposed / Exist, do so when we have silenced ourselves' (ibid. 26–7).

In the 'Author's Preface' to *A Necklace*, Tomlinson states his intention in 'according objects their own existence'. 'Observation of Facts' may appear to offer little to my proposed argument on metaphor given its approval of a plain style. However, Tomlinson's work begins to argue with itself and, in so doing, not only begins to look on metaphor more favourably, but does so in a manner that we might compare with Abram's perspective on metaphor and materiality. In 'The Art of Poetry', Tomlinson appears to pursue the former poem's argument: 'The fact being, that when the truth is not good enough / We exaggerate. Proportions // Matter. It is difficult to get them right.' (ibid.: 5–7). Tomlinson's instruction for 'proportions' resembles the 'detailed daily phenology' Petersen sets as an exercise. Likewise, the prescriptive tone of the poem evokes Christensen's rule regarding 'direct perception … not creative, but precise': a rule that once again suggests a kind of Puritan self-denial might be a common root in the formulation of certain environmental ethics. Yet, Tomlinson hesitates as to whether this is possible as another disturbing enjambment dislocates 'proportions' from 'matter' as if inviting a disruption between materiality and measurement. This disruption continues in the following isolated line: 'This green twilight has violet borders' (ibid.: 11). At odds with realistic 'proportions', such a sentence prompts the question as to whether this representation of twilight is a linguistic exaggeration, 'just for show'. Yet, simultaneously, this description might be true to phenomena relating to natural light. Skies are not often simply blue or grey, they might be pink, yellow, green. Perhaps, then, 'this green twilight' is one facet of the sky's 'facets of copiousness'.[4]

The question as to what kind of literary style affords an 'honest' representation of the environment looms larger in 'A Meditation on John Constable' in Tomlinson's second collection *Seeing Is Believing* (1960). The debate is initiated by the epigraph, a quotation from the nineteenth-century painter famed for working in situ: 'Painting is a science, and should be pursued as an inquiry into the laws of nature.' In uniting art and science, Constable's statement leads Tomlinson to describe how the painter 'replied to his own question' with 'the unmannered / Exactness of art' (1960: 1–2). Yet, in using language to record Constable's practice of painting, Tomlinson implicitly replies to a parallel question concerning artistic *language* and scientific understanding of environments. After setting out a practice applicable to both painting and writing, that of 'the labour of observation / In face of meteorological fact' (ibid.: 3–4), the following lines of 'A Meditation on John Constable' describe 'Clouds … scattered and mellowed shafts … raw fire … rags … gauze … a crescent crushed out … silvered-yellow' (ibid.: 4–19). After presenting this imagery, Tomlinson returns to the question raised in the earlier line with: 'Facts. And what are they?' (ibid.: 20). In his analysis that focuses on the influence that artworks have on Tomlinson's perception, Karl

Klein states that 'at the very moment when the objectivity of perception seems to be established, he puts it into question' (1996: 31). Yet, what is really questioned here is not the objectivity of the perception, but familiar definitions of objectivity that accompany definitions of fact. The timing of Tomlinson's question provokes a return to his lines only to discover that figurative language rather than fact has formed this detailed, vividly rendered representation of the sky.

Rather than writing 'cirrus' or 'stratocumulus' that might, within the poem, create detachment from the patterns and textures of the material environment, or an unhelpful shorthand for them, Tomlinson explores metaphor's capacity to represent the sky's sensuous detail. Such a practice helps to illustrate the irrelevance of the dualism concerning fact and figurative language that arises from the influence of natural history study. Metaphor can contain physical reality and detail. Dialogue between Christensen and a student on the environmental writing workshop at Green Mountain College touches on this very issue with excellent insight. A week after the class that concludes with Christensen's instruction that he wants students to see environments for what they are and so does 'not want to see a metaphor' in their writing, a paradoxically positive mention of metaphor arises. Discussing a student's poem in the weekly feedback session, Christensen draws attention to the description of 'a family of clovers' for the way it 'humanizes plants' through metaphor (2014a). His comment suggests that there is an anthropocentric quality to the writing that comes at the expense of the direct perception he has otherwise encouraged. A student responds by asking whether this humanizing is in fact problematic given that clovers do grow in clusters. Christensen concedes that perhaps this metaphorical expression is 'a form of ecological realism' (ibid.). While the brevity of the comment does not lend itself to further discussion in the class, it serves to acknowledge the referential capacity of metaphor. Just as Abram proposed that the 'howling wind' responds to sounds encountered in the environment, Christensen here admits that rather than 'family' being a fanciful attribution to the clovers, the material form of the plants informs the metaphor.[5]

Metaphor is not simply a solipsistic or exhibitionist device that risks overshadowing an environmental description. Rather, metaphor has the referential capacity to convey details about physical phenomena. Metaphorical description and literal description would seem, then, to be equally important. And yet, there is a case for arguing that metaphor goes further than literal description in its ability to draw out material particularities. 'A Meditation on John Constable' concludes with a witty remark: 'The artist lies / For the improvement of truth. Believe him' (1960: 51–2). Given the hope many teachers have that their students will become engaged, 'honest' writers, the notion that lying can generate an improvement of truth might seem inconceivable on an environmental writing course. Tomlinson's lying artist could be interpreted as an exaggerating artist who supposedly improves the truth by heightening it. Yet, this interpretation is not consistent with the poem that describes how art convinces 'As the *adequate* gauge, both of the passion / And its object' (ibid.: 50–1, emphasis added). Rather, Tomlinson's metaphorical use of language seems to underpin his sense of 'lying'. After all, philosophical approaches to metaphor, such as that by Donald Davidson in 'What Metaphors Mean' (1978), have emphasized that all metaphors are 'false' statements. The clouds are, after all, not rags. In turn, it is possible to interpret Tomlinson's 'lying' in terms of metaphor that, while making a false linguistic claim, improves truth by drawing attention to the particularity of its subject.[6] Instead of calling a bird a blackbird, calling it 'a small mad puritan with a banana in his mouth' draws attention to realities previously unseen: the shape and colour of the beak; the alert, slightly frenzied motion of its hop. With this development, is it possible to read a disparaging tone into Tomlinson's earlier 'Facts. And what are they?' that subsequently suggests that figurative language surpasses the referential capacity of fact by drawing attention to material detail that might be otherwise overlooked?

Metaphor's 'improvement of truth'

The naturalist's field journal takes a guiding role in Allison B. Wallace's article, 'The Place of Drawing in Nature Journaling' (2012). 'At the top of each entry' her students are expected to 'record the date; the time of day; the ambient temperature; the degree of cloud cover; and the direction and strength of the wind' (2012: 101). She explains, 'I acknowledge aloud, when introducing the assignment, the temptation students will surely feel to get some of these data off the web – after all, many of them carry smart phones – I urge them to set aside this crutch' (ibid.). The argument behind this decision fits with the experiential encounter teachers hope to foster: Wallace claims that 'being able to gauge accurately and unassisted the temperature, wind velocity, and other conditions is part of the sharpened powers of perception' she hopes to foster in her students (ibid.). As the exercise requires a student to make use of their senses to respond to the environment's palpable phenomena, it might be understood to embody some of Abram's phenomenologically inspired ecocritical thought. All the more surprising, then, is her choice: 'To help students identify their local tree, flower, bird, insect, and mammal species (beyond generic terms like "bug"), I lend out field guides such as the Audubon Society's guide to North American birds' (ibid.: 102). Instead of letting her students experience the diversity of species and notice differences between them as she did with the temperature, cloud cover and wind, Wallace lets a guide's pre-existing definitions lead the study and, put bluntly, do the work for them.

While telling a starling from a blackbird might be said to sharpen perception by asking the student to differentiate between the things they see, it shortens what could be more extensive, experiential engagements. With the 'crutch' of the field guide, are the students really as attentive as they could be? Wallace may state that 'we often do not truly see or hear something for which we have no name', but immediately providing these names and descriptions means that the students' opportunity to engage with materiality and its distinguishing features themselves is pre-emptively shaped (ibid.). As Wallace goes on to ask her students to draw what they see, she quotes ornithologist Roger Tory Petersen's claim that drawing goes 'beyond mere identification naming things [sic]; you begin to understand shape, function, movement, and behaviour' (ibid.: 103). The artistic component of Wallace's exercise is carefully considered, yet, in comparing linguistic identification of the environment to drawing the environment, Wallace does not apprehend how language might offer a similarly refined understanding. Rather than immediately noting a 'starling' in their journals, students might respond to the species by noting, say, its call like an auditory glitch, or the seaweed blush of its feathers in a process that could, if necessary, lead to the identification of the bird as a starling. By prompting students to generate their own metaphors, teachers can search for evidence that the students really have attended to materiality via their senses, allowing the authority of the field guide to take a secondary rather than primary position. Responding to the risk that the field guide might be used to simply 'match' a sighting of a bird to a pre-written summary, the exercise emphasizes active participation in appreciating physical distinction and selecting words to represent such.

As Tomlinson attended to the patterns and textures of clouds in 'A Meditation', so he moves towards the colours and shapes of environmental materiality in his poem 'Frondes Agrestes' (1960). The very title of the poem acknowledges the influence of John Ruskin. Many of the descriptions in Tomlinson's poem are taken directly from the Frondes Agrestes section in Ruskin's *Modern Painters* such as the first two lines: 'A leaf, catching the sun, transmits it: / "First a torch, then an emerald"' (ibid.: 1–2). Later in the poem Tomlinson uses another, even more concise metaphor belonging to Ruskin that draws out differences in colour and texture: 'a leopard-skin of moss' (ibid.: 12). The poem itself concerns Ruskin's style, admiring his use of metaphor to aid with physical specifics.[7] Tomlinson is, however, wary of Ruskin's potential to be an 'Organ voice dissolving among cloud-wrack', dominating the observation the way the 'voice / wearing a ruff' threatened to dominate in 'The Observation of Facts' (ibid.: 17). But metaphor is not symptomatic of this 'Sublimity' in 'Frondes Agrestes' (1960: 16). When 'the climber returns' from his lofty Romantic adventure, 'He brings / Sword-shaped, its narrowing strip / Fluted and green, the single grass-blade' (ibid.: 18, 18–20). What ultimately triumphs is a perception that participates with material distinction as the differing shapes of the grass-blade are perceived through the shapes of a sword and flute.

It is this process of perception that requires further investigation in view of Tomlinson's statement that 'The artist lies / For the improvement of truth'. After all, the grass-blade is not a sword, nor are lichens actually 'slow-pencilled, iris-dyed' as Ruskin strikingly says in *Modern Painters* ([1860] 2015). In each case, the writer is 'lying' in order to draw out physical differences in the environment. Tomlinson's use of 'sword' resuscitates the dead metaphor contained within the phrase 'blade of grass' to improve understanding of its shape. Likewise, the delicacy of the lichen's form alongside its colour come to the fore with the metaphorical use of 'iris' and 'slow pencilled'. The improvement Tomlinson refers to concerns the distinctions of environmental material that only become appreciated through metaphor. 'Distinctions' (1960) pursues this understanding. The poem opens with a disturbingly emphatic sibilance suggesting the blurring of waves: the seeming impossibility of definition. At first it appears that the sea is simply blue: 'Blue is blue', Tomlinson states (1960: 3). However, the homogenous marine landscape is not simply blue once the speaker acknowledges other entities within the environment, such as a pine-branch. Having perceived the branch, 'the eye / Returns to grey-blue, blue-black or indigo ' or 'To blue-after-the-pine-branch' (ibid.: 5–6, 8). Plainness of language, exemplified by Tomlinson's initial 'blue', fails to adequately respond to the particularity of the sea. In turn, the 'pine-branch' becomes a metaphorical vehicle that extends perception: the vehicle filters the tenor of the sea to draw out a more specific colour.

Like many teachers, Andrew Motion, whose 'Place, Environment, Writing' Master's Course at Royal Holloway I discussed in Chapter 3, is critical of his students' lack of interest or knowledge in naming different species of British flora and fauna (2013). Describing a week of the course entitled 'Journals and Field Guides', Motion explains that he gives his students a 'template of scientific knowledge as their basis so that when they went off to write their pieces about walking in the woods they'd know in a proper scientific way what they were looking at' (ibid.). 'The reason for that is very obvious', Motion goes on to state. 'It's that nothing we look at is innocent of living in a dangerous world – everything is doomed' (ibid.). His views can be taken as an extension of the ethical debate regarding identification and its ability to create writing that is 'more in the world', Motion claims that a scientific way of observing environmental phenomena suggests a certain level of responsibility: that by being aware of individual species we become aware of their potential loss. As he goes on to assert, 'we can't afford to be detached' (ibid.). So far, in this chapter, I have suggested, in contrast to Motion, that the 'proper scientific way' of identifying species risks detachment rather than engagement with the environment. Yet the logic underlying Motion's argument – that a greater attention to material diversity can result in an awareness of its potential loss – is worth pursuing, and I will do so using the principles central to Abram's ecocritical perspective as well as Tomlinson's attention to particularity in physical phenomena.

'Variegated excess'

Though many teachers, as we have seen, value scientific language above metaphorical language, its presence in environmental writing can be seen as problematic. The ecopoet and critic Terry Gifford asks: 'Does [the] artistic quality of writing have to be compromised to accommodate urgently needed data such as scientific content?' (2011: 10). 'For example', he adds, 'can percentages ever be used in poetry successfully?' He goes on to acknowledge that writing needs to respond to 'the culture of the public discourse of degrees: two, three, or six degrees of global warming … One metre or two meters sea-level rise' (ibid.: 12). Yet the phrasing of his question implies that scientific language is more likely to jeopardize literature than not. The danger in not including 'data' is that the writing may fail to explain complicated findings and do justice to the conditions in which such data was generated. But, on the other hand, the danger of including this scientific material is that of discordance between styles of expression. Gifford suggests that the latter risk is similar in effect to the danger of polemic that I discussed in Chapter 2. Writing on the poetry of Ted Hughes, Gifford draws attention to his poem 'Lobby from Under the Carpet'. After quoting Hughes's account of chemical pollution that results in 'a 40% drop / in the sperm count of all Western Males', Gifford suggests that the writing 'failed as poetry', while Hughes himself, according to Gifford, felt unconvinced about the propagandist quality of his own work (ibid.: 147).

There is a challenge here to the guidance given by teachers who hold scientific accuracy in high esteem. It seems, after all, that being too direct and too precise might not equal writing that is 'more in the world', but writing which wears its agenda uncomfortably on its sleeve. In an article recalling his teaching at Alma College in Michigan, Christensen argues that inputting scientific data into environmental writing incurs other risks too. Aiming to unite his students with their bioregion, Christensen initiates, as part of his 'Environmental Narratives', a project that will focus on the Pine River watershed. Explaining the watershed's formation, Christensen admits,

> We wrestled with problems like evoking geologic time or the massive size of glaciers. It would not be enough, we knew, simply to describe a glacier 10,000 feet thick, for numbers that large tend to remain abstract. We wanted people to *see* the glacier, and so we chose a trope that would be familiar to residents of central Michigan.
>
> (2003: 130)

The trope settled upon is one of houses: 'Imagine, though, that the snow keeps falling until it has covered the land to the height of a two-storey house – about twenty-five feet ... Eventually it accumulates to the height of four such houses – a hundred feet of snow' (ibid.). Finally, to convey the true size of the glacier, Christensen produces the image of '400 two-storey houses stacked atop one another' (ibid.). The risk that concerns him here is not that the inclusion of scientific data in collaborative non-fiction will produce discordance, polemic or misunderstanding, but that the information itself will become meaningless, since a figure such as '10,000 feet' is too difficult to visualize. Some may think figurative language showy or solipsistic, but this language fulfils a key function in communicating an otherwise intangible fact. The strategy Christensen turns to is, of course, central to the tradition of science communication in which metaphor is used to convey complex systems and interactions to non-expert audiences. Popular examples of this include the description of a genome as software, or an atom which is frequently depicted as a solar system.

Metaphor in Tomlinson's practice does not aim to communicate the scientific data that Gifford believes contemporary poetry is somewhat pressed to represent; it seems, after all, to be a way of finding new truths rather than representing existing ones. Yet, Tomlinson's reasoning points to a concept of environmental responsibility that deserves further attention. In the interview in which Tomlinson describes the importance of humility in perception – of being a 'servant' to the world – Bruce Meyer picks up the importance of Ruskin to Tomlinson. Speculatively, Meyer asks: 'Do you feel Ruskin was a necessary prerequisite training for your eye?' (1990: 439). Referring again to *Modern Painters* and Ruskin's ability to describe the 'peculiar and separating form' of clouds, water and vegetation, Tomlinson asserts,

> We live in a universe which goes beyond the merely human, is animate or inanimate, is vegetable, mineral – stone, clay, light, dark, what have you. We have so violently annexed that universe to our needs and our fantasies, literary, economic, political, we need to look again and find language for it and, in doing so, become more human, although *in* the finding of that language we are, say, putting to one side the ego, the personality, the what is *thought* to be 'human'.
>
> (ibid.: 440)

Tomlinson's charge that 'we need to look again' implies that it is not just a lichen that requires reconsideration, but the whole universe. In finding this new way of appreciating that which surrounds us, the concept of the human separates into two distinct categories. There is the 'human', a word he uses, with these scare quotes, to designate the assuming and egotistical personality that recurs as a concern in several of the poems discussed so far. As a way of resisting the impulse to annexe, appropriate or, more broadly, to act violently towards the universe, he turns towards the idea of another type of human who *does* look again and find language. It would seem from Tomlinson's split definition that to be 'more human' is to be committed to exploring new ways of perceiving and describing the world.

I have suggested that the experiential quality intended by much of pedagogical instruction to go out and write in the field might be compromised by a reliance on pre-existing guides. Tomlinson's reflection helps us to recognize that such instruction also risks compromising an experiential exploration of the capacities of language. It is interesting, then, to consider a text that occupies a space between field guide and poetry: Robert Macfarlane's *Landmarks* (2015b). The book was written partly in response to the publication of a new edition of the *Oxford Junior Dictionary* that replaced words such as 'buttercup' and 'conker' with 'broadband' and 'chatroom': a shift that Macfarlane, and many others, fear is representative of an increasing disassociation we have with the natural world. Celebrating unfamiliar words used for the landscape, gathered from maps, books, correspondence and conversations, *Landmarks* aims to 're-wild our contemporary language for landscape' (2015b: 9). For example, a glossary of terms relating to ice and snow includes 'aquabob' (meaning icicle in Kent), 'billow' (meaning snowdrift in East Anglia) and 'bleb' (a bubble of air in ice, coming from north-east Ireland and northern England) (ibid.: 87). Practised by particular generations of people and local communities, these words, Macfarlane argues, 'bring new energies to familiar phenomena' and a 'vibrancy of perception' – an argument that we might compare with Tomlinson's desire to look again and find language for the world (ibid.: 5, 9). By collating these glossaries of terms, Macfarlane produces a field guide of sorts, but one that showcases the creative potential for language to describe environments. Rather than one authority or one objective language to learn, here are several languages to explore. Indeed, *Landmarks* is not just about rediscovering language, but discovering it anew. For community groups in certain areas of the United Kingdom, the book has encouraged people to recall words used for the landscape in the local area, but also to invent their own (Macfarlane 2016b).

Many of the terms collected in *Landmarks* demonstrate how language can represent particular details and nuances in the landscape that might otherwise get overlooked. This relationship between language and landscape is pertinent to the subject of biodiversity. The need for an understanding and appreciation of the world's variety of plant and animal life is high. Reports suggest that the earth has entered 'a new period of extinction' and that biodiversity is under great threat from industrial agricultural practices, urban sprawl, pollution, the introduction of invasive species and climate change (Ceballos et al. 2017). Although it cannot be said that biodiversity is at the heart of Tomlinson's work, his stated intention to 'look again and find language' for the world is relevant. Approaching a vast seascape in 'Sea Change', Tomlinson acknowledges: 'To define the sea – / We change our opinions / With the changing light' (1966: 1–3). Consequently, he does not just look once but looks three times and in each case, each observation prompts a different use of metaphor: the sea is 'uneasy marble', then 'green silk' and lastly, 'blue mud' (ibid.: 8–10). Each instance of observation prompts a different use of metaphor. Later in the poem, this process of finding language becomes even more prominent: with the light of dawn, the sea is compared to different types of gemstone, before a hesitant decision is made on 'a leek – or apple-green chalcedony' (ibid.: 14). Tomlinson portrays a hashing of metaphorical language to represent the colour distinction he perceives in the sea. 'A leek – or apple-green chalcedony' mixes signifiers: one metaphorical vehicle is offered up and then another to produce a nuanced literary representation that tries to embody the particular colour of the ocean itself. Returning to Tomlinson's interview response that I discussed earlier in this chapter, could this series of comparisons embody 'servitude' to materiality? In this dramatization of the speaker's intention for precision, we could say that Tomlinson advocates a practice that encapsulates the idea that to be 'more human' is to be more engaged with exercising our sensorial and linguistic capacities.

One can imagine Tomlinson transferring his attention in 'Sea Change' from the colour of the sea to the colour, shape and movements of marine creatures found in rock pools, or the form and textures of shells washed up on the beach. Imagining this shift helps to illustrate how his practice of finding language might be used to reflect on biodiversity. In 'Northern Spring', he extends his argument on materiality and language even further. The poem begins with the declaration 'Nor is this the setting for extravagance' (1960: 1). And yet, as in 'The Art of Poetry', in which plainness of observation is advocated and exotic description responds, what Tomlinson goes on to write is a densely descriptive, arguably extravagant passage: 'Trees / Fight with the wind, the wind eludes them / Streaking its cross-lanes over the uneasy water / Whose bronze whitens (ibid.: 1–4). As personification and metaphor abound, Tomlinson reflects on the landscape he perceives: 'To emulate such confusion / One must impoverish the resources of folly / But to taste it is medicinal' (ibid.: 4–6). Like Abram, who writes of the environment's 'multiform strangeness' (2010: 3), Tomlinson sees movement, detail and capacity for change as 'confusion' and defends this quality as if disorientation were an antidote to an assuming ego. For such 'confusion' in the environment, the poem suggests, only a playfully creative language ('the resources of folly') is appropriate. As light 'deepens the scene' in 'Northern Spring', intensifying the confusion Tomlinson has already acknowledged, his speaker asks, 'Where should one look / In the profusion of possibilities?' (ibid.: 14–15). The attempt to represent his surroundings provokes a question that is posed both to perception as well as to language. Just as the definition of 'fact' was reconsidered in 'A Meditation on John Constable', Tomlinson redefines 'extravagance'. A literary quality that might exceed what is reasonable or appropriate – a quality that might even be associated with 'purple prose' – is needed in order to respond to what he calls the 'variegated excess' growing from the 'verdant ground' (ibid.: 19–20). To match a diversity in materiality, it appears that only a 'variegated excess' of language will do (19–20).

Re-identifying materiality

In this chapter I have questioned the ethical principles that emerge from the use of natural history tropes in environmental writing pedagogy. As I have discussed, many teachers associate fact with truth, and metaphor with solipsistic tendencies. Through my readings of Abram and Tomlinson, I have proposed an alternative argument. How, then, do we put that argument into practice? How can the perspective presented by Abram inform exercises that belong to a new ecocritical pedagogy? In his self-reflexive poetics that chart a movement from factual to figurative language, Tomlinson provides a creative model with which to consider the idea that metaphor can represent materiality in ways that more literal understandings of language cannot. Studied in this context, his poems introduce ways in which language might seek a closer fit to the diversity of physical phenomena. From an initial dismissal of literary 'frippery' in favour of plainness of fact, Tomlinson moves to a realization that the world is anything but plain, and a belief that metaphor improves truth. Ultimately, the need he sees is for metaphor to attend to the extravagance of materiality at hand. Fundamental to the journey Tomlinson makes is his own ethical stance that aims to put the ego to one side and become 'more human' in developing his response – perceptively and linguistically – to what is non-human. Such an approach in environmental writing aims to avoid the problematic effects that can arise from the use of scientific language, and to reflect creatively, rather than merely reporting, scientific fact.

An important exercise to start with is one which values unfamiliarity with the common names of species. The teacher could ask students to go out and search specifically for at least three plants, birds or insects that they cannot identify. Having found these examples, the students should make as many notes as they can to convey their material detail. In the manner demonstrated most distinctly in Tomlinson's 'A Meditation on John Constable', 'Sea Change' and 'Northern Spring', these notes should play with 'the resources of folly' in order to draw out the distinctions of, say, a particular type of bee or a butterfly. No language should be off limits in making these notes: mixed metaphor and personification included. Abram's understanding that sensory perception relies on an active reciprocity is relevant here: 'The terrain enters into us only to the extent that we allow ourselves to be taken up within that terrain' (58). A crucial part of the task is for students to prime the senses most appropriate to the entity they are observing. How can a simile rematerialize the colour, shape or texture of, say, a particular type of grass? How can language be made to embody the sound of a bird, the smell of a wildflower or the texture of a tree's bark? Informed by their notes, students can then consider what names they would give to the species they have studied. How does it feel to name this species? To develop the experiential element of the exercise, students might be asked to find another example of their species elsewhere. For example, if a wildflower were studied in a local wood in the first part of the exercise, is it possible to identify the same species in the local park? If successful, students might be asked whether the name they have chosen for that bird or tree is one which still seems relevant. Does this second observation of the species provide a material detail previously unseen? Is the colour of the bird's beak really banana-yellow or is it lemon-yellow?

Once they have written these notes and settled on a name, they should compare this work to the entry for the same species in a few different field guides. What similarities and differences can be observed? What is lost and what is gained in terms of sensory perception through these linguistic approaches? Stephen Moss, who leads the MA in Travel and Nature Writing at Bath Spa University, describes an approach that extends discussion of naming and draws attention to its shape-shifting nature. Comparing the different obstacles faced by practitioners in these two genres of writing, Moss suggests that writing about a foreign country can initially result in superficial representation, but, he states, 'You can remedy that by spending some time there' (2018b). The same cannot be said for wild nature: in contrast, 'It's like learning a language or learning to cook' (ibid.). This analogy, the comparison to language acquisition especially, stresses the idea that there is an objectively correct way of engaging with the environment. Moss acknowledges, however, the debate in which 'naming also has negative associations concerning control [and] human dominance' (ibid.). Thinking especially of 'twitchers', and contributing to the argument on passive versus active engagements with materiality, he critiques, 'A kind of male obsession with listing – now I've seen that bird I can tick it off. I've seen it now, though I might not have seen what it was doing' (ibid.) Extending these thoughts, Moss's own book, *Mrs Moreau's Warbler* (2018a) advocates identification but does so in a self-reflexive manner. The intention of his book is, after all, to explore the origins of bird names – often involving evolutionary linguistics, folklore and tales of competitive ornithologists – with the understanding that 'we need to know the origins of those names, as this unlocks a fascinating story of our long and deep relationship with birds and the rest of the plant and animal kingdoms.' (2018d).

Moss further blurs the line between fact and figuration in a way that recalls Tomlinson's question, 'Facts. And what are they?' In many cases, Moss's study helps to restore what Abram calls the 'sensuousness' of our engagement with bird species: with the Norman Conquest, came Middle English and the bird which had been known as 'red steort' (meaning red tail) turned into what is known today as the 'redstart' (2018a). Likewise, names such as cuckoo, finch and turtle dove, Moss explains, onomatopoeically reflect the birds' calls (ibid.). Students who have carried out the exercise I outlined above – the comparison between their own descriptions of species and those in the field guide – can deepen their engagement by following Moss's lead. What new understandings about a species can be brought to light by exploring its accepted name? What is the etymology of the name? What is the species called in other languages? How do these findings alter an understanding of the relationship between language and materiality? These tasks and questions can feed into different sorts of written assignment. For example, students can write essays reflecting on their experience of differentiating and naming species, as well as their research into the names provided by field guides. These various tasks can also be fruitful prompts for poems and short stories.

The tasks can also provide a foundation from which to approach the topic of biodiversity. Macfarlane celebrates lost or obscured words for landscapes in the belief that such words can bring us closer to the landscapes themselves and lead to a conservatory ethic. Tomlinson shows how finding new language for the world enacts a similar responsibility. What emerges from the studied poems in nearly every case is that Tomlinson's process of *finding* language is, in fact, a *making* of language through metaphor. With the same causal logic articulated by Macfarlane, it might be said that generating new terms with which to acknowledge and appreciate material distinctions raises consciousness about the ecological significance of these distinctions and a desire to protect them. To push this issue-led focus further, however, seminar discussion might focus on whether this approach communicates crucial information about biodiversity clearly enough. What alternatives are there? Must a poem about butterfly loss repeat newspaper stats announcing that 70 per cent of all species are experiencing decline? Using the results of the previous exercises in which students describe a species, or several species, through metaphor, students can experiment with techniques associated with found poetry in which an existing text is manipulated by the writer, resulting in a new text. For instance, a poem about the disappearance of butterflies might creatively materialize the loss by removing 70 per cent of its words. Likewise, in an essay that more broadly takes British wildlife as its subject, one in ten words could be eliminated in order to reflect the threat currently reported. The erasure form has been popularized by the contemporary American poet, Mary Ruefle, who selects deletions creatively in order to generate new meaning or effect from an original text. Alternatively, text can be inserted, rather than erased, in order to represent particular statistics. This text might be written afresh or it might come from a pre-existing source – perhaps associated with the causes of biodiversity decline; a government-approved register of pesticides, for example.

An interesting angle on environmental issues emerges when these techniques are applied to inorganic matter. In 'Ecopoetics', an undergraduate module offered at the University of Warwick, Jonathan Skinner and George Ttoouli introduce field guides to the classroom in order to question the 'object-oriented' emphasis of 'field pedagogy'. Their alternative is a creative process they see as receptive to 'change and metamorphosis' (Skinner 2014). Abram might add that the environment is also changeable, shifting and 'multiform'. Skinner and Ttoouli engage their students with field guides so that the naturalist's potentially reductive view can be reimagined and reapplied in the students' writing. 'I think the most successful response over the year was the student who started to identify the various names for cosmetic ingredients', Ttoouli offers (2014). 'Palm oil', he goes on to explain, is frequently 'obfuscated by various languages, sometimes translated, sometimes not' (ibid.). This discovery raises the question as to why the ingredient needs to be hidden – one of the bigger reasons is, of course, its detrimental impact on rainforest biodiversity. Such linguistic slipperiness challenges the field spotter's awareness and turns the student's writing into a political project. Ready meals and pesticide trade names could feature just as easily as cosmetics, and the technique might be applied to other concealed information. Sources of funding from companies known for environmentally unethical practices such as Shell and Coca Cola, easily qualify. As palm oil is confusingly also known as palm olein and glyceryl stearate, among other names, so big-name brands often operate as subsidiary companies. How can the process of identification discussed in terms of the naturalist's stance reveal the links between an 'oil major' and an international toymaker or a local university's investments?

How can writers approach this identity crisis? J. R. Carpenter's hybrid print and web-based work, *The Gathering Cloud* (2017), provides an innovative model. The work also demonstrates an effective balance between languages associated with literary creativity and scientific data. With lyric dexterity, Carpenter interweaves her own research on 'cloud computing' with Luke Howard's landmark scientific *Essay on the Modification of Clouds*, first published in 1803. In 'A Meditation on John Constable', Tomlinson draws new attention to the materiality of clouds by experimenting with metaphor. It is interesting to read Carpenter's poem alongside Tomlinson's: Carpenter similarly 'rematerializes' clouds but does so in order to reveal environmental damage. 'The Cloud is just someone else's computer', she writes and later refers to the 'tech giants' who 'power their twenty-first century clouds with / dirty nineteenth century coal energy' (2017: 76, 82). The material sensuousness at the heart of Tomlinson's poem gives way in

Carpenter's to the digital quotidian, which often exudes a kind of comic bathos, especially when Carpenter links such large-scale threats such as climate change to the number of cute cat photos stored on remote servers. Such work depends, of course, on a single metaphor – that of a cloud to signify data stored on remote servers. While this use of figurative language is very different to that discussed in relation to Tomlinson, this example of metaphor becomes a valuable bridge into thinking about identification and materiality with a greater emphasis on contemporary environmental issues. Students might explore similar phrases that signify both natural and cultural realms, such as 'Apple', 'Blackberry' and 'Amazon'; the task would be an opportunity for students to create their own piece of writing that questions the names we otherwise accept in today's world. The work would likely need to delve into related materialities including, say, Apple's environmentally destructive mineral mining. In creatively exploring different relationships between language and physical phenomena, these exercises gesture towards a revised ethics of representation for environmental writing.

5

'On the world's terms and not my own': Authenticity, self-reflexivity and otherness

'Write about an experience that was personally experienced', instructs John A. Murray in his *Nature Writing Handbook*. 'As you do, pay close attention to where you find it necessary to fictionalize in the interest of achieving structural unity, dramatic intensity, or character revelation' (1995: 104). Authenticity has long been a quality aspired to, and expected from, environmental writers. Resembling Murray's prescription of a self-regulating writing practice, Mark Cocker describes the need to write about the environment with 'some monitor, some tester of authenticity' (2014). Yet, crucially important as authenticity might be in depicting a wild swim or the changing colours of autumn, it remains a nebulous and complex term. What does it mean? 'The word authenticity is a funny word for sure', John Elder explains (2014). 'It has something to do with accuracy but it's not quite the same thing' (ibid.). Teaching at Bath Spa, Stephen Moss compares accuracy to truth, believing that the former is unachievable. He takes the example of a reproduced conversation: 'a) you've edited it, b) you've probably recorded it slightly wrong' (2018b). Consequently, the rule used by Moss is to ask, 'Have you captured the essence of that person?' (ibid.). However, this leaves us with another question, what is 'essence'? Of course, the risk of inauthentic writing is one which is not exclusive to environmental writing. If the weaponry in historical fiction or the relationship central to a romance novel seem unfeasible, the text becomes less immersive, the author less trustworthy and the whole endeavour less enjoyable. What differentiates the importance of authenticity in environmental writing is, then, its relationship to an ethics of representation. As this chapter explores, a certain pressure exists on writers to do justice to the environment. In what follows, I identify a series of tropes that aim towards authenticity in this context. Questioning the synthetic and often problematic character of these tropes, I explore creative alternatives that recognize the difficulty, if not the impossibility, of reliably identifying the world.

Authenticity is a difficult term to pin down. To be authentic can mean to express one's thoughts and feelings. Authenticity is, then, a quality that conveys one's 'true' inner self. However, the term is also understood to be more outward-looking. To create authentic representation is to create a representation that faithfully reflects real life. In *True West: Authenticity and the American West* (2004), Nathaniel Lewis looks at the importance of authenticity in texts about the American West that appeared in the first-half of the nineteenth-century. He explains, 'Authenticity (often coded in the words "fidelity," "accuracy," and "truth") implied factual representation of landscape, population, and historical record' (2004: 22–3). The author's aim was to create a 'faithful recording of region', and, in so doing, Lewis suggests, the author's role was reduced from that of a 'creative visionary' to a 'mere translator or observer' (ibid.: 32). This definition of authenticity, and its consequences for the author, guide my discussion in this chapter. As I argue later, the writer's attempt to avoid authorial manipulation of their subject in order to achieve a 'faithful recording' means that the writer's desire for their writing to be authentic may well be conceived of as a desire to create art that presents itself as 'non-art'.

By way of introduction to this definition and the manner in which it is enacted in environmental writing, it is useful to highlight the relationship between authenticity and several concerns I have focused on already in this book. Elder draws on the highly popular American writer Barry Lopez to plot the coordinates for authenticity. Basing his discussion in Lopez's essay, 'Landscape and Narrative', Elder summarizes Lopez's account in which he hears a story about the elusive wolverine from a group of native people in Alaska and tells this story to another indigenous group who recognize it, in the light of their experience, to be genuine. Authenticity is defined, in this case, by 'knowing and understanding natural patterns', Elder reflects in a manner that we might compare with the previous chapter's discussion of phenologies and fact (2014). Yet, turning to Lopez's essay itself reveals a slightly more complex set of criteria. 'The storyteller is obligated to … set forth a coherent and dramatic rendering of incidents – and to be ingenuous', states Lopez before he makes clear that the writing itself should concern a landscape local to the storyteller ([1984] 1988: 66). His argument is similar to those expressed by particular teachers discussed in Chapter 1. Lopez argues that credible depictions depend on local, perhaps even native conceptions of place: 'To violate *that* connection [between author and place] is to call the narrative itself into question' (ibid.: 68).[1]

A number of queries emerge from the argument on authenticity that Lopez provides. If a storyteller is 'obligated … to be ingenuous', how might their straightforward, natural manner be artificially constructed? Likewise, wouldn't a '*dramatic* rendering of incidents' suggest a certain level of manipulation antithetical to an authentic story (emphasis added)? Lastly, but perhaps most significantly, what are the repercussions of Lopez's association between authenticity and aboriginal culture? To generate authentic writing, must one be native to the landscape described? While Lopez's use of aboriginal culture to inform notions of authenticity might seem restrictive, it might also seem clichéd and exploitative. In *Unsettling the Literary West* (2003), Nathaniel Lewis draws attention to the romanticizing of Native Americans and its market value. Referring to the indigenous American writer N. Scott Momaday and his novel *House Made of Dawn,* Lewis expresses his unease at the book's promotional tagline: 'Almost unbearably authentic' (2003: 14).[2] Elder, in his pedagogical argument, seeks to take Lopez's idea of authenticity beyond its Native American context and apply it to the subject of environmental writing more broadly (as, indeed, Lopez himself seeks to do). However, his suggestion that the notion of authenticity not only relies on an indigenous culture, but a particular construction of that indigenous culture as more connected to nature than other cultures, throws its reliability and relevance into question.

When discussing authenticity, there is a danger of creating a reductively polarized argument over what is true and what is false. In *The Jargon of Authenticity* (1973), philosopher Theodor Adorno asks how we can judge between these qualities. His work is a critique of the rhetoric adopted by philosopher Martin Heidegger, and post-war Germany more broadly, that he sees as promulgating a sense of authenticity that relies on a series of tropes. In comparing authenticity's tropes to advertising, he draws attention to one of 'authenticity's funky commercials': a religious minister preaching on television (ibid.: 30). His behaviour is so earnest it becomes open to ridicule, Adorno states, and yet this is the very quality that allows it to be deemed authentic. His behaviour exudes a 'trustworthiness [that] supports the credibility of his statements' (ibid.). Ultimately, Adorno warns us of the dangers associated with the jargon of authenticity. He believes that as the jargon presents itself as 'natural' or 'true', it hides the contingencies of power that have constructed and maintained it, meaning that those who subscribe to it become complicit with certain ideologies. Along with advertising, Adorno associates the jargon of authenticity with fascist propaganda. While his warning may not be directly applicable to the context of environmental writing, Adorno's identification of authenticity is useful to my discussion because it demonstrates the ways in which the 'quality of truth' is not only frequently simulated, but simulated according to particular tropes. As I go on to show, some comparison might be made between the earnestness of Adorno's preacher and the writer who desires to represent the 'real' wild.

In his guide to environmental writing, David Petersen includes a chapter entitled 'A Nature Writer's Credo: Truth ... for Truth's Sake' that focuses on the practice of writing non-fiction. Opening with an epigraph by Edward Abbey, 'In writing, fidelity to fact leads eventually to the poetry of truth', Petersen explains that 'we live in a dishonest, self-serving, hypocritical culture, the pathology of which has spread even unto nature writing' (2001: 181). Consequently, in a rather threatening manner, Petersen insists: 'Everything you claim has happened, must in fact have happened, just as told' (ibid.: 182). He goes on to list what he calls 'morally conscionable narrative devices' such as the compression and coalescence of events and changing character names in the writing process (ibid.). Suggesting that the employment of such devices should be guided by the writer's conscience, he provides a few examples of good practice. In order to achieve 'the finest piece of American nature writing ever committed', according to Petersen, Edward Abbey 'compressed two full summers and several shorter expeditions ... into a single "Season in the Wilderness"' in *Desert Solitaire* (ibid.: 186). Petersen similarly defends Abbey's decision to have culled his second wife and first son from the story because, for the story to work, 'Ed had to be alone out there with the sandstone and snakes and lizards and blistering sun' (ibid.). Comparable to Henry David Thoreau's decision not to include mention of the home-cooked food he received from his mother in *Walden*, the reality of domestic life clearly has no place in generating a bona fide depiction of a man's connection with the harshness of Utahan land.

It is interesting to see how examples of environmental writing that do explore the more domestic and perhaps unappealing aspects of day-to-day life might also aim for a sense of 'authenticity' that is contrived. 'Between the laundry and the fetching kids from school, that's how birds enter my life', writes Kathleen Jamie in *Findings* (2005), a collection of essays that stands in contrast to Abbey's work in its decision to reflect the responsibilities of domestic life (2005: 32). Likewise, urbanity is acknowledged and admitted as rightful subject matter.[3] Tim Dee's *Landfill* (2018) and Richard Osmond's collection of poems, *Useful Verses* (2017), gesture towards an authentically human picture of the environment popularized by *Edgelands* (2011), co-written by Paul Farley and Michael Symmons Roberts. Preceding chapters dedicated to 'Sewage', 'Retail' and 'Canals', *Edgelands* begins with the explanation that, due to their childhoods in industrial Liverpool and Manchester, the countryside often seemed fictive;

landscapes 'lit and staged in the same way the moon landings a few years earlier had been confected' (2011: 2). Car parks and building sites are consequently perceived as very real landscapes. Providing environmental writing's answer to 'dirty realism', Farley and Symmons Roberts would seem to earn the stamp of authenticity. As if in direct competition with Robert Macfarlane's exploration of remote wildernesses in *The Wild Places*, the subtitle of *Edgelands* makes the claim that these are 'Journeys into England's *True* Wilderness' (emphasis added). Yet, could it be possible that such an understanding of truth is once again highly simulated?

Adorno challenges the value Heidegger posits in artisanal and pastoral life, or what Heidegger calls 'the splendor of the simple' (1973: 50). The authentic becomes a particular aesthetic, and a romanticized one at that. Although *Edgelands* appears to reverse this definition of authenticity, as well as that provided by Lopez (the authors explore and celebrate the idea of 'non-place' rather than indigenous roots), it is this very subversion which is used to package and sell the truth. The down-to-earth quality of works like *Edgelands* might seem immune to questions of fabrication, yet Macfarlane's review of the book suggests otherwise. While praising the authors for their refreshingly contrarian perspective, Macfarlane argues that Farley and Symmons Roberts have neglected to provide appropriate representation of the inhabitants of these edgelands (2011).[4] Additionally, he challenges the 'blitheness' of their attitude: 'Container yards are places of beauty and mystery', he quotes, and adds: 'Well, perhaps, but they are also places of crushed fingers and low wages. In the end, the love shown for the edgelands is too strong' (ibid.). The representation of England's true wilderness is, it seems, not true enough.

The challenges I have made to authenticity might have some relevance when discussing 'realism' – a term that ecocritic Lawrence Buell initially defines as 'transparent rendering' (1995: 87). Despite realism being dismissed by many scholars and writers as a 'highly stylized ideological or psychohistorical artifact', Buell wants to recover it, or at least a particular version of it (ibid.). In the light of Thoreau's revised drafts of a passage in *Walden*, Buell scrutinizes Thoreau's altered description of an encounter with a mouse. He recognizes that Thoreau's 'selective orchestration' of events does not make the passage less believable, but, quite the opposite: adding certain qualities provides texture, story and, consequently, an air of credibility (ibid.: 96). Like the authentic, the realistic is artificially constructed. This reading sets some of the foundations for Buell's main argument concerning mimesis in environmental representation. The mimetic strategies Buell favours are not strategies that aim to produce a carbon copy of a physical entity through words. Rather, he is interested in how mimesis and stylization, often thought antithetical to one another, can work together:

> We need to recognize stylization's capacity for what the poet-critic Francis Ponge calls *adéquation*: verbalizations that are not replicas but equivalents of the world of objects, such that writing in some measure bridges the abyss that inevitably yawns between language and object-world.
>
> (ibid.: 98)

Buell seems to suggest that this realist aesthetic is conscious of its status as a text. There is a hint here of a post-structuralist argument – that language cannot do justice to the world, that there is an 'abyss' between word and thing that 'yawns'. This, however, does not quite fit with Buell's aim to recover realism from theoretical critique. He wants to remain positive about the power of language to serve as a reconciliatory 'bridge'.

The examples provided by Buell continue this slightly disappointing line of thought. Although he suggests that examples of mimesis 'are as likely to dislocate the reader as to placate her' by drawing attention to the division between word and thing, his reading of Gerard Manley Hopkins is unreservedly appreciative (ibid.: 99). Hopkins's poem, 'Pied Beauty', conveys an 'exquisite responsiveness to environmental stimuli ... how delicately responsive the poem is to the stimuli it registers! ... There can be no question that this is a live trout shimmering for an instant in Hopkins's imaginary pool' (ibid.: 98). Have we returned to a rather idealistic notion of literary realism? Dana Phillips believes so. Published eight years after Buell's *The Environmental Imagination,* Phillips's *The Truth of Ecology* (2003) provides an extensive critique of his revival of realism. Phillips explains

> If ecocriticism were limited to reading realistic texts realistically, it would have to scant not only nature (ironically enough) but a lot of literature as well ... An ecocriticism pledged to realism will be hamstrung in another way: its practitioners will be reduced to an umpire's role, squinting to see if a given depiction of a horizon, a wildflower, or a live oak tree is itself well-painted and lively.
>
> (2003: 163–164)

As if these reasons for dismissing a realist aesthetic were not enough, Phillips suggests that 'the pursuit of realism in the depiction of nature has produced a surfeit of kitsch' (ibid.: 164). He gives the example of wildlife art depicting a 'leaping largemouth bass gazing at the art and nature lover with a flat, fishy eye' (ibid.).

Phillips's mention of kitsch is worth pursuing as I would argue that it can apply to both concepts of realism and authenticity. After all, in the context of this discussion, both realism and authenticity often attempt to dissolve the boundary between art and non-art, or even suggest the former as the latter. This dissolution is central to Timothy Morton's discussion of kitsch in *Ecology without Nature* (2007). Here, Morton devises the term 'ecomimesis' to identify the ways in which writers attempt to generate transparent renditions of environments. The aim of ecomimesis is to provide a representation that is recognizably genuine. In a similar manner to Phillips, Morton associates ecomimesis with the cheesy, unfashionable (yet popular) qualities of kitsch (2007: 132). Although Morton does not give much in the way of illustrative example, he does reference Aldo Leopold's *A Sand County Almanac* which, by using an almanac form, 'tries to escape the pull of the literary' and present itself as non-art (ibid.: 31). Leopold resembles 'a minimalist painter who puts an empty frame in an art gallery' (ibid.). Later, Morton also argues that the sentimentalism frequently central to kitsch 'wants to make us love nature' (ibid.: 152). He describes how Leopold's illustrated prose attempts to 'melt our hearts' (ibid.).[5] Although Morton finds much of interest in kitsch, it is ultimately antithetical to his overall intention to relinquish the very idea of nature. After all, he seeks aesthetic modes that value hesitation and non-identity (ibid.: 151). Non-identity is a concept that reaches Morton from Adorno's *Negative Dialectics* in which Adorno argues that thought is not identical with its subject, that subjects exist beyond our attempts to define them. As I will return to explain, non-identity has interesting repercussions when it comes to Morton's reimagining of kitsch.

Morton is not alone in searching for alternative strategies to art that presents itself as non-art. Kate Rigby highlights and challenges Heidegger's view that language can 'give voice to the song of the earth', and challenges, thereby, its ecocritical adoption in Jonathan Bate's *Romantic Ecology* and *Song of the Earth* (2004a: 123). In essence, Heidegger's view affirms the ability for language to disclose the being of entities, which in turn may help us to live in a more ecologically respectful manner. Combining post-structuralist argument with environmental ethics, Rigby wants to protect 'the otherness of the earth from disappearing into a humanly constructed world of words' (ibid.: 119). She not only believes that when language speaks for an environment it imposes its own logic upon the earth and, in that way, 'may well open the way to exploitation' (ibid.: 124), but she also proposes that the earth is 'unsayable' in the sense that its otherness cannot be identified through human words. (2004b: 437). If language is a threat to the environment, or perhaps, as her latter point suggests, entirely meaningless, we might want to eliminate it altogether, causing the end of environmental writing. Rigby, however, grants some leeway for writers. She pursues Heidegger's idea that poets might 'save' the earth. It is important to note that 'save' has a specific Heideggerian meaning that notions towards setting the earth 'free in its own presencing' (2004a: 89). Continuing her thoughts on the limitations of language, Rigby revises Heidegger's argument and asks: 'How then does the work of art "save" the earth by disclosing it as unsayable? It does so, I would suggest, precisely to the extent that it draws attention to its own status as text and hence as a mode of enframing' (ibid.: 437). She goes on to call this 'negative ecopoetics'. One way of performing this new creative strategy is, she explains, through textual 'moments of incoherence' in which writers fail to put the world into words (ibid.).[6]

Although Morton is concerned that such strategies may alienate us from our familiarity with environments and thus re-establish distance between ourselves and the environment (a distance which currently leads many to feel justified in inflicting damage upon the natural world), his own proposal for 'radical kitsch' demonstrates some interesting parallels with Rigby's argument. In contrast to the kitsch resulting from ecomimesis, 'radical kitsch' means 'invoking the underside of ecomimesis, the pulsing, shifting qualities of ambient poetics' (2007: 159–60). For Morton, 'ambience' refers to the illusion of a palpable environment that ecomimesis can generate. If this ambience begins to pulse and shift, it begins to not only show itself as unreliable, but, in doing so, also draws attention to itself as an aesthetic construction. Indeed, instead of trying to melt dualism away, it is possible that radical kitsch, which is radical because it uses garish or sentimental tropes ironically, can exploit dualism, the difference between 'I' and 'slimy things'. (ibid.: 160). Rather than being magicked away by ecomimesis, the division that exists between writer and environment should be explored.

While their perspectives are different, both Rigby and Morton appear driven by a desire for a representational mode that is self-conscious or self-reflexive. If the pedagogical instruction to be authentic previously seemed unstable, the idea becomes untenable in the light of such ecocritical departure. How, then, might these theories influence a new ecocritical pedagogy that encourages students to acknowledge the limits of representation? In spite of his concern for authenticity discussed above, Cocker's pedagogical stance incorporates something of this self-reflexive approach. He recalls an exercise he believes Ted Hughes first deployed to 'fight against cliché and received ideas' (2014). Cocker describes Hughes instructing students to 'look at a cow until the word cow became utterly meaningless, until they had moved beyond the word to the thing itself' (ibid.). There is a hint here of Morton's sense of dualism between writer and environment. How might the difficulty of the relationship between word and thing, 'I' and 'slimy things' be pursued on the page to productive effect?

'I have wandered down the lane to a stream at the edge of the fen wood', Richard Mabey writes before describing the 'bubbling tremolo' of a nightingale who 'holds it for more than 10 seconds … I want to clap – and with barely credible timing, a shooting star arcs over the bush in which he is singing' (2003). Mabey, a renowned British nature writer, immediately questions the truth of his own description and suggests that he is 'guilty of "staging"', that he is too self-conscious (ibid.). 'Yet', he writes, 'trying not to be would have written me – a self-aware human – out of the relationship' (ibid.). Mabey does not want his piece to be regarded as non-art. Rather, the 'staginess' of the piece is crucial as it reflects the role of the writer, and, in the words of Rigby, 'draws attention to its own status as text'. This is a version of what Viktor Shklovsky called 'laying bare the device' ([1921] 1990). The more staged a representation is, the more opportunity it gives us to reflect on the distance between representation and reality. Such a thought evokes the words of American poet Richard Wilbur, 'I like the world to resist my ordering of it, so that I can feel it is real and that I'm honoring its reality' ([1968] 1990: 51).

To explore these questions and ideas through close reading, I will focus now on Canadian poet Don McKay and British poet Jen Hadfield. Each of these writers exhibits a refreshing approach to the relationship between language and environment, honesty and artifice. 'Poetry is when language, which usually is our supreme tool for controlling and manipulating the world, reverses itself and becomes a listening post', claims McKay in an interview (2012b). He makes this reversal by means of metaphor, anthropocentrism and a kind of comic absurdism. Using such styles and devices, both McKay and Hadfield conjure a self-reflexivity in their language that deliberately undermines their representational aim, resulting in a heightened recognition of environmental otherness.

'Between yes and no, so / and not so'

A prize-winning poet with sixteen poetry collections to his name, and a well-regarded essayist, Don McKay is suspicious of the 'romantic poet (or tourist for that matter)' who 'desires to be spoken to' by the environment (2001). The passivity of Romantic inspiration is not to be trusted. Focusing on the role of the writer in *Vis à Vis* (ibid.), McKay is particularly worried by the Romantic idea that perception flows into language 'without a palpable break' (ibid.: 27). Though he recognizes that such 'aeolian harpism' is compelling given its ability to 'restore a coherent reality', he seeks a practice of poetic attention that values the 'wilderness of the other' (ibid.). Hugh Dunkerley has provided a useful introduction to reading McKay in the context of Rigby's theory of negative ecopoetics. Dunkerley's chapter 'Translating Wilderness' focuses on the way in which McKay challenges a Romantic idealization of nature in order to problematize the language of description (2013: 213). Well founded as it is, the breadth of Dunkerley's study means that it does not focus in on any particular techniques used by McKay to explore tensions between language and environment. I will look closely at McKay's use of metaphor, in order to develop my argument in Chapter 4, and also build on Dunkerley's study.

'As If', collected in *Paradoxides* (2012a), contemplates otherness. Describing a coastal scene, McKay writes of seeing a Milky Way in the cove. Once McKay's speaker has picked up a pair of binoculars, however, the scene changes: the Milky Way is not the Milky Way but eider ducks that dip and dive under the water

> like this: as if, as if, as
> if that surface were the border –
> suddenly porous –
> between yes and no, so
> and not so
>
> (2012a: 17–21)

Trustworthy depiction becomes an impossible act. The twinkling stars are not stars but ducks, and yet the ducks themselves are hard to define as they slip between the waves. The slipperiness of the world McKay's speaker perceives seems only to be grasped at via the slipperiness of language. Instead of a seamless, persuasive description, the poem is full of the 'palpable breaks' otherwise concealed in the Romantic approach he distrusts. 'As If' draws attention to simile as a literary device that aims for identification of its subject, but fails – the relationship between subject and representation is only ever tenuously based on likeness. Far from being 'grounded', as Elder desired, with McKay's description we are all at sea.

McKay's argument concerning simile's hinge of 'yes and no' – of identity and non-identity – applies more broadly to his work. 'Metaphor, and its related figures, use language's totalizing tendency against itself', he asserts, before going on to explain that the consequence of such is that metaphor 'un-name[s] its subject, reopening the question of reference' (2001: 69).[7] It would seem that as metaphor questions linguistic identity with its environmental counterpart – coming down more heavily on the 'no' or 'not so' of metaphor's hinge – it becomes a reflexive device with which to consider not only our attempt to put the world into words, but also the world's 'unsayability'. Often, McKay appears to choose metaphors that are visually compelling, but which only fit momentarily before the object evades them. Opening with a strangely comical scene in which God urges a seemingly idle Adam to name some of Earth's creatures, McKay's 'Twinflower', collected in *Apparatus* (1997), is a useful example in exploring how metaphor might 'un-name its subject'. Adam begins with the plant *Linnaea borealis* or 'Twinflower', easily recognized by its small, usually pink, paired flowers. Testing God's patience, Adam takes his time:

> Engrossed in their gesture,
> the two stalks rising, branching, falling back
> into nodding bells, the fading arc
> that would entrance Pre-Raphaelites and basketball.
> Maybe he browsed among the possibilities of elves
>
> (1997: 15–19)

Comprised of sections, the poem moves from Adam's rather eccentric nomenclature to formal botanical taxonomies as McKay finds the twinflowers in a 'field guide' where 'the bright / reticulated snaps of system will occur / as the plant is placed, so, among the honeysuckles' (ibid.: 39–41). Understandably, 'snaps' does not seem a particularly promising word when describing a delicate plant, and, explaining the subtle threat contained within his description, McKay states that the act of identification brings up the 'same old problem, / how to be both / knife and spoon' (ibid.: 32–4). While the 'spoon' suggests a certain openness, the 'knife' is clearly violent, evoking, at least in part, William Wordsworth's conviction that 'We murder to dissect' in his famous poem 'The Tables Turned' ([1798] 1994: 28). As if suggesting a certain amount of inevitability, however, both descriptions enable something to be eaten.

Comparing two different ways of identifying a plant, 'Twinflower' appears to suggest that the field guide's preconceived classifications are possessive, restrictive, and might even result in death for the species involved (especially when considering those picked for botanical study). The 'snaps of system' stand in contrast, then, to the figurative associations made by Adam between the twinflower and 'Pre-Raphaelites', 'basketball' and 'elves'. These associations continue later in the poem as McKay describes the twinflower as 'a shy / hoister of flags, a tiny lamp to read by, one / word at a time' (ibid.: 35–7). The proliferation of comparisons might initially suggest the impossibility of fixing one stable description to the plant and, thus, of turning 'language's totalizing tendency against itself'. Yet, focusing upon the anthropocentric quality within the metaphors also helps to identify how metaphor becomes expressive of the environment's 'unsayability'. Despite the variety of figurative associations, each is radically disassociated from the natural world and consistent, instead, with Western popular culture. The zaniness of each juxtaposition illustrates McKay's idea that metaphor 'reopen[s] the question of reference' through a metaphorical 'leap' that 'always says (besides its fresh comparison) that language is not commensurate with the real, that leaps are necessary if we are to regain some sense of the world outside it' (2001: 69). Although it might be thought that all metaphors contain a leap by their very nature, McKay suggests that the leap can be exaggerated in order to question the description it is making. A sports hall collides with woodland as we compare a twinflower with basketball. Jarring in its effect, the leap prompts a moment of reflection as to whether the real world eludes the words we have for it. In direct contrast to the 'snaps of system', the leap performs a liberating linguistic act as it apprehends the environment's non-identity with language.[8]

In her essay, 'The Case against Metaphor' (2004), Brenda Miller leads her pedagogical argument about representing the environment with a personal anecdote. She describes her observation of migratory birds and her perception of 'their restlessness', before confessing 'already I can feel it, like a tickle in my throat, that strangled mandate: *Must ... Make ... Metaphor*' (2004: 116). Challenging this impulse, she writes, 'I don't want to make that inevitable connection between migratory fervor and my own vast restlessness' (ibid.). Such a metaphor is 'too assembled, and I want the world to just remain as it is, firmly itself' (ibid.: 117). The argument here is not dissimilar to Buell's suggestion that a description should be formed through 'disciplined extrospection ... an affirmation of environment over self' (1995: 104). Miller understands metaphor as anthropocentric and thus disrespectful of the environment's 'real' character. She asks, if 'my job is to pay attention, why can't I do it on the world's terms and not my own?' (ibid.). Miller provides a useful illustration of what Morton means by 'ecomimesis' as she advocates a kind of non-art. The anthropocentric nature of her immediate response to the birds is, in her opinion, appropriative. Appearing to resist what Petersen called 'self-serving' nature writing, Miller pits metaphor against 'the world's terms' (ibid.). And yet what exactly is meant by 'the world's terms'? Comparable to my earlier discussion of phenologies, fact and authenticity, she goes some way in (problematically) defining 'the world's terms' via anecdotes about her guide, Rich, whose more scientific way of knowing the birds 'seems more guileless' (ibid.). McKay's poems would seem to suggest exactly the opposite argument. Contrary to the foundations of Miller's argument, McKay would seem to be practising his belief that 'nature poetry should not be taken to be *avoiding* anthropocentrism, but to be enacting it, thoughtfully' (2001: 29). Contrived, perhaps to the point of kitsch, his metaphors provoke a struggle with the subjects they aim to describe and thus prompts in the reader a self-reflexive examination of the relationship between language and reality.

Anthropocentric self-reflexivity

Reviewers and interviewers engaging with Jen Hadfield's work have criticized the anthropocentric quality often found in her poems. Yet, in the light of McKay's defence of anthropocentrism, discussed above, and his technique of deploying it in 'Twinflower', we might ask whether these criticisms could be overlooking a similarly nuanced strategy in Hadfield's writing? A Shetland-based poet, Hadfield is author to three poetry collections that engage with place and its non-human inhabitants. When she won the T. S. Eliot Prize in 2008 with her book *Nigh-No-Place*, Hadfield was described by Judge Andrew Motion as having a 'jaunty, energetic, iconoclastic – even devil-may-care' attitude. Hadfield's playfulness is, however, far from reckless. Her anthropocentric explorations are central to her interest in exploring 'those places where we overlap with the wilderness doing its own thing, messily usually' (2009b). Hadfield believes it is important to reflect on her own human perspective while being attentive to the independence of the environment, a principle partly owing to the writers who influence her: Scottish poets such as Edwin Morgan and Norman MacCaig whom Hadfield sees as 'honest and humane' (2009a). 'Daed-traa', collected in *Nigh-No-Place*, introduces Hadfield's approach through her rather complex figurative comparison of a rockpool with the qualities of poetry that is undertaken through the medium of popular culture. Like McKay, in his eccentric selection of basketball and Pre-Raphaelites, Hadfield moves between Shakespeare, cult cinema and Hollywood icons in order to describe the non-human.

'Daed-traa' is a Shetland dialect term that refers to the 'slack of the tide'. It titles one of Hadfield's poems, which is also a meditation on the writer's practice:

It has its theatre –
hushed and plush.

It has its Little Shop of Horrors.
It has its crossed and dotted monsters.

It has its cross-eyed beetling Lear.
It has its billowing Monroe.

(2008: 5–10)

Hadfield's mixed metaphors are difficult to determine. The cinematic reference of the 'Little Shop of Horrors' suggests a comic violence to be found in the rockpool's creatures, perhaps in sea anemones specifically. The 'crossed and dotted monsters' invite consideration of the patterns of rockpool plant and animal life, yet it also refers to writing, with its crossing of t's and dotting of i's. The ambiguity and anthropocentricity of these metaphors increases: the 'cross-eyed beetling Lear' suggests a crab in the rockpool as well as madness in the writing practice that in turn evokes Shakespeare's Lear, Gloucester's speech on vision and blindness during the Dover Beach scene in *King Lear*, or even Edward Lear's love of nonsense. As Hadfield goes on to conjure what might be a jellyfish through a reference to Marilyn Monroe in the famous billowing dress in *The Seven Year Itch*, her poem increasingly becomes the antithesis of Miller's pedagogical instruction to write 'on the world's terms and not my own'.

Hadfield defends her use of such cultural reference points in her poems, arguing that it is important to be 'honest about the present tense that you live in' when looking at the environment (quoted by Ben Wilkinson 2009). In contrast to Miller's attempt at self-effacement, Hadfield suggests that disregarding the human point of view (perhaps involving Monroe and the *Little Shop of Horrors*) is dishonest and inauthentic. However, criticism of Hadfield's approach prevails. In an interview, Zoe Brigley asks Hadfield, 'How close do you think human beings are to nature? In poems like "Daed-traa" … nature seems to be a microcosm of human worlds?' (Hadfield 2010). Understanding this question as a critique of anthropocentrism in her work, Hadfield responds: 'That makes it sound like an inexcusable (on my part) extension of the pathetic fallacy' (ibid.). Answering Brigley more fully, Hadfield is keen to explain that

> I certainly don't think of nature as a microcosm of the human world. But we maybe meet it as we do people from other cultures. We ask each other about

our likenesses and our differences. We are obsessed with our likenesses and differences. At least when we are not afraid; and get beyond taking advantage.

(ibid.)

Distinguishing between exploring likeness and 'taking advantage', Hadfield's cultural analogy for the act of analogizing echoes McKay's interest in the hinge between identity and non-identity in metaphor. Where there is likeness there is also difference, and metaphor can bring both to our attention.

Returning home, slightly drunk, from a night out, the speaker in 'Hedgehog, Hamnavoe' stumbles upon a hedgehog. The creature is described as 'flinching' in their hands, and later as 'a kidney flinching on a hot griddle / a very small Hell's Angel' (2008: 4–5). Ali Alizadeh, reviewing *Nigh-No-Place*, comments that in this poem 'Hadfield's speaker has absolute power over the animal, and treats the powerless mammal like a plaything' (2010). He goes on to claim that the coddling of the hedgehog is enough to 'make anyone remotely sympathetic to animal rights cringe' (ibid.). While hedgehogs are increasingly subject to what might be called 'cute-ification' across the globe, given the presence of hedgehog memes, YouTube videos and hedgehog cafes in Japan, surely Hadfield's metaphor of the hedgehog 'flinching' on the 'hot griddle' of her hands already implies an uncomfortable dynamic at work between the human and the non-human. The hedgehog is later made into 'a very small Hell's Angel' by Hadfield and while this might be interpreted as a quirky, endearing gesture (assisted by Hadfield's accidental sanitation of the phrase via an unnecessary apostrophe), the metaphor's associations with counter-culture should not be dismissed (ibid.: 5). We might say that the identification proposed between the hedgehog and the Hells Angel is based on the 'studded' leather jackets often associated with biker culture, but could it also be that the identification hints at unpredictability and possible rebellion?

The anthropocentric description continues, but, crucially, the anthropocentrism begins to invalidate itself as it does so. By the third tercet of the poem, the creature is not a kidney or a Hells Angel, but a crystal ball. The imagined size and possible curled shape of the spiny mammal affords the comparison as does the suggested curiosity of the person holding it. Nevertheless, the following lines reveal that this curiosity is thwarted: the 'I' of the poem stares into the animal 'hellbent the realistic mysteries / should amount to more than guesswork // and fleas.' (ibid.: 8–10). By extending the figurative comparison between the hedgehog and the crystal ball, Hadfield allows the comparison to become questionable. The metaphor conceptually breaks down (and physically breaks out of the otherwise consistent tercet form) as the hedgehog resists further comparison to Hadfield's crystal ball. Rather than mysticism or epiphany a bathetic engagement with the reality of the hedgehog, represented by 'guesswork // and fleas', ensues. Alizadeh argues that with such metaphors that liken animals to man-made things, Hadfield is expressing a 'desire to capture, own and control the wildlife for her, and her reader's amusement'. However, by pushing the anthropocentric metaphor as far as it will go, Hadfield actually generates the opposite effect. Invalidating itself, the metaphor draws attention to the different and unknowable reality of the hedgehog.

In his guide to writing about the environment, *Writing Naturally*, David Petersen is wary of metaphor. Though not as ethically minded as Miller or Alizadeh, he sees the device as an obstacle to authentic representations of environments. Though it can 'add spice to the stew', no sooner than conceding the value of metaphor Petersen warns: 'Beware the temptation to over-season … Beware the metaphorical color purple … Too many writers, reaching too far too fast … Beware the mixed metaphor' (2001: 117–18). Petersen's warnings echo those of Jim Perrin who, as discussed in Chapter 4, criticized the 'new nature writing' for using 'forced images'. Such unfavourable accounts of metaphor are, of course, nothing new: they present concerns about bad writing. It is possible that 'over-seasoning' a piece of writing with metaphor makes the writing difficult to understand, or produces an overly fantastic quality. However, as 'Hedgehog, Hamnavoe' demonstrates, metaphors that are 'forced' or 'reaching too far' between the natural world and the human world have productive potential. Such metaphors can disassemble the notion of authenticity by generating a self-reflexivity that prompts awareness of language as a representational medium and its limitations in capturing reality. Breaking under the strain of an incompatible vehicle and tenor, such uses of figurative language are consistent with the arguments of both Rigby and Morton. With regard to Rigby, Hadfield's metaphor can be seen to enact 'a moment of incoherence' as the parts of the metaphor no longer marry. Being unlike rather than like, the two subjects of hedgehog and crystal ball become ever more distinct from one another. In so doing, the failed metaphor would seem to, in the words of Morton, 'exploit dualism'. The initial charm and sentimentality of Hadfield's depiction that may well resemble kitsch gives way to a recognition of the difference between 'I' and, in this case, spiky things. In this discussion, however, something has been missed: humour. After all, a silliness exists in McKay's attempt to describe a twinflower through Pre-Raphaelites and basketball. There is a funny cuteness to the 'crossed and dotted monsters' of Hadfield's rockpool, and, of course, a bathetic humour in recognizing that our anthropocentric image of a hedgehog and the reality of a hedgehog are irreconcilable. If this humour encourages self-reflexivity to take place, then could the sometimes too sober and earnest genre of environmental writing find a useful role for absurdism?

Laughable descriptions?

'Are they birds or fish / in these nets of moonlight? ... At what does the watermelon laugh when it's murdered?', asks Pablo Neruda in *The Book of Questions*. Using Neruda's poetry, Mary Edwards Wertsch outlines a children's pedagogical exercise based on writing poems about the environment. The exercise would seem to contrast the belief that a writer should be held accountable for the representation they provide, as if a text should (and could) mirror reality, as Wertsch makes clear that she wants students to write a poem 'made of questions' (2000: 168). Likewise, far from encouraging them to identify what they see with a field guide, she instructs her students to go outside, explore their environments, and return with 'questions that are exciting, that get you to think. The kind of questions I mean are wondering questions that spin a bit in your head, perhaps surprise you, and are certainly not easy to answer' (ibid.: 169). Clearly, the exercise is not interested in conjuring 'immediacy' – the quality Morton links to the authenticating device of ecomimesis. Instead of seeking to capture what they observe, students explore the environment's elusiveness, valuing hesitation and, perhaps, non-identity.

The parallel between Wertsch's pedagogical approach and the ecocritical argument I am developing could, of course, be emphasized. Further explanation of Neruda's Surrealist influences might help students to realize that rather than the questions being 'not easy to answer', the questions are likely to be impossible to answer. In turn, this recognition might prompt a greater exploration of how Neruda's questions actually *question*. Wertsch asserts that it is the 'compelling form of a question' that prompts an 'invitation to the reader to reflect on the words' in Neruda's lines (ibid.: 171). And yet, this is not quite accurate. After all, Neruda's question is not simply 'Are they birds or fish?' but 'Are they birds or fish / in these nets of moonlight?' It would seem to be the figurative nature of his description that provokes reflection by generating curious juxtapositions that verge on incompatibility and incoherence. Extending the sample that Wertsch provides of Neruda's work helps to reveal another factor contributing to the power of the question form. When Neruda writes 'where did the full moon leave

/ its sack of flour tonight?', the question mark clearly acts a catalyst for the act of reflecting upon his imagery, but the subtly humorous tension between the full moon with its associations of romance and lyricism and quotidian flour provokes reflection in itself ([1974] 1991: 1). 'Why do leaves commit suicide / when they feel yellow?', similarly contrasts societal preconceptions regarding colour and mood with the environment, creating comic tension between human terms and 'the world's terms' (ibid.: 5).

Humour is hard to find in environmental writing. The sincerity of trying to create an authentic representation means that opportunity for comedy is scarce, reduced, perhaps, to a self-critical scoff at mistaking a dunnock for a sparrow. The gravity of current environmental crises similarly makes any comic gesture, apart from satire, seem inappropriate. However, writing on Don McKay's poetry and criticism, Sophia Forster offers a refreshing perspective on comedy's importance. She claims that McKay's sense of humour serves to expose anthropocentric arrogance and deflate literary pretence. The key to creating this effect, argues Forster, is McKay's 'outlandish metaphors' (2002: 127). His uses of figurative language 'remind us that we are not *discovering* meaning in, but *making* meaning of the world around us.' (ibid.). Here it might be possible to take Forster's argument a step further and suggest that through such metaphors comes the recognition that we *impose* meaning on the world. Alongside the self-conscious and thus amusing definition McKay provides of himself as 'Mr Nature Poet' in *Vis à Vis*, Forster picks out examples such as 'scrawny owlets like brainy bespectacled three-year-olds' in 'But Nature Has Her Darker Side' (ibid., Forster quotes McKay 1983, 2001). Self-conscious of its artifice, such a description seems to poke fun at the very intention to portray the environment through words.

In 'Morning Prayer Ending with a Line Borrowed from the Holiday Inn', collected in *Birding, or Desire* (1983) McKay describes 'a treeful of starlings, speckled and / oily as comic book germs or high school wiseguys, mocks / the whole dumb enterprise – / words!' (1983: 11–14). The metaphors are without doubt outlandish. Comparing starlings to germs and teenagers might already seem a bit ridiculous, but the tongue-in-cheek language of 'wiseguys' and '*comic book* germs' exaggerates the depiction's absurd quality (emphasis added). The starlings may well mock the dumb (i.e. mute) enterprise of words because of their garrulous sounds. And yet, given the discussion so far that has concerned McKay's desire to challenge language's appropriating nature by creating self-reflexive anthropocentrism, could 'dumb' be synonymous with stupid? The slightly ridiculous description of the birds as 'comic book germs' thwarts the reliable, authentic relationship we might expect between language and environment. The description finds the starlings to be beyond the bounds of language. Our tools for representation become the object of ridicule. Words are dumb! In his aforementioned essay 'Baler Twine', McKay describes his belief that nature poetry should involve 'an extra metaphorical stretch and silliness of language as it moves toward the other, dreaming its body' (2001: 31). The humour, or 'silliness' involved in McKay's anthropocentric 'leaps' is, then, central to the process of reopening the question of reference. For all its serious, meaningful work, the acknowledgement of non-identity and extra-linguistic otherness is ultimately conducted through a joke.

Calls for authenticity dismiss artifice and anthropocentrism as antithetical to their project. For poets such as McKay and Hadfield, however, the strategy of taking these modes to a comic extreme helps us to reflect on the tensions involved in trying to represent reality. James Seitz, in *Motives for Metaphor* (1999), makes an argument that develops this line of thought regarding the effect of self-reflexivity, though his work does not directly address the subject of environmental writing. Seitz's ideas raise the possibility that the humour presented by Hadfield and McKay brings with it another environmental lesson that moves beyond the questions of language's limitations. As a teacher of composition in the United States, Seitz explains his frustration with the pedagogical instruction for students to learn 'seamless coherence': a concept that resonates with the aesthetic mode of ecomimesis that imparts a sense of immediacy (1999: 49). He explains:

> If the act of identification 'goes all the way', without any recognition of the differences between this and that, then the dialogue between reader and text has ended before it even begins, with no space for the exploration of further relationships: this simply *is* that – and nothing more need be said.
>
> (ibid.: 125)

Though Seitz's study focuses exclusively on metaphor, his argument easily applies to textual representation more broadly. Influenced by Roland Barthes, Seitz explores the possibility of a pedagogy that values fragmentation, incoherence and thus multiple interpretations. According to Seitz, if more attention were drawn to incompatibility and incoherence within metaphors, students would be allowed greater participation with the text. Students would be prompted to think about where they see the metaphor working and where they see the metaphor going 'too far', of where it is apt and where it is inappropriate. In other words, students would become spectators of their own reading.

What Seitz contributes to the argument I have been developing is the notion that this interruption to narrative flow or image prompts a more personal self-reflexivity within the reader, which challenges the politics of how they relate to the text and its subject. In one of McKay's shortest poems, '–deer' (1975), included in its entirety below, a deer is pictured fleeing into the woods:

> And came that morning down the dusty road
> into the deer's
> virginity –
>   gone, white flag flashed
> did you see it flashed
> like a
> like a fridge left crisp & clean in the mind
> all day
>
>   (1975)

Rather than the giggle-inducing depiction of starlings like 'high school wiseguys', McKay's portrayal of the deer is more likely to produce a nervous laugh. The 'white flag flashed' presumably refers to the deer's white tail, but why is a fridge like a deer? Is the fridge meant to emphasize the whiteness of the image? If so, why not choose something else that is more fitting to the size and shape of a deer? With no further lines to serve as explanation, the brief lyric moment becomes uncomfortable, as the domestic chafes against the wild, or as Méira Cook puts it, 'collides' (2006: xv). The simile is 'funny strange', not 'funny ha-ha'.[9] While this peculiar juxtaposition of subjects once again suggests that the deer has escaped linguistic definition, there is a residual awkwardness that emerges from the incongruity of the description.

To begin making sense of this awkwardness, we need an understanding of where we disagree with the image. It would be an example of the participation or spectatorship Seitz recommends. In the case of McKay's description of the deer, the reader is led to reflect on where they think human terms dominate and conflict with the environmental subject of the poem. Could it be that, light-hearted and bizarre as they may seem, the anthropocentric styles exhibited by Hadfield and McKay deliver a rather more sobering reflection on today's relationship between 'I' and 'slimy things'? In the representation of environmental matters, a deliberately excessive anthropocentric perspective might have the potential to function as an analogy for the way in which societal behaviour clashes with, or imposes upon, ecology itself. The analysis of Juliana Spahr's exploration of 'the problems of analogy' in Chapter 1 has some bearing here. As I examined, Spahr reveals the capacity of analogy to assume likeness and neglect difference and records the detrimental effects of this in the context of Hawai'i's colonization. The online translation machine is central to her enactment of analogy and its distortive power. From my reading of Hadfield and McKay, it becomes possible to see how an anthropocentric absurdism in environmental writing might take a deliberately provocative view of the world in order to think about the power dynamics involved in terrestrial exploitation. The absence of resolution between the natural and artificial terms in McKay's description of the fridge-like deer not only undermines our expectation that language will directly express reality, but also summons the ubiquity of fly-tipping: the old sofa or broken television dumped among junipers and firs.

Writing self-reflexively

In 'The Human Condition' by René Magritte, a painting of a landscape stands on an easel in front of a window that looks out upon the landscape that the painting depicts. The assumption that the view from the window contains the 'real' landscape is disrupted because, of course, this view, being part of Magritte's artwork, is fabricated too. This work can be seen as an inversion of the *trompe l'oeil* tradition in which landscapes and objects appear three-dimensional and 'deceive the eye'. In turn, Magritte draws attention to art as art. M. C. Escher's famous 'Drawing Hands' serves as another example. One hand draws another and in so doing, draws attention to two-dimensional representation versus three-dimensional reality. The deliberate flatness of depiction in works by Henri Matisse, especially 'Basket with Oranges', similarly functions as a self-reflexive device; the work declares itself a painting of gathered fruit and not the genuine article. The effect of such artwork resonates with Richard Mabey's thought that, for all its artifice, the 'staging' quality within environmental writing is crucial in its acknowledgement of the 'self-aware human' involved in each act of representation. Rather than support the idea that the environment can be authentically represented on the page, an ecocritical pedagogy might encourage reflection on the act of representation and its limitations in the light of environmental otherness and 'unsayability'. In what follows, particular strategies that teachers can give to their students, or for students to pursue independently, are proposed.

In much contemporary non-fiction about the environment, authors reflect on their literary predecessors in a way that could be said to prompt acknowledgement of the representational act. In *Eating Stone*, for example, Ellen Meloy questions T. H. White's depiction of the goshawk. Robert Macfarlane cites Nan Shepherd frequently across his works. Instances of intertextuality in fiction, such as Cormac McCarthy's *Blood Meridian* that borrows structural as well as aesthetic motifs from Herman Melville's *Moby-Dick*, may, to the vigilant reader, also serve as self-referential gestures almost like Magritte's painting of a canvas within a canvas. McKay and Hadfield are clearly more overt in their exposure of the writing process, underlining the limitations – even the impossibility – of conveying in language wildflowers, jellyfish, hedgehogs, starlings and deer. Before moving on to suggest writing exercises that share in these poets' techniques, I will explore a few more examples of writing that complicate the notion of literary authenticity and the desire to write on the 'world's terms'. After all, the idea of creating through words a realistic world that amounts to a literary form of virtual reality relies on many of the tropes I have challenged in previous chapters. A fixed sense of local place, as intimated through Lopez's engagement with indigenous peoples, appears to be one ingredient in the recipe for authenticity. Likewise, first-person narration in environmental writing is frequently understood to give voice to real experiences – the 'I' is an intimate presence who is often trusted to tell it as it is. What techniques, then, might be used to create a self-reflexive sense of place and voice in order to undermine their associations with authenticity?

'All voices should be read as the river's mutterings', writes Alice Oswald in the preface to her book-length poem, *Dart* (2002). And yet, the marginal notes in the text signify the participants she spoke to when beginning her project – a naturalist, a walker, a salmon netsman, a fisherman and others who, in one way or another, interact with the Devonshire river. Appropriately fluid, the voice shifts between registers with often incoherent syntax. Though seemingly attributed to the eel-watcher, the lines provoke doubt: 'I depend on being not noticed, which keeps me small and rather nimble, I can swim miles naked with midges round my head' (ibid.: 7). Who is speaking here? Collectively, the voices constitute a rather unusual example of an unreliable narrator. Rather than one perspective on the environment, Oswald provides a Cubist rendition of the river in which multiple subjectivities blur into one another or jostle for attention. No one sense of reality is proffered above another. The notion of voice as an authenticating device is undermined. Following Oswald's *Dart* as an example, students can explore the idea of a shifting narrator. Having written a paragraph focused on a landscape using a personal perspective, how might a student write another using a different voice? A voice, perhaps, from a different genre? A piece of dialogue? How might these seeming intrusions put the original description given by the first-person 'I' into question?

A voice can, of course, be unreliable in different ways. 'As I write this, I am sitting on the seashore', writes Morton before challenging the ecomimetic device with 'No – that was pure fiction, just a tease' (2007: 29–30). On her reading list for 'Writing on Location' at Newman University, Elizabeth-Jane Burnett (2019) includes video artists such as Janet Cardiff and Sophie Calle in order to disrupt her students' expectations about the form that environmental writing takes and introduce the potential of performance. Cardiff's audio walks are particularly useful here as they attempt a consistent sense of place despite obvious (and deliberate) discrepancies between video and the environment in which the viewer of the video stands. As in 'Alter Bahnhof Video Work' by Cardiff and George Bures Miller, fantasy mixes with reality. Burnett explains that after engaging with Cardiff's work, one student wrote a script for a fake guided tour (ibid.). Rather than creating 'seamless coherence', how might an account of a coastal landscape or woodland create incoherence and incongruity? A piece of writing, or a script for a fake guided tour, might begin by evoking Hampstead Heath, its grand trees and eccentric flock of parakeets, only to slip into description of scarlet macaws in the Amazon rainforest and end on a description of the gift shop on the way out of a zoo.

Descriptions of place might foreground their own subjectivity, personal, cultural and historical, by making more pronounced juxtapositions between fact and fiction. Matthew Francis's collection of poems, *Mandeville*, written after Sir John Mandeville's fourteenth-century travel memoir, includes 'Of the Vegetable Lamb'. Twenty-one lines describe the plant scientifically and where it is likely to be found, before revealing that the fruit is a 'sweet, chewable' lamb, tasting 'like liver / scented with honey' (2008: 11, 20–1). The effect is reminiscent of Edward Lear's *Nonsense Botany*. The poems emerge from texts that appeared authentic to their medieval audiences but were at least in part invented. Today, such clearly fictitious descriptions have bearing on the discussion of surreal humour and literary self-reflexivity. Students might invent their own species and create a field guide entry for it, or they may experiment with describing native species found in their own local neighbourhoods in unexpectedly foreign or fantastical terms, thereby troubling the association that arises between a 'rooted' sense of place and authenticity.

While these models and exercises disturb ideas of ecomimesis, revealing non-art as art, and consequently emphasizing the gap between representation and subject, they do not directly question the medium of representation – language – or its limitations. For this necessitates a return to McKay and Hadfield. In his poem in which the Milky Way is revealed to be a scattering of eider ducks, McKay enacts a kind of hesitant stutter on the page as an appropriate word is sought. 'As if' is repeated three times which, while conveying the uncertainty of the perception, troubles the act of representation, prompting doubt as to whether language can deliver the matter it pursues. 'Like a / like a' similarly reveals the obstacle McKay finds between signified and signifier in '– deer'. Expanding on these examples, doubt and indecisiveness in the act of writing itself can be explored in several directions. Having written a paragraph of environmental description, students could write another discussing the choices they have made in terms of language, image, narrative and tone and aim to 'correct' the description. The wind didn't really skip across the ground, it was faster and I lost my hat. Perhaps I shouldn't have described the sea anemone as pink, but red, or somewhere between. Was the sky really sad or was it me (and my lost hat)? Such commentaries would escape the idea of a finished piece of writing that produces virtual reality on the page. They would enact McKay's stutter on a larger scale. Reflecting on the fallibility of the narrator, such an exercise would also begin to suggest that language is unable to identify the real.

A text that reveals itself as a draft, full of false starts, mistakes and reservations, 'draws attention to its own status as text' as Rigby suggests, while simultaneously renouncing the 'controlling and manipulating' power McKay attributes to language. Other techniques are also worth exploring in terms of their effect. Scare quotes, as suggested by the phrase itself, point to unusual, inappropriate or inaccurate use of language. Likewise, italicization distinguishes phrases for emphasis or further scrutiny. In Jorie Graham's poem 'Afterwards', as we saw in Chapter 2, the word 'happened' is italicized, casting doubt on the finality of the past tense conveyed in the poem. Text is italicized or put into quotation marks in Elisabeth Bletsoe's *Pharmacopoeia* ([1999] 2010), a sequence of poems that describe particular species such as the stinging nettle and the foxglove. The latter, for example, is depicted as 'glistening with excitement' and able to '*purgeth the body both / upwards and down*' ([1999] 2010: 1, 6–7). These relatively subtle techniques might be considered by students alongside those above given their potential to raise questions as to the authority or source of the text presented.

I have argued so far that traditionally undesirable literary qualities or devices, such as anthropocentrism and 'forced' metaphor, may, in fact, be productive in their capacity to provoke self-reflexivity. Another such device is cliché. Inflated, seemingly grand, and yet, simultaneously, trite and banal, hackneyed terms or phrases can serve to question the relationship between language and matter. Students might explore the potential of a description of water that uses a limited palette of words ('sparkling', 'glittering'), or of familiar personifications (a 'threatening' mountain), or the phrase 'to be at one with nature'. As deliberate cliché self-consciously falls short of its subject, so hyperbole self-consciously overindulges in the act of representation. After writing a paragraph of description about an environmental subject – a lake, a disused quarry, a sparrow – students can rewrite it initially with cliché and again on more exaggerated or theatrical terms.

Students might read Morton on 'radical kitsch' and then make a caricature of their own environmental writing. This exercise might come close to the far-fetched and comical anthropocentrism exhibited in the poems by Hadfield and McKay. After all, rather than attempting to be non-art, these poems wear their artifice on their sleeve. Describing the issues involved in teaching environmental writing, Chris Kinsey explains that her students often 'cute-sify things and I will challenge that' (2014). She explains this problem further as 'seeing things in human terms or appropriating or giving qualities that aren't there' and goes on to give the example of the student who responded to an image of a wolf with 'aw, cute' (ibid.). The conventional assumption that to 'cute-sify' is to produce bad writing. Yet, McKay and Hadfield show how an ironical use of these human terms, which takes them to an extreme, can prompt reflexivity that refocuses upon the physical environment, exploring the conflict that can be introduced with human terms and the ecological damage humans do. A simple exercise based on metaphor helps to explore this opportunity. On one scrap of paper, students write down a 'natural' subject and on another they write down an 'artificial' subject. In pairs, the students must then swap their natural subject with one another and attempt to compare this natural subject to their existing artificial subject in as many ways possible: how is a woodlouse like a telephone, a seagull like a crisp packet, a waterfall like an email? Strained, problematical and likely farcical, the act of forced comparison affords students not only the opportunity to recognize how language can invalidate itself and produce non-identity, but also the opportunity to recognize the incongruous and uncomfortable nature of an anthropocentric perspective.

In his essay, 'Education by Poetry' ([1931], 2007), the poet Robert Frost turns his attention to the provisional nature of metaphor. His argument is similar to the one Seitz has made more recently. Frost asserts that metaphor should not be taken at face value. Indeed, metaphor should not be wholly trusted because 'all metaphor breaks down somewhere' ([1931] 2007: 107). Yet, as the title of his essay suggests, these concerns tackle more than just the figurative device. Metaphor represents the accepted truths and practice of learning taught by education. Like metaphor, these accepted truths passed down from generation to generation should not be immediately accepted. The student should question what is being said. Frost values the process of reading between the lines, of exploring incongruity and of searching for different answers and opinions. If you do not understand the metaphor in 'its strength and its weakness', then 'you are not safe with science; you are not safe in history', he declares (ibid.: 106). In this chapter I have argued for an ecocritical recognition of the relationship between text and environment that values, in a manner not dissimilar to Frost's, incoherence and failure in textual representation in order to challenge the power that the idea of authenticity holds in environmental writing. Indeed, in fostering self-reflexivity through metaphor, anthropocentrism and humour, students can begin to find that they are 'not safe' in the communicative medium we have no choice but to use as writers: language.

Afterword

In 2016, the *Journal of Creative Writing Studies* published 'Our Discipline: An Ecological Creative Writing Manifesto', written by Jeremy Schraffenberger. The manifesto begins with an explicit nod to Walt Whitman, 'Our discipline contains multitudes' (2016: 1). These multitudes take the form of a list. They concern subject matter, perspective and aesthetic: 'Our discipline is mountainous, oceanic, cavernous … Our discipline is grounded in place … Our discipline flirts with science, longs for science, dreams of science' (2016: 2–4). In one instance, Schraffenberger denounces nostalgia and romantic inspiration. In another, pre-emptively defending the ecological writer from being typecast as a Luddite, he asserts that those practising under the banner of ecological writing are 'comfortable with computers', and, better yet, the internet. The manifesto spans five pages and this length owes, at least in some part, to the fact that the statements are often expressed with much nuanced backpedaling. Mountains and oceans are great subject matter, but so are 'sidewalks and streets, alleys and highways' (ibid.: 2). We dream of science, but 'our discipline resists the mechanistic' (ibid.: 4). Ecological writers use computers but 'we all need to cut back on our screen time' (ibid.: 2). Although there is some risk here of the manifesto seeming less like a manifesto and more like a parody of one, this rather unwieldy list of principles would seem to successfully embody the multitudes Schraffenberger believes intrinsic to ecological creative writing. There is a feeling here that such writing is diverse, accessible and open-minded. But there are exceptions. When it comes to the question of theory, he writes,

> Our discipline is not afraid of critical theory and will even use it sometimes, but often it prefers to be more or less atheoretical. Our discipline is not naïve. Our discipline has read those books, too, sure. Our discipline understands and appreciates what you're saying but would sometimes rather talk about something else. Our discipline will be over here.
>
> (2006: 4)

Schraffenberger's statement is rich in qualifiers and defensive in tone. It is also unclear as to exactly why writers prefer to be 'atheoretical', though we might be reminded of the teachers I discussed in the Introduction who believe ecocriticism – specifically ecocriticism that adopts critical theory – might compromise or alienate a student's approach to environmental writing.

It is time to reconsider this line of thought. Focusing on current pedagogical approaches to environmental writing, this book has sought to counter the belief that ecocritical theory is irrelevant or, at worst, antagonistic to creative practice by demonstrating how dialogue between the two can develop new understandings of environments and bring to light thought-provoking modes of representation. My discussion of Ursula Heise's theory of eco-cosmopolitanism in Chapter 1 functioned as a catalyst for developing place-based approaches with an awareness of globalization. My reading of Juliana Spahr's poetry through Heise's theory demonstrated the range of creative techniques and forms that might be used to express environmental comprehension on a global scale. Chapter 2 posed similar questions concerning some recurring instructions in pedagogy for students to write in the first-person. I applied Rob Nixon's argument that seeks engagement beyond the 'here and now' in order to perceive 'slow violence' to poems by Jorie Graham to show how the first-person can be adapted through a practice of perspective-taking that affords both insight and empathy concerning environmental issues. I continued this work on perspective-taking by focusing on pedagogical approaches to representing nonhumans in Chapter 3. As I demonstrated, teachers frequently warn against anthropomorphism, believing it to be unethical. Arguments by Donna Haraway and Timothy Morton, however, suggest nuanced perspectives that resemble those found in poems by Les Murray and Roy Fisher. Through an ecocritically inflected pedagogy, then, Chapter 3 explained the importance of returning to and experimenting with anthropomorphism.

Having addressed subject matter and perspective in the first three chapters, I focused more emphatically on language in the final two chapters. The belief that scientific modes of language correspond to an ethical relationship with environments is often found in discussions of environmental writing, including those between teachers and students. Through readings of the ecocritical work of David Abram and poems by Charles Tomlinson, I questioned the importance placed on natural history in some current pedagogy. These sources helped me to propose a different relationship between literary aesthetic and moral ethic; one which showed how metaphor (often distrusted in a similar manner to anthropomorphism) has the potential to deepen experiential engagements with environmental materiality, particularly in the context of biodiversity. In Chapter 5, I attended to the topic of authenticity that arises in pedagogical instruction that suggests the dissolving of the boundaries between art and non-art. As such suggests an equivalence between word and subject, the breach between the practice of environmental writing and ecocriticism influenced by post-structuralism becomes particularly noticeable. Yet, rather than pitching camp and stating 'Our discipline will be over here' as Schraffenberger does in his manifesto, the chapter explored the ways in which 'authenticity' might be replaced with ecocritical concepts of 'unsayability' in order to expand creative opportunities for environmental writing. I showed how poets Don McKay and Jen Hadfield provide inventive literary models for such opportunities. Their work demonstrates how anthropocentrism can be explored to comic and thus self-reflexive effect, prompting the reader to recognize that the reality of environments lies beyond language.

'Our discipline thinks aesthetics and ethics should get to know each other and talk on a regular basis', writes Schraffenberger (2016: 4). Given the gravity and urgency of the environmental crisis, this dialogue is understandably important. But it is also important to be aware of how particular relationships between aesthetics and ethics can become dominant in approaches to environmental writing and consequently obscure other possibilities. I have shown how an emphasis on local conceptions of place has the potential to eclipse thought on global connection, and how a preference for scientific language in, say, the description of a species of bird might hinder awareness of ways in which metaphor can convey new relationships to materiality. The ecocritical arguments that I have used to query and revise some instances of pedagogical instruction in this study have been crucial in demonstrating how the dialogue between ethics and aesthetics can change and adapt. We might, however, take this further.

The ethical standpoint that current pedagogy frequently encourages is one in which egotism is 'quashed' and environments are revered. This is clearest in my discussions concerning certain pedagogical approaches to the first-person 'I', anthropomorphism and metaphor. Surely, however, our moral compasses do not always conform to this model. What of an environmental ethics that is hypocritical or inadequate? In her recent book, *Bad Environmentalism* (2018), Nicole Seymour questions whether 'reverence is required for ethical relations to the nonhuman' (2018: 5). She argues that 'earnestness, seriousness, and didacticism' are not always productive approaches to environmental subject matter given that such approaches do not reflect our often flawed or inconsistent attitudes to the environment (ibid.: 17). In turn, Seymour finds irony, absurdity, irreverence and playfulness to be productive aesthetic strategies in expressing 'uncertain or awkward' positions rather than positions that are confident 'as to what is right and wrong' (ibid.: 32). My encouragement of comic anthropocentrism in Chapter 5 shares in some of Seymour's interests, but more work here may be valuable. It is worth considering, for example, how moral approaches to the environment will often be inherited through texts set on the reading list, or through dominant modes of thought associated with environmentalism. How might pedagogy help students to reflect on their own position regarding the environment that may be neither straightforwardly 'good' nor 'bad'?

The relationship between ethics and aesthetics means that as we become aware of, and inhabit, different ethical positions, our modes of representation will diversify too. As I have shown, early pedagogy focused on environmental writing closely aligned itself with science, which led to the association between environmental writing and non-fiction. By examining poetry, I have aimed to draw attention to a range of creative approaches that aim to disrupt the dominant idea that 'literal' modes of representation are more ethical than those which are 'literary'. My argument, however, has not suggested that poetry should be the preferred form of environmental writing. Rather, my discussion of poetry has led to proposals for particular creative exercises that have demonstrated, among others, the environmental possibilities of writing in translation, science fiction, confessional journals and epistolary modes.

Increasingly, universities in Britain and America offer creative writing modules, classes and specialized pathways – not to mention doctoral study – with staff who focus on environmental themes. Workshops, one-off classes and residential courses are similarly plentiful outside higher education. Beyond the UK and US context, other countries are also beginning to offer comparable routes of study. As part of a Master's degree in creative writing, The University of Melbourne in Australia offers a module in 'Genealogies of Place'. 'Ecology and Writing' is also offered as a module on a postgraduate course delivered by the University of the Western Cape, South Africa. Although I could never have composed an exhaustive study of how environmental writing is taught, this study is the first book-length critical appraisal of the phenomenon in education.

As well as an appraisal, this book serves as a proposal for a new ecocritical pedagogy. Broadly speaking, creative writers and critical theorists never have been the best of friends. Tracing the disconnection, J. T. Welsch (2015) goes as far as to reference Plato's binary opposition between poetry and philosophy in the *Republic*, whereas Paul Dawson (2005) asserts that some teachers have used this division to strengthen disciplinary identity and ensure institutional support. The specific relationship between ecocriticism and environmental writing pedagogy is, however, an unusual one. As I explained in my Introduction, the beginnings of environmental writing pedagogy were bound with those of early ecocriticism. The fact that writers, teachers and ecocritics (and individuals who occupy all three roles) continue to rub shoulders, particularly via conferences and publications associated with the Association of Study for Literature and the Environment and its international iterations, is testament to the potential for a renewed dialogue between creative and critical practices.

Environments do not stay the same. Rainforests are cut down for cattle ranches and palm oil plantations. Marshes are drained and land is built upon. Only in a few cases do we see the reverse, when environments are recovered and turned into protected sites. While new species are sometimes discovered, sadly it is more common to read of species that have become extinct. As environments change, so does our language. The 'dodo' lives on, but only as a symbol for our destructive tendencies and as a metaphor for that which has become obsolete. The thawing of permafrost, owing to a rise in global temperature, displaces trees from their vertical standing: a phenomenon we currently call 'drunken trees' or 'drunken forests'. With new publications each year, the practice of environmental writing is changing too. The same can be said of ecocriticism. Seymour's work might be considered one such example. Broader trajectories currently undertaken by scholars in, say, queer theory and posthumanism, provide further evidence. If pedagogy is to reflect changes in environmental thought, and, moreover, if it is to help create thinkers who will participate in the future of such thought, it is essential that pedagogy also adapts.

Notes

Introduction

1 https://www.essex.ac.uk/courses/pg00845/1/ma-wild-writing-literature-landscape-and-the-environment.
2 https://engl.iastate.edu/graduate-students/mfa-program-in-creative-writing-and-environment/.
3 It is also worth noting that in some cases students become teachers of the same subject. According to Iowa State University's alumni website, between 2012 and 2017 eight alumni of the MFA Programme in Creative Writing and Environment went into teaching roles and academic fellowships, half of which were in Iowa State itself.
4 Any attempt to define such writing is uneasy: as Daniel J. Philippon states, 'Taxonomies give the appearance of stasis to a world in constant motion' (2014: 394). No labels are immune to interrogation. As noted, 'environmental' is often understood to be synonymous with 'activist' given its proximity to 'environmentalism' suggesting a literature that is science-focused and potentially polemical in character. Adding to these concerns, David Mazel suggests 'the environment' as a term creates division: it 'separates the environment from the speaker who is environed' (2000: xvi), raising similar concerns as those associated with the phrase 'nature writing'. Ultimately, however, it is necessary to commit to a term. 'Environmental writing' not only helps to open discussion, but reflects this study's application of ecocriticism to pedagogy, which in turn may be associated with Education for Sustainable Development that prioritizes ideas concerning 'environment' over 'nature' as suggested by later discussions in this Introduction.
5 Historical accounts of creative writing in US higher education by D. G. Myers (1996) and Mark McGurl (2009) may have some bearing on this preference for factual engagements (and consequent wariness concerning the imagination) as they describe how US classes in creative writing emerged from classes in composition taught in the nineteenth century. Reflecting on the injunction to 'write what you know', McGurl finds the history of composition significant in establishing 'the dominant position of realism (whether regionalist, ethnic, or domestic) in the postwar creative writing establishment' (2009: 95).
6 Along with the distinctions I have argued for, including the challenge to the nature/culture binary, second-wave ecocriticism was also marked by the environmental justice movement in which questions of race, gender and class became prominent. Many scholars use the wave metaphor, and Laurence Buell (2005) provides

a particularly useful account of it. I employ the wave metaphor to aid my identification of the divergences between ecocritical and pedagogical practice, but it is worth considering how the metaphor suggests a straightforward sense of progress that at times obscures a more complex, dialectic dynamic.

7   Among these more particular points, it is also worth noting that the historical relationship between theory and broader studies of creative writing has been similarly fraught. Reflecting on the mid-twentieth century expansion of creative writing and New Criticism, Paul Dawson suggests that creative writing 'became entrenched in opposition to it as a means of retaining disciplinary identity' (2005: 4). Although his argument differs in breadth when compared to this study focused on environmental writing, Dawson makes a similar case as to how theory can invigorate creative writing and play a significant role in the production of new writing that contributes to the development of literary culture (see Dawson's chapter 'Negotiating Theory').

8   There is also surprising provision in terms of ecocritical pedagogy for school pupils including *Teaching Secondary English as if the Planet Matters* (2010) by Sasha Matthewman which concentrates on secondary school education and *Teaching Environments: Ecocritical Encounters* (Bartosch and Grimm 2014) that provides a wide-ranging exploration of teaching English at all educational levels.

9   Magazines dedicated to environmental writing have proliferated in recent years both in print and online. British publications include *Caught by the River*, *Zoomorphic*, *Elementum*, *The Clearing* and up until recently *Earthlines*, whereas America offers *Orion*, *Ecotone*, *Canary*, *Terrain.org*, *Flyway* and *Fourth River* (the latter two coincidentally arising from environmental writing courses in Iowa State and Chatham universities). Similarly healthy is prize culture with the Wainwright Prize and Ginkgo Prize in the United Kingdom and the Orion Book Award and the John Burroughs Award in the United States. Little Toller and the Dark Mountain Project have been successful in the United Kingdom as publishers specializing in environmental writing, and, likewise, Green Writers Press, set up in America in 2015.

10 This question is, of course, also applicable to geographies *within* the United States and the United Kingdom. Laird Christensen explains how his past experiences in the wildernesses of Oregon initially meant that when he moved to Vermont to teach at Green Mountain College he taught students to 'bracket off the human element' (2018). Reading the work of 'Easterners' such as Bill McKibben and Janisse Ray helped Christensen to see the value in incorporating 'social components' to his Environmental Writing Workshop (ibid.).

11 For a sustained look at how geography has influenced writing in the United Kingdom, see Graham Huggan's essay 'Back to the Future: The "New Nature Writing", Ecological Boredom, and the Recall for the Wild'.

12 In 'A Short History of Creative Writing in British Universities', Graeme Harper argues that creative writing existed in Britain long prior to the 1970s but in a less formalized manner. He looks as far back as the sixteenth century, to Jasper Heywood and Thomas Carew, who studied at the University of Oxford, but did not attend 'classes with titles anything like "Creative Writing" … however … [the] writer was influenced, educated and developed at university and went on further to this to work as a creative writer' (2012: 10). He also argues that adult education programmes and the proliferation of polytechnics in the 1960s and 1970s were crucial to the establishment of creative writing as a distinct discipline.
13 Paralleling familiar teaching and learning practices in creative writing pedagogy, classes in environmental writing frequently comprise discussion of set reading as well as writing 'prompts' or 'exercises'. These 'prompts' request students to write to a brief that may be based on a particular subject matter, narrative voice or literary style. These prompts are generally used to give students an opportunity to experiment in their writing and to instruct them on certain valuable techniques.
14 It is also worth noting that in many cases, interviewees shared samples of their teaching materials and generously allowed follow-up email correspondence, all of which have contributed to this survey.

1 'Where you are': Place writing

1 Taking the British and American courses and modules where interviews were conducted as an indicative sample, 73 per cent included Thoreau's *Walden* as either set reading or as influential to the course design.
2 And yet the connection between close attention to place and the identification of species in Dillard's writing has been questioned. When it was revealed that the frog-sucking giant water bug was not experienced first-hand as she describes in *Pilgrim at Tinker Creek*, but taken from a book, some degree of controversy ensued that queried whether Dillard's writing was an authentic portrayal of place.
3 As Chapter 2 highlights, an approach to place which values wilderness and solitude might be considered a 'retreat narrative' in the words of Randall Roorda who studies the intentions and ethical implications of American writers from Thoreau onwards. Roorda comments on the origins of this ritual in relation to British and American writing: 'To tap Thoreau as the retreat narrative's progenitor is in no way to deny his relatedness to the likes of Gilbert White; but it does involve claiming that it's the Walden story, not the Selborne one, that consumers of the genre want most to recapitulate' (1998: 7).
4 For more on Jim Perrin's perspective of the 'new nature writing' and its metropolitan flavour, see 'The Condry Lecture' (2010).

5 One particular example to keep in mind during analysis of Spahr might be found in Stein's *Lectures in America,* in which Stein argues that British literature of the nineteenth century began to favour the 'phrase' (over the eighteenth-century 'sentence'), which was invented 'by those living a daily island life and owning everything else outside' ([1935]1988: 40). For more on Stein's influence on Spahr, see Spahr's critical work on reading; *Everybody's Autonomy* (2001).

6 Given the length and prose-like quality of Spahr's work, all quotations from her collections are cited in terms of page number rather than line number.

7 Map-making activities as place-based pedagogical strategies can be found in *Stories in the Land* (1998), particularly in 'Finding Home: A Map Making Activity'.

8 A number of scholarly works address similar concerns. David Sobel's landmark *Beyond Ecophobia: Reclaiming the Heart in Nature Education* (1996) argues for the importance of a child's bond with nature before engaging with the issues that jeopardize such environments. Sobel's more recent titles, such as *Childhood and Nature* (2008), pursue these ideas. Finding a way through the emotional consequences of engagements with environmental issues, Joanna Macy and Molly Young Brown (2014) discuss the importance of 'despair work'.

9 For more on Spahr and entanglement, see Tana Jean Welch's ecocritical argument in her essay 'Entangled Species: The Inclusive Posthumanist Ecopoetics of Juliana Spahr' (2014) in which Welch situates Spahr in Timothy Morton's ecocritical theory of 'the mesh'.

10 Another creative model that might be considered alongside Spahr's when exploring causal chains and associations is Tadeusz Różewicz's *recycling* (2001): a series of poems that juxtapose capitalism, the BSE crisis, and the Holocaust. Perhaps most relevantly to the exercise suggested, in 'Gold', Różewicz describes the resurfacing of Nazi gold, but the vault he describes 'contains gold teeth / gold caps gold rings / with diamond eyes / spectacle frames hair / fountain pens breaths' (ibid.: 35).

2 The 'I-me-my voice': The first-person in environmental writing

1 *The Wild Places* has featured on James Canton's 'Wild Writing' course at the University of Essex, Andrew Motion's 'Place, Environment, Writing' Master's course at Royal Holloway (University of London) and Jon Gower's 'Nature Writing' module at Swansea University. Kathleen Jamie's review in the *London Review of Books* is a talking point in most, if not all, environmental writing courses in the United Kingdom. The review has been set reading at the University of Essex, on Miriam Darlington's 'Places and Journeys' undergraduate module at the University of Exeter, and the 'Place, Environment, Writing' Master's course at Royal Holloway, University of London. In David Cooper's undergraduate module 'Writing and

Place' at Manchester Metropolitan University, he asks students to undertake psychogeographic exercises (discussed in Chapter 3) in groups. In so doing, students 'aren't walking alone: walking is seen as a collective act. It's getting away from the idea of the 'lone, enraptured male' (2018).

2. Evans's statement is reminiscent of Thoreau's opening statement in *Walden* quoted at the beginning of this chapter. With thought on his own early writing that aimed for self-effacement in order to create an 'unmediated' environmental representation, Laird Christensen similarly questions its feasibility. Remembering a time in which he received a poetry rejection from an editor that criticized his poems on the basis that they expressed 'no sense of the speaker', he explains how more mediated representations of the environment can help instill plot, action and make the writing more engaging (2014c).

3. Gower's analogy deserves some attention. Though the comparison between environmental writing and biography serves his argument about the need for an unobtrusive narrator, it also suggests that an environment, like a person, is a living entity with a story to be told.

4. The title of 'reductive propaganda' is attributed to Gary Snyder's widely anthologized poem, 'Mother Earth: Her Whales' (Gifford [1995] 2011: 11). Rather than representative of the whole genre, this poem might be thought of as an exemplary model of the dangers associated with polemic. Snyder's poem receives further criticism in Jonathan Bate's ecocritical work *Song of the Earth* in which Bate finds it lacking in imagination and craft: beyond rhetoric, the 'language is not being asked to do ecological work' (2000: 200).

5. Certain trends in scholarship on Graham's work might be consulted to extend discussions on the subject of self-consciousness, perception and representation. Willard Spiegelman's chapter on Graham in his book *How Poets See the World* (2005) focuses upon how Graham enacts description and, in doing so, questions the character of seeing in such collections as *Materialism*. The act of seeing (and more broadly, the way the world is experienced) also becomes the central focus of Thomas Gardner's collection of essays, *Jorie Graham: Essays on the Poetry* (2005). Collected by Gardner, Helen Vendler's essay on the length of, and disruption in, Graham's lines foregrounds the way in which Graham tackles the 'excess' of experience. Gardner's collection of essays also emphasizes the way in which Graham's poems problematize the act of writing. James Logenbach's chapter draws attention to poems that attempt to describe particular locations at particular times but, recognizing the temporal act of recording these locations, these poems 'simultaneously conjure and disperse locations' (2005: 206).

6. For greater theoretical commentary, the work of Jonathan Culler in *Theory of the Lyric* (2015) speaks to apostrophe's relevance to presence and absence, self and other, as well as temporality. His closing remarks in his chapter, 'Lyric Address', suggest that apostrophe performs an ecological function in the way it permits entities to

'exercise agency, resisting our usual assumptions about what can act and what cannot' (2015: 242).

7 Following Thomashow's interest in collective responsibility, thought might be given to reimagining the 'I' as a collective pronoun. Students might read the opening discussion in Chapter 1 that studies Juliana Spahr's pronoun play between 'I' and 'we', and then experiment further with narrative perspective. In 'Gentle Now, Don't Add to Heartache', Spahr suggests that 'becoming individuals' is symptomatic of disconnection with an environment. In turn, students might try to identify which situations prompt them to use a collective pronoun and, in contrast, which situations might prompt them to identify as an individual.

8 'Burning the Shelter' is, coincidentally, one of the essays included in the anthology section of *Environmental and Nature Writing*. Prentiss and Wilkins identify the text as a valuable example of 'activist-writing' that reveals the false dichotomy between nature and culture, but they provide no further comment or analysis as to how it could influence new writing (2016: 109).

3 'I am not a swift': Approaching non-humans

1 My argument corresponds to John Simons's discussion in *Animal Rights and the Politics of Literary Representation* (2002) which distinguishes 'strong anthropomorphism' from 'fable' and 'trivial' anthropomorphism as that which prompts 'profound questions in the reader's mind as to the extent to which humans and non-humans are really different' (2002: 120). However, this taxonomy of anthropomorphism only arrives halfway into Simons's study and comprises such a whirlwind analysis of a variety of texts (Kenneth Grahame's *Wind in the Willows*, Jonathan Swift's 'A Modest Proposal' and *Gulliver's Travels*, John Coetzee's *The Lives of Animals*, Eleanor Akinson's *Greyfriar's Bobby* and *Babe*) that a clear argument as to how 'strong anthropomorphism' might be achieved becomes difficult to recognize. Furthermore, Simons offers no subsequent analysis as to the potential effect of apprehending non-human difference. This chapter aims to address both of these issues.

2 For further explanation of the relationship between Les Murray's poetry and Australian Aboriginal culture as well as other influences, see Michael Malay's *The Figure of the Animal in Modern and Contemporary Poetry* (2018: 159–208).

3 *Translations* has informed several scholarly studies on animal representation. Gillian Beer (2005) identifies Murray's use of the figurative device but shows minimal close reading of the poems themselves, preferring to establish, at a safe distance, that the poems 'warp language' (ibid.: 319). Her analysis does, however, address the effect of this strange language: it 'pays respect to the ways of being that lie beyond language' (ibid.: 321). This perspective is adopted in ecocriticism as Greg Garrard briefly turns

to Murray's works and states that 'every poem is a vivid testament to the difficulty, if not impossibility, of the representational work it undertakes' (2004: 168). Hugh Dunkerley (2001) takes a more obvious post-structuralist approach as he states that each poem uses 'signs to point towards this being, which is itself beyond language' (2001: 81). Yet, in immediately arguing that Murray's language invalidates itself in order to point towards the animal outside language, these critics omit close readings of how Murray creates subtle contrasts in sensorial and conceptual meaning, which I address.

4   Haraway illustrates her argument with Nancy Farmer's novel, *A Girl Named Disaster*, that features Baba Joseph: a character who oversees a lab experiment. With the aim to learn more about sleeping sickness and its prevention, guinea pigs are held in baskets and wire cages full of biting flies are placed over them. Haraway focuses on the moment Baba Joseph puts his bare arm into the cage as an attempt to share in the guinea pigs' suffering. Although the character's actions suggest mimetic sharing (his flesh is bitten as the animal's flesh is bitten), Haraway contends that another outcome is non-mimetic: 'Baba Joseph's bitten arm is not the fruit of a heroic fantasy of ending all suffering … but the result of remaining at risk and in solidarity in instrumental relationships that one does not disavow' (2008: 69). Sharing in the guinea pigs' suffering does not provide closure, conversely it draws attention to the unresolvable and uncomfortable complexity of response.

5   The New Materialist angle of Bennett's study is recognizable in David Abram's proposal of modern-day animism in *Becoming Animal*. Examined in Chapter 4, Abram argues for the importance of returning to oral culture in participating with 'an animate, expressive world' (2010: 4). Object-Oriented Ontology also forms a large part of this movement in its study of 'thinghood', which is discussed, albeit briefly, with regard to Ian Bogost's concept of 'alien phenomenology' in this chapter.

6   Bennett's definition of agency is influenced by Bruno Latour's definition of the 'actant' in *Politics of Nature*. Bennett says 'an actant is a source of action that can be either human or nonhuman; it is that which has efficacy, can *do* things, has sufficient coherence to make a difference, produce effects, alter the course of events' (2010: viii). She explains that her concept of 'distributive' agency depends on ad hoc groupings of material entities that she calls 'assemblages' after Deleuze and Guattari's term. This argument leads Bennett to question common understandings of causality as one entity causing an effect in isolation, and to suggest that causality 'is more emergent than efficient, more fractal than linear' (ibid.: 33).

7   All in-text citations of *A Furnace* refer to the page rather than line number due to the book-length form of the poem. Literary scholarship has gone some way in identifying an animist quality in *A Furnace*. Ralf Pite (2000) studies the influence of the late Romantic novelist, John Cowper Powys in Fisher's writing. However, consumed by this parallel with Powys, Pite does not question how, unlike Powys,

Fisher applies this literary style to the context of an industrial city. William Wootten (2005) pays further attention to the city environment in *A Furnace*, yet, providing another Powysian reading, he spends most of his study contextualizing passages from *A Furnace*. Wootten makes the point that Powys's understanding of 'fetish' affords 'interaction with the dead ... and the notion of timeless extra-human entities to emerge' and while this is relevant to the subject of 'lively' matter and anthropomorphism (2005: 88), Wootten's interest in delineating the theoretical complications of 'fetish' rather than identifying exactly what 'the dead' and the 'extra-human entities' are, means that the latter remain to be addressed. Clair Wills (2000) approaches this 'interaction with the dead' in more detail. Examining Fisher's conjurations of the life of the dead in terms of 'gothic', she describes *A Furnace* as 'being haunted by a buried past' (ibid.: 261). However, as will be shown, Wills interprets life only in human terms, thereby overlooking the entanglement of human and non-human identities I go on to discuss.

4 Writing 'more in the world': Fact and figuration

1 The Martian school of poetry, emerging from Britain in the 1970s, might be brought into comparison here. Originating with Craig Raine's poem 'A Martian Sends a Postcard Home', this school frequently deployed metaphor in order to make the familiar strange. Although parallels might be drawn between Martianism and Viktor Shklovsky's theory of *ostranenie* or 'defamiliarization', scholars have suggested that where 'Surrealist imagery at its best aggregates in an attempt to discredit or undermine quotidian logic ... "Martian" imagery seems usually to have no significant animating principle other than the display of amusing ingenuity' (Jackaman 1989: 277–8).
2 Gilcrest's argument is influenced by William Bevis, a modernist literary scholar, who praises meditative detachment in the poetry of Wallace Stevens. He states 'metaphorical perception is rooted in a Romantic sensibility' and while 'meditative perception ... encounters a new world by means of less self ... imaginative perception creates a new world by means of more self' (Gilcrest 2002: 127, quotes Bevis 1989: 9, 11). It is noteworthy in the context of the discussion on religious association that Bevis connects this 'meditative consciousness, or no-mind' to the passive states of Buddhism (1989: 11, but also see 11–14, 92–104).
3 The exact subject of Tomlinson's criticism remains open to interpretation. In *Passionate Intellect*, Michael Kirkham suggests that 'Observation of Facts' maintains an Objectivist stance and responds to 'the neo-romantic subjectivist poetic of Dylan Thomas and others in the 1940s and 50s' (1999: 217).
4 In *Passionate Intellect*, Michael Kirkham pursues the role of reality and imagination in Tomlinson's poems beyond the two collections studied in this chapter. Though

relatively brief, Kirkham's study touches on an environmental theme by suggesting that Tomlinson shared Wordsworth's belief in a 'participatory consciousness' between mind and world (1999: 53). In a passage which provides an interesting angle on Abram's ecocritical argument, Kirkham quotes a discussion between Ian Hamilton and Tomlinson in which the latter is said to have conjectured 'the world of Wordsworth … allied with the insights of the phenomenologists, might have given us back a human universe' (ibid.: 15).

5   For an extensive discussion on the referential capacity of metaphor, see Norrman and Haarberg's semiotic study, *Nature and Language* (1980). Paralleling the claim that the physical quality of clovers determines its role in metaphor, Norrman and Haarberg propose, 'When a man is called a pumpkin … the sign "pumpkin" in the metaphor … preserves its pumpkiness, which again means that to understand its meaning it is necessary not only to study language but to study reality as well' (1980: 5).

6   Max Black's 'interaction theory' of metaphor, influenced by I. A. Richards and elucidated in his two articles, 'Metaphor' (1955) and 'More about Metaphor' (1977), is a valuable theoretical touchstone when considering Tomlinson's idea: 'The artist lies / For the improvement of truth'. Proposing that metaphor can 'generate new knowledge and insight', Black provides a thorough investigation with which to situate and extend interpretation of Tomlinson's practice (1977: 35). Indeed, the later interpretation of Tomlinson's 'pine branch' follows Black's argument: that to describe a battle using vocabulary drawn from chess means that 'the chess vocabulary filters and transforms: it not only selects, it brings forward aspects of the battle that might not be seen at all through another medium' (1955: 289).

7   In 'Tomlinson, Ruskin, and Moore: Facts and Fir Trees' (1989), Ruth Grogan provides a useful examination of Ruskin's influence on Tomlinson that, anticipating Meyer's later question on Tomlinson's eye, parallels current discussion concerning metaphor and materiality. Turning to one particular anecdote, Grogan writes of a visit Canadian literary scholar, Hugh Kenner, made to Tomlinson in 1956. During his visit, Tomlinson read Kenner a passage from Ruskin's *Seven Lamps of Architecture* that describes a common black spruce fir in the terms of a 'chandelier', 'solid tables', 'strong arms' and 'shields' before concluding that 'it is vain to endeavor to paint the sharp, grassy, intricate leafage, until this ruling form has been secured' (1989: 184). As Grogan goes on to suggest, Tomlinson's appreciation for Ruskin's highly figurative style of observation informs his own practice that rebels against convention.

5   'On the world's terms and not my own': Authenticity, self-reflexivity and otherness

1   It is interesting to note that authenticity is often said to possess health-giving properties. Elder, for example, finds authenticity 'instructive, nourishing, and, in the

case of nature writing or "the poetry of earth", grounding' (2014). Lopez, too, finds the 'skilful invocation of unimpeachable sources' leads to a text that can 'nurture and heal ... repair a spirit in disarray' ([1984] 1988: 69). To some extent, to be authentic is to express one's inner thoughts and feelings, as opposed to concealing or repressing them. We might understand authenticity to be healthy in this sense. However, there seems to be a broader, moral argument at work here concerning the authentic as opposed to artifice and commodification. Using Wendell Berry's argument in *The Unsettling of America*, Elder associates the 'inauthentic' with television advertising (2014). This argument is reiterated in terms of technology and virtual reality in Lawrence Buell's thoughts on realism, which I later discuss. Here, Buell argues that 'the humble aspiration of environmental mimesis ... is far healthier ... than the arrogance of cyberspace' (1995: 114).

2 The authenticity of Momaday's novel has, furthermore, been disputed. See Mark McGurl's discussion of Karl Kroeber's criticism that *House Made of Dawn* is not a real example of Native American art because, among other reasons, it is indebted to white modernist writers (2009: 239–44).

3 The possibility that urban subject matter may well appear more frequently in British writing about the environment than American writing reflects the extent to which even wild places in Britain are small enclaves, highly managed and manipulated. The popularity of psychogeography in 1990s Britain may also play a role here. However, several US examples can be found, such as A. R. Ammons's *Garbage*, Jenny Price's essay 'Thirteen Ways of Finding Nature in LA' and *Unseen City* by Nathanael Johnson.

4 As discussed in Chapter 2, Kathleen Jamie finds Macfarlane guilty of the same offence. Macfarlane, according to Jamie, fails to include the inhabitants of the landscapes he explores and represents in *The Wild Places*.

5 It is also worth noting that Robert Macfarlane has suggested that, in the context of the Anthropocene, 'categories such as the picturesque or even the beautiful congeal into kitsch' (2016a). He also suggests that in 'an age of mass extinction it has become hard to tolerate notions of nature as an external or salvific "other", except as forms of cute or kitsch' (2017).

6 Rigby elucidates her theory of negative ecopoetics through a few diverse examples. Robert Gray's poem 'Early Morning' that recalls a walk in a park is useful to Rigby given Gray's nod to unsayability: 'And what is really here no words can tell' (2004b: 437). Rigby admits that such moments are also present in Romantic literature: for example, William Wordsworth's failure of expression in 'Home at Grasmere' when he writes 'but I cannot name it' (2004a: 125). More broadly, she notes that the 'phonetic and metrical patterning ... foregrounds the sonority of the linguistic medium', and so presumably the linguistic medium itself (ibid.: 125–6).

7   This argument about metaphor shares in the idea presented in Chapter 4 that metaphor is by its very nature a false linguistic claim.
8   McKay's proposal of the leap might be compared with that proposed by Robert Bly, a US poet who redeveloped the Deep Image Movement into a school of poetry marked by its intense imagery that often has a dreamlike progression. In *Leaping Poetry* ([1975] 2008) Bly argues for literature to return to leaping 'from the known part of the mind to the unknown part', and illustrates this with Surrealist writers such as Federico García Lorca and Pablo Neruda (ibid.: 1).
9   In his thorough and engaging investigation of comedy, *The Philosophy of Laughter and Humor* (1987), John Morreall proposes three types of humour: the superiority theory, the relief theory and, lastly, the incongruity theory. For more detail on the latter theory, see his chapter 'Funny Ha-Ha, Funny Strange, and Other Reactions to Incongruity', as well as my ecocritical reading of Morreall's theories in 'A Dark Ecology of Comedy: Environmental Cartoons, Jo Shapcott's Mad Cow Poems and the Motivational Function of the Comic Mode' (2013).

Bibliography

Abbey, E. ([1968] 1990). *Desert Solitaire*. New York: Simon & Schuster.
Abram, D. (1996). *The Spell of the Sensuous: Perception and Language in a More-Than-Human World*. New York: Pantheon Books.
Abram, D. (2010). *Becoming Animal: An Earthly Cosmology*. New York: Pantheon Books.
Adelson, G., and J. Elder (2006). 'Robert Frost's Ecosystem of Meanings in "Spring Pools"'. *Interdisciplinary Studies in Literature and Environment*, 13(2): 1–17.
Adorno, T. (1973). *The Jargon of Authenticity*, trans. K. Tarnowski and F. Will. Evanston: Northwestern University Press.
Adorno, T. ([1973] 1990). *Negative Dialectics*. London: Routledge.
Alizadeh, A. (2010). 'Ali Alizadeh Reviews Jen Hadfield'. *Cordite Poetry Review*, 11 January. Available online: http://cordite.org.au/reviews/alizadeh-hadfield/ (accessed 15 September 2017).
Arigo, C. (2008). 'Notes toward an Ecopoetics: Revising the Postmodern Sublime and Juliana Spahr's *This Connection of Everyone with Lungs*'. *How2*. Available online: https://www.asu.edu/pipercwcenter/how2journal/vol_3_no_2/ecopoetics/essays/arigo.html (accessed 23 July 2016).
Arthur, N. (2003). 'Day of the Dolphin'. *Washington Post*, 31 January. Available online: https://www.washingtonpost.com/archive/lifestyle/2003/01/31/day-of-the-dolphin/493063d2-ef69-42d5-952a-73e7a8b4c20b/?utm_term=.5ebc709b8ea3 (accessed 3 April 2016).
Astley, N. (ed.). (2007). *Earth Shattering: Ecopoems*. Tarset: Bloodaxe.
Atkin, P. (2019). 'Why Is It always a Poem Is a Walk?'. *New Welsh Reader*, 120: 41–54.
Atkins, W. (2014). *The Moor: Lives, Landscape, Literature*. London: Faber and Faber.
Bahrani, R. (dir.). (2009). 'Future States: Plastic Bag'. *Independent Television Service: Future States*. Available online: https://www.pbs.org/video/futurestates-plastic-bag/ (accessed 5 September 2018).
Baker, J. A. ([1967] 2015). *The Peregrine: The Hill of Summer & Diaries: The Complete Works of J.A. Baker*, ed. J. Fanshawe. London: William Collins.
Barkham, P. (2016). 'Being a Beast by Charles Foster Review: The Man Who Ate Worms Like a Badger'. *The Guardian*, 3 February. Available online: https://www.theguardian.com/books/2016/feb/03/being-beast-charles-foster-review-man-whoate-worms-like-badger (accessed 6 March 2016).
Bartosch, R., and S. Grimm (2014). *Teaching Environments: Ecocritical Encounters*. Frankfurt am Main: Peter Lang.

Bate, J. (1991). *Romantic Ecology: Wordsworth and the Environmental Tradition*. London: Routledge.
Bate, J. (2000). *The Song of the Earth*. London: Picador.
Battersby, E. (2014). 'Bird Tale That Fails to Fly: H Is for Hawk by Helen Macdonald'. *Irish Times*, 6 September. Available online: https://www.irishtimes.com/culture/books/bird-tale-that-fails-to-fly-h-is-for-hawk-by-helen-macdonald-1.1917840 (accessed 15 March 2019).
Beckwith, M. (1972). *The Kumulipo, a Hawaiian Creation Chant*. Honolulu: University Press of Hawaii.
Beer, G. (2005). 'Animal Presences: Tussles with Anthropomorphism'. *Comparative Critical Studies*, 2(3): 311–22.
Beigel, J. (1996). 'Literature and the Living World'. *Interdisciplinary Studies in Literature and Environment*, 2(2): 105–18.
Bevis, W. (1989). *Mind of Winter: Wallace Stevens, Meditation, and Literature*. Pittsburgh: University of Pittsburgh Press.
Bennett, J. (2010). *Vibrant Matter: A Political Ecology of Things*. Durham, NC: Duke University Press.
Black, M. (1955). 'Metaphor'. *Proceedings of the Aristotelian Society*, 55: 273–94.
Black, M. (1977). 'More about Metaphor'. *Dialectica*, 31(3–4): 431–57.
Bletsoe, E. ([1999] 2010). *Pharmacopoeia and Early Selected Works*. Bristol: Shearsman Books.
Bly, R. ([1975] 2008). *Leaping Poetry: An Idea with Poems and Translations*. Pittsburgh, PA: University of Pittsburgh Press.
Bogost, I. (2012). *Alien Phenomenology, or, What It's Like to Be a Thing*. Minneapolis: University of Minnesota Press.
Bryant, P. T. (1985). 'Nature Writing: Connecting Experience with Tradition', in F. O. Waage (ed.), *Teaching Environmental Literature: Materials, Methods, Resources*. New York: Modern Language Association of America, 93–101.
Buell, L. (1995). *The Environmental Imagination: Thoreau, Nature Writing, and the Formation of American Culture*. Cambridge, MA: Belknap Press of Harvard University Press.
Buell, L. (2005). *The Future of Environmental Criticism: Environmental Crisis and Literary Imagination*. Oxford: Blackwell.
Burnett, E. J. (2018). Interviewed by I. Galleymore. 20 February. Unpublished.
Burnett, E. J. (2019). Email correspondence with I. Galleymore. 21 June. Unpublished.
Burroughs, J. ([1903] 1998). 'Real and Sham Natural History', in R. H. Lutts (ed.), *The Wild Animal Story*. Philadelphia, PA: Temple University Press, 129–43.
Burroughs, J. ([1922] 2016). *The Last Harvest*. Boston: Houghton Mifflin.
Campbell, S. (2006). 'Layers of Place'. *Interdisciplinary Studies in Literature and Environment*, 13(2): 179–83.
Canton, J. (2013). Class shadowing notes by I. Galleymore. 6 February. Unpublished.
Canton, J. (2018). Interviewed by I. Galleymore. 10 January. Unpublished.

Carpenter, J. R. (2017). *The Gathering Cloud*. London: Penned in the Margins.
Carson, R. ([1962] 2012). *Silent Spring*. London: Penguin Classics.
Cave, S. (2016). '"Being a Beast", by Charles Foster'. *Financial Times*, 29 January. Available online: https://www.ft.com/content/f79a521c-c395-11e5-808f-8231cd71622e (accessed 15 March 2016).
Ceballos, G., P. R. Ehrlich and R. Dirzo (2017). 'Biological Annihilation via the Ongoing Sixth Mass Extinction Signaled by Vertebrate Population Losses and Declines'. *PNAS*, 114(30): 89–96.
Chandler, K. (2003). 'Can't See the Forest or the Trees: Finding Focus', in H. Crimmel (ed.), *Teaching in the Field: Working with Students in the Outdoor Classroom*. Salt Lake City: University of Utah Press, 103–23.
Christensen, L. (2003). 'Writing the Watershed', in H. Crimmel (ed.), *Teaching in the Field: Working with Students in the Outdoor Classroom*. Salt Lake City: University of Utah Press, 124–36.
Christensen, L. (2011). Course description. Unpublished.
Christensen, L. (2014a). Class shadowing notes by I. Galleymore. 26 September. Unpublished.
Christensen, L. (2014b). Class shadowing notes by I. Galleymore. 3 October. Unpublished.
Christensen, L. (2014c). Interviewed by I. Galleymore. 6 October. Unpublished.
Christensen, L. (2014d). Class shadowing notes by I. Galleymore. 7 October. Unpublished.
Christensen, L. (2018). Email correspondence with I. Galleymore. 12 February. Unpublished.
Christensen, L., and H. Crimmel (eds). (2008). *Teaching about Place: Learning from the Land*. Reno: University of Nevada Press.
Clare, H. (2016). 'Charles Foster: "I Need to Be More of a Badger"'. *The Spectator*, 20 February. Available online: https://www.spectator.co.uk/2016/02/charles-foster-i-need-to-be-more-of-a-badger/ (accessed 12 March 2016).
Cocker, M. (2008). *Crow Country*. London: Vintage Books.
Cocker, M. (2014). Interviewed by I. Galleymore. 9 January. Unpublished.
Cocker, M. (2015). 'Death of the Naturalist: Why Is the "New Nature Writing" So Tame?' *New Statesman*, 17 June. Available online: https://www.newstatesman.com/culture/2015/06/death-naturalist-why-new-nature-writing-so-tame (accessed 20 June 2017).
Cook, I., T. Angus and J. Evans (2010). 'A Manifesto for Cyborg Pedagogy?'. *International Research in Geographical and Environmental Education* (10)2: 195–201.
Cook, M. (2006). *Field Marks: The Poetry of Don McKay: Selected with an Introduction by Méira Cook*. Ontario: Wilfrid Laurier University Press.
Cooper, D. (2018). Interviewed by I. Galleymore. 24 July. Unpublished.

Cornell, J. B. (1979). *Sharing Nature with Children: A Parents' and Teachers' Nature-Awareness Guidebook*. Nevada City, CA: Ananda.

Cowley, J. (ed.). (2008). 'The New Nature Writing'. *Granta*, 102. Available online: https://granta.com/issues/granta-102-the-new-nature-writing/.

Crimmel, H. (2003). *Teaching in the Field: Working with Students in the Outdoor Classroom*. Salt Lake City: University of Utah Press.

Crimmel, H. (2014). 'Rafting, Walking, and Hiking in the Canyons of Dinosaur National Monument'. *Asle.org Syllabi*. Available online: https://www.asle.org/syllabi/rafting-writing-hiking-canyons-dinosaur-national-monument/ (accessed 12 April 2019).

Croke, V. C. (2016). 'I Want to Know What It Is Like to Be a Wild Thing'. *The New York Times*, 13 July. Available online: https://www.nytimes.com/2016/07/17/books/review/being-a-beast-charles-foster.html (accessed 4 September 2016).

Culler, J. (2015). *Theory of the Lyric*. Cambridge, MA: Harvard University Press.

Davidson, D. (1978). 'What Metaphors Mean'. *Critical Inquiry*, 5(1): 31–47.

Dawson, P. (2005). *Creative Writing and the New Humanities*. London: Routledge.

Dee, T. (2018). *Landfill*. Dorset: Little Toller.

Deleuze, G., and F. Guattari ([1980] 2003). *A Thousand Plateaus: Capitalism and Schizophrenia*, trans. B. Massumi. London: Continuum.

Derrida, J. ([1997] 2008). *The Animal That Therefore I Am*, ed. M. L. Mallet, trans. D. Wills. Ashland, OH: Fordham University Press.

Dickinson, E. ([1868] 1975). '1129', in T. H. Johnson (ed.), *The Complete Poems of Emily Dickinson*. London: Faber.

Dillard, A. ([1974] 1998). *Pilgrim at Tinker Creek*. New York: Harper Perennial.

Dobrin, S. I., and C. R. Weisser (2001). *Ecocomposition: Theoretical and Pedagogical Approaches*. New York: State University of New York Press.

Doty, M. (2008). *Theories and Apparitions*. London: Cape Poetry.

Dunkerley, H. (2001). 'Unnatural Relations? Language and Nature in the Poetry of Mark Doty and Les Murray'. *Interdisciplinary Studies in Literature Environment*, 8(1): 73–82.

Dunkerley, H. (2013). 'Translating Wilderness: Negative Ecopoetics and the Poetry of Don McKay', in S. Norgate (ed.), *Poetry and Voice: A Book of Essays*. Newcastle: Cambridge Scholars, 210–21.

Elder, J. (1985). *Imagining the Earth: Poetry and the Vision of Nature*. Urbana: University of Illinois Press.

Elder, J. (1998). *Stories in the Land: A Place-Based Environmental Education Anthology*. Great Barrington, MA: Orion Society.

Elder, J. (2014). Interviewed by I. Galleymore. 10 October. Unpublished.

Engelhardt, J., and J. Schraffenberger (2015). 'Ecological Creative Writing', in A. Peary and T. C. Hunley (eds), *Creative Writing Pedagogies for the Twenty-First Century*. Carbondale: University of Southern Illinois Press, 475–505.

Evans, P. (2014). Interviewed by I. Galleymore. 10 July. Unpublished.

Farley, P., and M. S. Roberts (2011). *Edgelands: Journeys into England's True Wilderness*. London: Jonathan Cape.

Felstiner, J. (2009). *Can Poetry Save the Earth?: A Field Guide to Nature Poems*. New Haven, CT: Yale University Press.

Fisher, R., J. Rasula and M. Erwin (1975). *Roy Fisher, Nineteen Poems and an Interview*. Pensnett: Grosseteste.

Fisher, R. (1986). *A Furnace*. Oxford: Oxford University Press.

Fisher, R. (2008). Interviewed by J. Kerrigan. 'Come to Think of It: The Imagination', *Jacket*, Available online: http://jacketmagazine.com/35/iv-fisher-ivb-kerrigan.shtml (accessed 14 June 2015).

Fisher, R. ([1991] 2012). 'Texts for a Film', in *The Long and the Short of It: Poems 1955–2005*. Tarset: Bloodaxe.

Forster, S. (2002). 'Don McKay's Comic Anthropocentrism: Ecocentrism Meets "Mr. Nature Poet"'. *Essays on Canadian Writing*, 77: 107–35.

Foster, C. (2016). *Being a Beast: Adventures across the Species Divide*. London: Profile Books.

Fowkes Tobin, B. (1996). 'Imperial Designs: Botanical Illustration and the British Botanic Empire'. *Studies in Eighteenth-Century Culture*, 25: 265–92.

Francis, M. (2008). *Mandeville*. London: Faber.

Fritzell, P. A. (1990). *Nature Writing and America: Essays upon a Cultural Type*. Ames: Iowa State University Press.

Frost, R. ([1931] 2007). 'Education by Poetry', in M. Richardson (ed.), *The Collected Prose of Robert Frost*. Cambridge, MA: Belknap Press of Harvard University Press, 102–12.

Fürstenberg, U. (2004). *'Les Murray Country': Development and Significance of an Australian poetic Landscape*. Tubingen: Gunter Narr Verlag.

Galleymore, I. (2013). 'A Dark Ecology of Comedy: Environmental Cartoons, Jo Shapcott's Mad Cow Poems and the Motivational Function of the Comic Mode'. *Green Letters*, 17(2): 151–63.

Galt, M. F. (2000). 'Nature as Teacher and Guide', in C. McEwen and M. Statman (eds), *The Alphabet of the Trees: A Guide to Nature Writing*. New York: Teachers & Writers Collaborative, 249–60.

Gardner, T. (2005). *Jorie Graham: Essays on the Poetry*. Madison: University of Wisconsin Press.

Garner, D. (2016). 'Review: In "*Being a Beast*", Charles Foster Eats Roadkill and Channels Otters'. *New York Times*, 14 June. Available online: https://www.nytimes.com/2016/06/15/books/review-in-being-a-beast-charles-foster-eats-roadkill-and-channels-otters.html (accessed 8 July 2016).

Garrard, G. (2004). *Ecocriticism*. London: Routledge.

Garrard, G. (2007). 'Ecocriticism and Education for Sustainability'. *Pedagogy*, 7(3): 359–83.

Garrard, G. (2010). 'Prospects and Problems in Ecocritical Pedagogy'. *Environmental Education Research*, 16(2): 233–45.

Garrard, G. (2012). *Teaching Ecocriticism and Green Cultural Studies*. Basingstoke: Palgrave Macmillan.

Gifford, T. (2003). 'Teaching Environmental Values through Creative Writing with School Children', in H. Crimmel (ed.), *Teaching in the Field: Working with Students in the Outdoor Classroom*. Salt Lake City: University of Utah Press, 137–51.

Gifford, T. (2011). *Green Voices*. Nottingham: Critical, Cultural and Communications Press.

Gifford, T. (2016). 'Towards a New Multi-Dimensional Ecopoetics of Place', in A. Goodbody and C. F. Junquera (eds), *Sense of Place: Transatlantic Perspectives*. Universidad de Alcalá: Servicio de Publicaciones, 215–28.

Gilcrest, D. W. (2002). *Greening the Lyre: Environmental Poetics and Ethics*. Reno: University of Nevada Press.

Gower, J. (2013). Interviewed by I. Galleymore. 18 February. Unpublished.

Graham, J. (1980). *Hybrids of Plants and of Ghosts*. Princeton, NJ: Princeton University Press.

Graham, J. (1987). *The End of Beauty*. New York: Ecco Press.

Graham, J. (1993). *Materialism*. Hopewell, NJ: Ecco Press.

Graham, J. (1998). *The Errancy*. Manchester: Carcanet.

Graham, J. ([1996] 2000). Interviewed by M. Wunderlich. 'The Glorious Thing: Jorie Graham and Mark Wunderlich in Conversation', *Poets.org*. Available online: https://poets.org/text/glorious-thing-jorie-graham-and-mark-wunderlich-conversation (accessed 12 April 2019).

Graham, J. (2002). *Never*. New York: Ecco.

Graham, J. (2003). Interviewed by T. Gardner. 'The Art of Poetry No. 85', *Paris Review*. Available online: http://www.joriegraham.com/interview_gardner (accessed 21 April 2013).

Graham, J. (2008). *Sea Change*. Manchester: Carcanet.

Graham, J. (2010). Interviewed by K. Grubisic. 'Jorie Graham: Instructions for Building the Arc', *The Fiddlehead*. Available online: https://www.joriegraham.com/node/201 (accessed 3 May 2013).

Graham, J. (2012a). *Place*. Manchester: Carcanet.

Graham, J. (2012b). Interviewed by Sharon Blackie. 'Interview with Jorie Graham', *Earthlines*. Available online: http://www.joriegraham.com/earthlines-interview (accessed 14 May 2013).

Graham, J. (2014). Interviewed by D. Wengen. 'Imagining the Unimaginable', *Poets.org*. Available online: https://poets.org/text/imagining-unimaginable-jorie-graham-conversation (accessed 12 April 2019).

Graham, J. (2017). *Fast*. Manchester: Carcanet.

Greenwell, G. (2008). 'To a Green Thought: Beauty's Canker: On Jorie Graham'. *West Branch*, 63: 115–34.

Grogan, R. (1989). 'Tomlinson, Ruskin and Moore: Facts and Fir Trees'. *Twentieth Century Literature*, 35(2): 183–94.
Hadfield, J. (2005). *Almanacs*. Tarset: Bloodaxe.
Hadfield, J. (2008). *Nigh-No-Place*. Tarset: Bloodaxe Books.
Hadfield, J. (2009a). Interviewed by AbeBooks. 'T.S. Eliot Prize-Winner Jen Hadfield'. *AbeBooks Blog*. Available online: https://www.abebooks.co.uk/books/jen-hadfield.shtml (accessed 3 November 2015).
Hadfield, J. (2009b). Interviewed by S. Mansfield. 'Northern Light', *The Scotsman*. Available online: https://www.scotsman.com/lifestyle-2-15039/jen-hadfield-interview-northern-light-1-832298 (accessed 7 August 2014).
Hadfield, J. (2010). Interviewed by Zoe Brigley. Available online: https://blogs.warwick.ac.uk/zoebrigley/entry/interview_with_the/ (accessed 2 August 2014).
Haraway, D. (2003). *The Companion Species Manifesto: Dogs, People, and Significant Otherness*. Chicago, IL: Prickly Paradigm.
Haraway, D. J. (2008). *When Species Meet*. Minneapolis: University of Minnesota Press.
Harper, G. (2012). 'A Short History of Creative Writing in British Universities', in H. Beck (ed.), *Teaching Creative Writing*. London: Palgrave Macmillan, 9–16.
Heise, U. (2008). *Sense of Place and Sense of Planet: The Environmental Imagination of the Global*. Oxford: Oxford University Press.
Heise, U. (2011). 'Developing a Sense of Planet: Ecocriticism and Globalisation', in G. Garrard (ed.) *Teaching Ecocriticism and Green Cultural Studies*. London: Palgrave Macmillan, 90–103.
Hess, S. (2015). 'Nature and the Environment', in A. Bennett (ed.), *William Wordsworth in Context*. Cambridge: Cambridge University Press, 207–14.
Hooker, J. (2017). *Ditch Vision*. Stroud: Awen.
Huggan, G. (2016). 'Back to the Future: The "New Nature Writing", Ecological Boredom, and the Recall for the Wild'. *Prose Studies*, 38(12): 152–71.
Hughes, T. ([1967] 2008). *Poetry in the Making: A Handbook for Writing and Teaching*. London: Faber and Faber.
Jackaman, R. (1989). *The Course of English Surrealist Poetry Since the 1930s*. Lampeter: Mellen.
Jamie, K. (2005) *Findings*. London: Sort of Books.
Jamie, K. (2008). 'A Lone Enraptured Male'. *London Review of Books*, 30(5): 25–7.
Jamie, K. (2012). *The Overhaul*. London: Picador.
Jefferies, R. ([1884] 2011). 'The Pageant of Summer', in *The Life of the Fields*. Cambridge: Cambridge University Press Online, 41–64.
Karwoska, S. (2000). 'White Clouds and the BQE', in C. McEwen and M. Statman (eds), *The Alphabet of the Trees: A Guide to Nature Writing*. New York: Teachers & Writers Collaborative, 17–29.
Keith, W. J. (1975). *The Rural Tradition: William Cobbett, Gilbert White and Other Non-Fiction Prose Writers of the English Countryside*. Hassocks: Harvester Press.

Kerridge, R., and N. Sammells (eds). (1998). *Writing the Environment: Ecocriticism and Literature*. London: Zed Books.

Kerridge, R. (2012). Interviewed by I. P. Ramos. 'Interview with Richard Kerridge', *Ecozon@* 3(2): 135–44.

Kinsey, C. (2014). Interviewed by I. Galleymore. 22 July. Unpublished.

Kirkham, M. (1999). *Passionate Intellect: The Poetry of Charles Tomlinson*. Liverpool: Liverpool University Press.

Klein, K. (1996). 'Poetry: An Art of Lying. Reflections on Charles Tomlinson', in D. Gohrbandt and B. v. Lutz (eds), *Self-Referentiality in 20th Century British and American Poetry*. New York: Peter Lang, 23–42.

Knickerbocker, S. (2012). *Ecopoetics: The Language of Nature, the Nature of Language*. Amherst: University of Massachusetts Press.

Lakoff, G., and M. Johnson (1980). *Metaphors We Live by*. Chicago, IL: University of Chicago Press.

Leopold, A. ([1949] 2001). *A Sand County Almanac*. Oxford: Oxford University Press.

Lewis, N. (2003). *Unsettling the Literary West: Authenticity and Authorship*. Lincoln: University of Nebraska Press.

Lewis, N. (2004). 'Truth or Consequences', in W. R. Handley and N. Lewis (eds), *True West: Authenticity and the American West*. Lincoln: University of Nebraska Press, 21–37.

Logenbach, J. (2005). 'The Place of Jorie Graham', in T. Gardner (ed.), *Jorie Graham: Essays on the Poetry*. Madison: University of Wisconsin Press, 206–18.

Long, W. J. ([1903] 1998). 'The Modern School of Nature-Study and Its Critics', in R. H. Lutts (ed.), *The Wild Animal Story*. Philadelphia, PA: Temple University Press, 144–52.

Lopez, B. H. ([1984] 1998). 'Landscape and Narrative', in *Crossing Open Ground*. New York: Scribner's.

Mabey, R. (1973). *The Unofficial Countryside*. London: Collins.

Mabey, R. (2003). 'Nature's Voyeurs'. *The Guardian*, 15 March. Available online: https://www.theguardian.com/books/2003/mar/15/featuresreviews.guardianreview1 (accessed 24 February 2017).

Macdonald, H. (2014). *H Is for Hawk*. London: Vintage Books.

Macdonald, H. (2014). '"Grief Shatters Narratives": Helen MacDonald on H Is for Hawk'. *London Review Bookshop Blog*. Available online: https://www.londonreviewbookshop.co.uk/blog/2014/8/grief-shatters-narratives-helen-macdonald-on-h-is-for-hawk (accessed 18 September 2015).

Macfarlane, R. (2003). 'Call of the Wild'. *The Guardian*, 6 December. Available online: https://www.theguardian.com/books/2003/dec/06/featuresreviews.guardianreview34 (accessed 19 July 2018).

Macfarlane, R. (2007). *The Wild Places*. London: Granta Books.

Macfarlane, R. (2011). 'How to Be a Nature Writer'. *BBC Wildlife Magazine*. Available online: http://www.discoverwildlife.com/competition-article/how-be-nature-writer (accessed 14 February 2014).
Macfarlane, R. (2015a). 'Robert Macfarlane: Why We Need Nature Writing'. *New Statesman*, 2 September. Available online: https://www.newstatesman.com/culture/nature/2015/09/robert-macfarlane-why-we-need-nature-writing (accessed 5 June 2018).
Macfarlane, R. (2015b). *Landmarks*. London: Hamish Hamilton.
Macfarlane, R. (2016a). 'Generation Anthropocene: How Humans Have Altered the Planet Forever'. *The Guardian*, 1 April. Available online: https://www.theguardian.com/books/2016/apr/01/generation-anthropocene-altered-planet-for-ever (accessed 10 April 2019).
Macfarlane, R. (2016b). 'What's a "Chuggypig"? Robert Macfarlane's Word Search'. *The Guardian*, 14 May. Available online: https://www.theguardian.com/books/2016/may/14/robert-macfarlane-readers-letters-words (accessed 20 July 2018).
Macfarlane, R. (2017). 'Violent Spring: The Nature Book That Predicted the Future'. *The Guardian*, 15 April. Available online: https://www.theguardian.com/books/2017/apr/15/the-peregrine-by-ja-baker-nature-writing (accessed 7 September 2017).
Macy, J., and M. Y. Brown (1998). *Coming Back to Life: Practices to Reconnect Our Lives, Our World*. British Columbia: New Society.
Malay, M. (2018). *The Figure of the Animal in Modern and Contemporary Poetry*. Basingstoke: Palgrave Macmillan.
Matthewman, S. (2010). *Teaching Secondary English as if the Planet Matters*. Oxon: Routledge.
Mazel, D. (2000). *American Literary Environmentalism*. London: University of Georgia Press.
McEwen, C., and M. Statman (eds). (2000). *The Alphabet of the Trees: A Guide to Nature Writing*. New York: Teachers & Writers Collaborative.
McFadden, M. (1985). '"The I in Nature": Nature Writing as Self Discovery', in F. O. Waage (ed.), *Teaching Environmental Literature: Materials, Methods, Resources*. New York: Modern Language Association of America, 102–7.
McGurl, M. (2009). *The Program Era: Postwar Fiction and the Rise of Creative Writing*. Cambridge, MA: Harvard University Press.
McKay, D. (1975). *Long Sault*. London: Applegarth Follies.
McKay, D. (1983). *Birding, or Desire*. Toronto: McClelland and Stewart.
McKay, D. (1997). *Apparatus*. Toronto: McClelland and Stewart.
McKay, D. (2001). *Vis à Vis: Fieldnotes on Poetry & Wilderness*. Wolfville: Gaspereau Press.
McKay, D. (2012a). *Paradoxides*. Toronto: McClelland & Stewart.
McKay, D. (2012b). Interviewed by CBC Radio-Canada. 'Spring Collections'. Available online: https://www.cbc.ca/books/2012/04/spring-collections-paradoxides-by-don-mckay.html (accessed 23 July 2014).

Meeker, J. (1997). *The Comedy of Survival: Studies in Literary Ecology*. Tucson: University of Arizona Press.
LeMenager, S., S. Siperstein and S. Hall (eds). (2017). *Teaching Climate Change in the Humanities*. Oxon: Routledge.
Miller, B. (2004). 'The Case against Metaphor: An Apologia'. *Fourth Genre: Explorations in Nonfiction*, 6(2): 115–18.
Morreall, J. (1987). *The Philosophy of Laughter and Humor*. New York: State University of New York Press.
Morton, T. (2007). *Ecology without Nature: Rethinking Environmental Aesthetics*. Cambridge, MA: Harvard University Press.
Morton, T. (2010a). *The Ecological Thought*. Cambridge, MA: Harvard University Press.
Morton, T. (2010b). 'Thinking Ecology: The Mesh, the Strange Stranger, and the Beautiful Soul'. *Collapse*, 6: 265–93.
Morton, T. (2013). *Hyperobjects: Philosophy and Ecology after the End of the World*. Minneapolis: University of Minnesota Press.
Moss, S. (2018a). *Mrs Moreau's Warbler: How Birds Got Their Names*. London: Guardian Faber.
Moss, S. (2018b). Interviewed by I. Galleymore. 27 March. Unpublished.
Moss, S. (2018c). 'Assignment Brief Handout'. Unpublished.
Moss, S. (2018d). Email correspondence with I. Galleymore. 2 July. Unpublished.
Motion, A. (2013). Interviewed by I. Galleymore. 25 February. Unpublished.
Murphy, P. D. (2000). *Farther Afield in the Study of Nature-Oriented Literature*. Charlottesville: University Press of Virginia.
Murphy, P. D. (2009). *Ecocritical Explorations in Literary and Cultural Studies: Fences, Boundaries, and Fields*. Lanham: Lexington Books.
Murray, J. A. (1995). *The Sierra Club Nature Writing Handbook: A Creative Guide*. San Francisco, CA: Sierra Club Books.
Murray, L. (1992). Interviewed by Barbara Williams. 'An Interview with Les A. Murray'. *Westerly*, 37(2): 45–56.
Murray, L. (1992). *Translations from the Natural World*. Manchester: Carcanet.
Murray, L. (2009). Interviewed by J. M. Smith. 'A Conversation with Les Murray'. *Image Journal*, 64. Available online: https://imagejournal.org/article/conversation-les-murray/ (accessed 3 July 2015).
Myers, D. G. (1996). *The Elephants Teach: Creative Writing Since 1880*. Englewood Cliffs, NJ: Prentice Hall.
Nagel, T. ([1974] 2012). 'What Is It Like to Be a Bat?', in *Mortal Questions*. Cambridge: Cambridge University Press, 165–80.
Neruda, P. ([1974] 1991). *The Book of Questions*, trans. W. O'Daly. Washington, DC: Copper Canyon Press.
Nixon, R. (2011). *Slow Violence and the Environmentalism of the Poor*. Cambridge, MA: Harvard University Press.

Nixon, R. (2018). 'The Swiftness of Glaciers: Language in a Time of Climate Change'. *Aeon*. Available online: https://aeon.co/ideas/the-swiftness-of-glaciers-language-in-a-time-of-climate-change (accessed 20 April 2019).

Nolan, A. J. (2010). 'Not Your Grandfather's Nature Writing: The New "Nature" Journals'. *Fiction Writers Review*, 11 August. Available online: https://fictionwritersreview.com/essay/not-your-grandfathers-nature-writing-the-new-nature-journals/ (accessed 16 November 2018).

Norrman, R., and J Haarberg (1980). *Nature and Language: A Semiotic Study of Cucurbits in Literature*. London: Routledge and Kegan Paul.

Oppermann, S. (2018). 'Storied Matter', in R. Braidotti and M. Hlavajova (eds), *Posthuman Glossary*. London: Bloomsbury, 411–13.

Osmond, R. (2017). *Useful Verses*. London: Picador.

Oswald, A. (2002) *Dart*. London: Faber.

Owens, L. (1998). 'Burning the Shelter', in *Mixedblood Messages: Literature, Film, Family, Place*. Norman: University of Oklahoma Press, 214–36.

Perrin, J. (2010). The Condry Lecture by Jim Perrin. *The Condry Lecture*. Available online: http://www.thecondrylecture.co.uk/_/pdf/Condry-Lecture-2010.pdf (accessed 7 October 2014).

Perrin, J. (2014a). Interviewed by I. Galleymore. 15 August. Unpublished.

Perrin, J. (2014b). 'Alarm Call from the Plover, as the Wildfowling Season Approaches'. *The Guardian*, 15 August. Available online: https://www.theguardian.com/environment/2014/aug/15/alarm-call-golden-plover-talsarnau-gwynedd-wildfowling (accessed 1 October 2014).

Petersen, D. (2001). *Writing Naturally: A Down-to-Earth Guide to Nature Writing*. Boulder, CO: Johnson Books.

Phillips, D. (2003). *The Truth of Ecology: Nature, Culture, and Literature in America*. New York: Oxford University Press.

Philippon, D. J. (2014). 'Is American Nature Writing Dead?', in G. Garrard (ed.), *The Oxford Handbook of Ecocriticism*. Oxford: Oxford University Press, 391–407.

Pite, R. (2000). '"Coming into Their Own": Roy Fisher and John Cowper Powys', in J. Kerrigan and P. Robinson (eds), *The Thing about Roy Fisher: Critical Studies*. Liverpool: Liverpool University Press, 231–56.

Plumwood, V. (2008). 'Shadow Places and the Politics of Dwelling'. *Australian Humanities Review*, 44: 139–50.

Prentiss, S., and J. Wilkins (2016). *Environmental and Nature Writing: A Writer's Guide and Anthology*. London: Bloomsbury.

Price, J. (2006). 'Thirteen Ways of Seeing Nature in L.A.' *The Believer*, 1 April. Available online: https://believermag.com/thirteen-ways-of-seeing-nature-in-la/ (accessed 14 May 2015).

Rigby, K. (2004a). *Topographies of the Sacred: The Poetics of Place in European Romanticism*. Charlottesville: University of Virginia Press.

Rigby, K. (2004b). 'Earth, World, Text: On the (Im)possibility of Ecopoiesis'. *New Literary History*, 35(3): 427–42.

Roorda, R. (1998). *Dramas of Solitude: Narratives of Retreat in American Nature Writing*. Albany: State University of New York Press.

Roosevelt ([1907] 1998). 'Nature Fakers', in R. H. Lutts (ed.), *The Wild Animal Story*. Philadelphia, PA: Temple University Press, 192–8.

Rueckert, W. (1978). 'Literature and Ecology: An Experiment in Ecocriticism'. *Iowa Review*, 9(1): 71–86.

Ruskin, J. ([1860] 2015). *Modern Painters* (Vol. 5). Project Gutenberg. Available online: http://www.gutenberg.org/ebooks/44329 (accessed 7 February 2017).

Różewicz, T. (2001). *Recycling*, trans. T. Howard and B. Plebanek. Lancashire: Arc.

Schraffenberger, J. (2016). 'Our Discipline: An Ecological Creative Writing Manifesto'. *Journal of Creative Writing Studies*, 1(1): 1–5.

Scigaj, L. M. (1999). *Sustainable Poetry: Four American Ecopoets*. Lexington: University Press of Kentucky.

Seitz, J. (1999). *Motives for Metaphor: Literacy, Curriculum Reform, and the Teaching of English*. Pittsburgh: University of Pittsburgh Press.

Seymour, N. (2018). *Bad Environmentalism: Irony and Irreverence in the Ecological Age*. Minneapolis: University of Minnesota Press.

Shklovsky, V. ([1921] 1990). 'The Novel as Parody: Sterne's *Tristram Shandy*', in *Theory of Prose*, trans. B. Sher. Champaign, IL: Dalkey Archive Press, 147–70.

Simons, J. (2002). *Animal Rights and the Politics of Literary Representation*. Basingstoke: Palgrave.

Skinner, J. (2014). Interviewed by I. Galleymore. 17 January. Unpublished.

Smyth, R. (2017). 'Plashy Fens: The Limitations of Nature Writing'. *Times Literary Supplement*, 11 July. Available online: https://www.the-tls.co.uk/articles/public/nature-writing-richard-smyth/ (accessed 6 August 2017).

Snow, C. P. ([1959] 1998). *The Two Cultures*. Cambridge: Cambridge University Press.

Sobel, D. (1996). *Beyond Ecophobia: Reclaiming the Heart in Nature Education*. Great Barrington, MA: Orion Society.

Sobel, D. (2008). *Childhood and Nature: Design Principles for Educators*. Portland, OR: Stenhouse.

Soper, K. (1995). *What Is Nature?: Culture, Politics and the Non-Human*. Oxford: Blackwell.

Spahr, J. (2001). *Everybody's Autonomy: Connective Reading and Collective Identity*. Tuscaloosa: University of Alabama Press.

Spahr, J. (2005a). *This Connection of Everyone with Lungs*. Berkeley: University of California Press.

Spahr, J. (2005b). Interviewed by M. Boyko. 'A Brief Q&A with Juliana Spahr', *Tarpaulin Sky*, 3(2). Available online: http://www.tarpaulinsky.com/Summer05/Spahr/Juliana_Spahr_Q-n-A.html (accessed 4 May 2015).

Spahr, J. (2007). *The Transformation*. Berkeley, CA: Atelos.

Spahr, J. (2011). *Well Then There Now*. Boston, MA: David R. Godine.
Spahr, J. (2015a). Interviewed by J. Charles. *Entropy Magazine*, 11 December. Available online: https://entropymag.org/interview-with-juliana-spahr/ (accessed 7 May 2016).
Spahr, J. (2015b). *That Winter the Wolf Came*. Oakland, CA: Commune Editions.
Spiegelman, W. (2005). *How Poets See the World: The Art of Description in Contemporary Poetry*. Oxford: Oxford University Press.
St Germain, S. (2014a). Interviewed by I. Galleymore. 6 October. Unpublished.
St Germain, S. (2014b). 'Conjuring Place Handout'. Unpublished.
Stein, G. ([1935] 1988). *Lectures in America*. London: Virago.
Stenning, A., and T. Gifford (2013). 'Twentieth-Century Nature Writing in Britain and Ireland'. *Green Letters*, 17(1): 1–4.
Stewart, F. (1995). *A Natural History of Nature Writing*. Washington, DC: Island Press for Shearwater Books.
Swander, M. (2014). Interviewed by I. Galleymore. 25 July. Unpublished.
Tallmadge, J. (2000). 'A Matter of Scale: Searching for Wilderness in the City', in C. McEwen and M. Statman (eds), *The Alphabet of the Trees: A Guide to Nature Writing*. New York: Teachers & Writers Collaborative, 60–5.
Thomashow, M. (1995). *Ecological Identity: Becoming a Reflective Environmentalist*. Cambridge, MA: MIT Press.
Thomashow, M. (2002). *Bringing the Biosphere Home: Learning to Perceive Global Environmental Change*. Cambridge, MA: MIT Press.
Thoreau, H. D. ([1854] 2008). *Walden*, ed. S. A. Fender. Oxford: Oxford University Press.
Tomlinson, C. (1960). *Seeing Is Believing*. Oxford: Oxford University Press.
Tomlinson, C. (1966). *The Necklace*. Oxford: Oxford University Press.
Tomlinson, C. (1985). 'The Poet as Painter', in *Eden: Graphics and Poetry*. Bristol: Redcliffe Poetry, 9–22.
Tomlinson, C. (1990). Interviewed by B. Meyer. 'A Human Balance: An Interview with Charles Tomlinson'. *Hudson Review*, 43(3): 437–48.
Tomlinson, C. (2009). *New Collected Poems*. Manchester: Carcanet.
Trimble, S. (1995). *Words from the Land*. Reno: University of Nevada Press.
Ttoouli, G. (2014). Interviewed by I. Galleymore. 5 June. Unpublished.
Uexküll, J. v. ([1934] 2010). *A Foray into the Worlds of Animals and Humans: With a Theory of Meaning*, trans. J. D. O'Neil. Minneapolis: University of Minnesota Press.
Umphrey, M. (2008). 'A Hunger for Reality: Writing an Essay of Place'. *Asle.org Syllabi*. Available online: https://www.asle.org/syllabi/hunger-reality-writing-essay-place/ (accessed 14 May 2018).
Vendler, H. (2005). 'The Moment of Excess', in T. Gardner (ed.), *Jorie Graham: Essays on the Poetry*. Madison: University of Wisconsin Press, 42–59.
Vico, G. ([1744] 1999). *New Science: Principles of the New Science Concerning the Common Nature of Nations*, trans. D. Marsh. London: Penguin Books.

Waage, F. O. (1985). *Teaching Environmental Literature: Materials, Methods, Resources*. New York: Modern Language Association of America.

Waage, F. O., L. Christensen and M. Long (eds). (2008). *Teaching North American Environmental Literature*. New York: Modern Language Association of America.

Wallace, A. B. (2012). 'The Place of Drawing in Place Journaling'. *Honors in Practice*, 8: 101–7.

Welch, T. J. (2014). 'Entangled Species: The Posthumanist Ecopoetics of Juliana Spahr'. *Journal of Ecocriticism*, 6(1): 1–12.

Welsch, J. T. (2015). '"Critical Approaches to Creative Writing": A Case Study'. *Writers in Practice*, 1. Available online: https://www.nawe.co.uk/DB/current-wip-edition-2/articles/critical-approaches-to-creative-writing-a-case-study.html (accessed 19 March 2019).

Wertsch, M. E. (2000). 'What Is the Voice That Whispers? Writing Nature Poems Based on Pablo Neruda's *Book of Questions*', in C. McEwen and M. Statman (eds), *The Alphabet of the Trees: A Guide to Nature Writing*. New York: Teachers and Writers Collaborative, 168–72.

Wheeler, W. (2016). *Expecting the Earth*. Chadwell Heath: Lawrence and Wishart.

White, G. ([1789] 1996). *The Natural History of Selborne*, ed. G. Allen. Hertfordshire: Wordsworth Classics.

Wilbur. R. ([1968] 1990). Interviewed by J. Hutton, in W. Butts (ed.), *Conversations with Richard Wilbur*. Jackson: University of Mississippi, 46–55.

Wilkinson, B. (2009). 'Jen Hadfield: British Council Critical Perspective'. Available online: https://literature.britishcouncil.org/writer/jen-hadfield (accessed 14 May 2015).

Williams, R. (1973). *The Country and the City*. New York: Oxford University Press.

Williams, R. (1976). *Keywords: A Vocabulary of Culture and Society*. London: Croom Helm.

Williams, T. T. (1991), *Refuge: An Unnatural History of Family and Place*. New York: Vintage Books.

Wills, C. (2000). *A Furnace and the Life of the Dead*. Liverpool: Liverpool University Press.

Wootten, W. (2005). 'Romanticism and Animism in Roy Fisher's *A Furnace*'. *Cercles*, 12: 79–93.

Wordsworth, W. ([1798] 1994). 'The Tables Turned', in *The Collected Poems of William Wordsworth*. Hertfordshire: Wordsworth Editions.

Wordsworth, W. ([1798] 2006). 'Lines Composed a Few Miles above Tintern Abbey', in S. Greenblatt (ed.), *The Norton Anthology of English Literature, Eighth Edition* (Vol. 2). New York: Norton.

World Economic Forum (2016). 'The New Plastics Economy: Rethinking the Futures of Plastics'. *WE Forum*, 19 January. Available online: http://www3.weforum.org/docs/WEF_The_New_Plastics_Economy.pdf (accessed 6 June 2017).

Zwinger, A., and S. Zwinger (2008). 'Learning Nature through the Senses', in L. Christensen and H. Crimmel (eds), *Teaching about Place: Learning from the Land*. Reno: University of Nevada Press, 20–36.

Index

Abram, David 123–4, 128, 136–8, 140
activism
    environmental writing 5, 10, 62–3
    polemic 44–5, 62–5, 81–5, 132
Adorno, Theodor 145–7, 149
analogy 46–8, 110–11, 157, 162
anthropocentrism 155, *see also* egotism
    challenges to 105, 157–63, 167–72
    problems of 8, 92, 154–6
anthropomorphism
    of animals 9, 89–100, 110–12
    of materials 93–4, 100–9, 112–15
anthropocene 108
apostrophe 77–81, 85
Association for the Study of Literature and the Environment 10, 23
authenticity 30, 34, 143–50, 158–9, 161, 164, *see also* ecomimesis *and* truth

Baker, J. A. 16, 117, 120–1
Bate, Jonathan 17, 61, 149
Bennett, Jane 101–5, 112–13
biodiversity 135–6, 139–40, *see also* extinction
bioregionalism 26–8, 33, 54, *see also* place-based education
Bogost, Ian 110–11, 113
Buell, Laurence 11, 147–8, 154
Burnett, Elizabeth-Jane 12, 119–20, 165
Burroughs, John 6, 9, 16, 89–91, 120

Campbell, SueEllen 30, 76–7
Canton, James 13, 30, 121
Carpenter, J. R. 140–1
Carson, Rachel 6, 31
Chandler, Katherine R. 27, 42
Christensen, Laird 13, 68–9, 85, 118–19, 128, 133
climate change
    communication 132–3
    language of 86
    representations of 51, 74–77, 141

Cocker, Mark
    pedagogy 119, 143, 150
    writing 28, 31, 81, 92, 121
colonialism 15, 45–8, 51
Cooper, David 29, 83, 114, 178
Crimmel, Hal 3, 7, 12

Deleuze, Gilles, and Guattari, Félix, *A Thousand Plateaus* 94–5
Derrida, Jacques 11, 94
Dillard, Annie 26–8, 31, 58, 69
Doty, Mark 1–5, 8

ecocriticism
    first-wave and second-wave 12–14, 17
    recent developments 171–3
ecoliteracy 27, 33, 118, *see also* natural history
ecomimesis 11, 149–150, 154, 159, 161, 165
edgelands 29, 146–7, *see also* urban environments
egotism 59–61, 81, 119–22, 126, 134–7, 171, *see also* anthropocentrism
Elder, John
    ecocritical writing 10–11, 19
    pedagogy 26–7, 57–8, 72–3, 90, 117, 143–5
empathy 77–8, 81–2, 84, 86–7, 90, 98
Evans, Paul 61
extinction 51, 70, 74, 135, *see also* biodiversity

field work 7–8, 27, 117, 129–32, *see also* natural history
Fisher, Roy *A Furnace* 103–8, 113–14
Foster, Charles 92
Frost, Robert 19–20, 167–8

Galt, Margot Fortunato 49–51
Garrard, Greg 14, 16
Gifford, Terry 30, 54, 132–3

Gilcrest, David W. 11, 122–3
globalization 32–43, 49–56, 76
Gower, Jon 28, 32, 61
Graham, Jorie
   Fast 86–7
   Hybrids of Plants and Ghosts 66
   Never 69–72
   Place 77–9
   Sea Change 73–6, 77–8

Hadfield, Jen
   Nigh-No-Place 155–8
Haraway, Donna 94–5, 97–8, 108, 110
Heise, Ursula 32–7, 41, 49, 54
Hooker, Jeremy 28–9
Hughes, Ted 17, 91, 132–3, 150
humour 55, 141, 158–62

indigenous cultures 49–50, 95, 124, 144–5
industrialization, *see also* edgelands *and* urban environments
   city 105–7
   farming 99–100
   pollution 37, 132–3
interdisciplinarity 3, 5–8, 114, 169

Jamie, Kathleen 60–1, 146

Karwoska, Susan 106–7
Keith, W. J. 8–9, 28
Kinsey, Chris 62–3, 91, 98–9, 167
kitsch 148–50, 167
Knickerbocker, Scott 124–5

Mabey, Richard 29, 151
Macdonald, Helen 91–2
Macfarlane, Robert 16–17, 19, 25, 59–60, 81, 134–5, 139, 147
McFadden, Margaret 58–60, 66
McKay, Don
   Apparatus 153–4,
   Birding, or Desire 160–1
   Long Sault 162–3
   Paradoxides 152
   Vis à Vis 151–5, 161
map-making 28, 39–41
metaphor 110–11, 117–41, 152–8, 160–1, 166–8
Momaday, N. Scott 49, 145

Morton, Timothy
   'non-identity' 149
   'radical kitsch' 150
   'strange stranger' 95, 100–2, 108
Moss, Stephen 29, 138–9, 143
Motion, Andrew 91, 98, 108, 131–2, 155
Murphy, Patrick D. 4–5, 119
Murray, John A. 7, 11, 20, 57, 68, 72, 143
Murray, Les
   Translations from the Natural World 95–101, 110, 112

Nagel, Thomas 94, 110–11
narrative
   confessional 53–4, 84–5
   objective versus subjective 20, 67–9, 110, 117, 120, 135
   unreliable 111, 150, 164–5
natural history, *see also* field work
   influence of 28, 118, 120–2
   naming 122, 129–30, 138–40
nature fakers 89–90
new materialism 101, 104, 110, 123
new nature writing 17–19, 30, 91–2, 121
Nixon, Rob 58, 64–65, 69–70, 72, 76, 81–2

Oswald, Alice 164
Owens, Louis 61, 84

Perrin, Jim 30, 44, 62–3, 121–2
perspective taking
   animals 92, 95–99, 109–12
   humans 64–5, 75–9
   materials 102, 108, 112–14
Petersen, David 8, 15, 21, 58–63, 66–7, 118–19, 146, 158
Phillips, Dana 11–12, 19, 148
place-based education 26–8, 31–3, 39–40, 58, 68, 73, 76, 117–18, *see also* bioregionalism
Plumwood, Val 32
Prentiss, Sean, and Wilkins, Joe,
   Environmental and Nature Writing 40, 62–3, 117
psychogeography 114–15
purple prose 119, 136, 158

responsibility 31, 4, 50, 84, 97, 105, 115, 134, *see also* stewardship

Rigby, Kate 149–52, 158, 166
romanticism 17, 60–1, 107, 124, 149, 151–2
Roorda, Randall 28, 69, 83
Ruskin, John 125, 130–1, 134

St Germain, Sheryl 3, 13, 27, 31, 39–40, 42, 44
Schraffenberger, Jeremy 15, 30, 169–71
Scigaj, Leonard 11–12
Seitz, James 161–2
self-effacement 68–9, 83, 154–6
self-reflexivity 20, 42, 84, 125, 150–1, 154–68
sentimentalism 16, 20, 62, 149, 158, *see also* kitsch
Seymour, Nicole 171–3
Skinner, Jonathan 19, 140
Spahr, Juliana
  This Connection of Everyone with Lungs 37–44
  Transformation, The 51
  That Winter the Wolf Came 44
  Well Then There Now 36–7, 45–8, 50–1
spiritualism
  connection 3, 14, 31, 49
  creation myth 97, 106–7
  self-discovery 58–9
stewardship 27, 31, 39–40, *see also* responsibility
surrealism 114, 122, 159

Tallmadge, John 101–2
Thomashow, Mitchell 33–4, 73, 84
Thoreau, Henry David 9, 26, 57–8, 146–7
Tomlinson, Charles
  Necklace, The 126–7, 135–6
  Seeing Is Believing 127–31, 136
transcendentalism 10, 17, 26, 28, 58–9, 62–3
travel writing
  and environmental writing 29–30
  tourism 45–6, 61, 151
truth 7, 9, 20, 118–19, 127–8, *see also* authenticity
Ttoouli, George 140

urban environments 101–2, 114–15, 146, *see also* edgelands *and* industrialization

Waage, Frederik O. 5–8
Wallace, Alison B. 27, 30–2, 46, 118, 129
Wertsch, Mary Edwards 159
White, Gilbert 9, 120–1
wilderness 16, 28, 147
Williams, Raymond 4, 9,
Williams, Terry Tempest 61, 63
Wordsworth, William 2, 16, 60–1, 153

www.ingramcontent.com/pod-product-compliance
Lightning Source LLC
Chambersburg PA
CBHW072236290426
44111CB00012B/2123